PENETRATING THE INTERNATIONAL MARKET

The Political Economy of International Change
John Gerard Ruggie, General Editor

PENETRATING THE INTERNATIONAL MARKET

Theoretical Considerations and a Mexican Case Study

David R. Mares

Columbia University Press

NEW YORK   1987

Library of Congress Cataloging-in-Publication Data

Mares, David R.
Penetrating the international market.

(The Political economy of international change)
Bibliography: p.
Includes index.
1. Produce trade—Mexico.   2. Produce trade—
United States.   3. Vegetable trade—Mexico—Sinaloa
(State)   4. Agriculture and state—Mexico.
5. Agriculture and state—United States.   6. Competition,
International.   I. Title.   II. Series.
HD9014.M62M38   1987   382'.415'097232   87-6358
ISBN 0-231-06346-6

Columbia University Press
New York   Guildford, Surrey
Copyright © 1987 Columbia University Press
All rights reserved
Printed in the United States of America

To Jane

CONTENTS

TABLES

ACKNOWLEDGMENTS

Any serious academic and intellectual endeavor is heavily influenced by the myriad of professional and personal relationships which develop in the course of analysis of a complex subject.

I wish to thank Jorge I. Domínguez, friend and adviser. I benefited immeasurably from his patience, which helped to bring my analytic capacity to the surface and his refusal to allow me to lapse into easy or uncritical thoughts. From Jorge I have taken so much that I will never begin to repay it.

In Mexico, three people in particular were fundamental to this study. Mario Ojeda, friend and tutor, provided me with three years at El Colegio de México, first as visiting researcher and then as professor of the Centro de Estudios Internacionales. In addition, he took special interest in helping this Chicano toward a deeper understanding of Mexican society and politics, for which I will always be grateful. I would also like to thank Carlos Salinas de Gortari for his encouragement and support in the writing stages. I am especially thankful for the opportunity to further my knowledge of Mexican agriculture and trade by working with him at the Ministry of Planning and Budget and elsewhere. Finally, but not least, Manuel Ortega deserves mention for his friendship and the months he spent trying to explain Sinaloa's reality to me. We oftentimes disagreed, but the richness of the study is in no small part due to his concerns.

In San Diego I benefited tremendously from discussions with two colleagues in the political science department, Peter F. Cowhey and, most especially, David L. Laitin. David's infinite patience and unselfish attention to drafts is responsible for this manuscript's attempt to break out of a simple case study and make a theoretical contribution to the field. I thank him greatly and wish that all young professors could find someone like David to inspire them, guide them, and be their friend.

Nathaniel Beck, Refugio Rochín, F. Lamond Tullis, Van Whiting, and, in particular, John Odell, read and commented on various versions of the manuscript. The Program on Interdependent Political Economy at the University of Chicago provided an opportunity to present my argument about the political economy of international competitiveness. Charles Lipson and John Coatsworth were especially helpful.

The concluding chapter benefited greatly from the comments of Tun-jen Cheng, Stephan Haggard, and David B. Yoffie.

As series editor, John Gerard Ruggie provided stimulating criticism and welcome encouragement from the time I submitted the manuscript to Columbia University Press until its publication. I am also grateful to Kate Wittenberg, Executive Editor at the Press, for helping me to navigate the editorial process. At San Diego, Betsy Faught, Lee Dewey, and Kelly Charter provided vital staff support.

Funding for this study came from a variety of sources. The now-defunct Graduate Fellowship Program for Mexican-Americans, once funded by the Ford Foundation, provided initial support for field research in Mexico. The Latin American Program of the Woodrow Wilson Center for International Scholars, Smithsonian Institution, provided me with a summer in Washington, D.C., to carry out research on the trade aspects of the study. The University of California's Consortium on U.S.-Mexico Studies and Stanford's Project on U.S.-Mexico Relations supported further research into the international aspects of Mexico's trade relations. Writing was facilitated by two summers of support provided by the University of California's Affirmative Action Faculty Career Development program. The Center for Advanced Study in the Behavioral Sciences provided editorial and graphic support and, most importantly, time to devote to the final stages of publication.

I gratefully acknowledge permission to reproduce sections of work published elsewhere. Chapter 2 builds on "The U.S.-Mexico Winter Vegetable Trade: Climate, Economics, and Politics," published in Bruce F. Johnston et al., eds., *U.S.-Mexico Relations: Agriculture and Rural Development* (copyright © 1987 by Stanford University Press, Stanford, Calif.). Sections of chapter 4 appeared in "La articulación nacional y local y el desarrollo rural: La irrigación" *América Indígena* (July-September 1980), vol. 4, no. 3; "Agricultural Trade: Domestic Interests and Transnational Relations" in Jorge I. Dominguez, ed., *Mexico's Political Economy: Challenges at Home and Abroad* (copyright © 1982 by SAGE, Beverly Hills, Calif.) contains the early version of my argument in chapter 8.

No one deserves more credit for the completion of this study than Jane Milner-Mares, intellectual companion and partner in life. She put up with tarantulas in the living room, helped me think through various versions of each chapter, withstood repeated separations, and played both mother and father to Alejandro for most of his first year.

Although everyone mentioned above, and others whom I have thanked in private, contributed to the study, I take full responsibility for what is written and thank all who were involved.

ABBREVIATIONS

AARC	Asociación de Agricultores del Río Culiacán
CAADES	Confederación de Asociaciones Agrícolas del Estado de Sinaloa
CAM	Consejo Agrario Mexicano
CDA	Comité Directiva Agrícola
CIOAC	Confederación Independiente de Obreros Agrícolas y Campesinos
CNC	Confederación Nacional Campesina
CNPP	Confederación Nacional de la Pequeña Propiedad
CNTA	Comisión Nacional Tripartita Agraria
CROC	Confederación Revolucionaria de Obreros y Campesinos
CTA	Comisión Tripartita Agraria
CTM	Confederación de Trabajadores Mexicanos
DAAC	Departamento de Asuntos Agrarios y Colonización
DFI	Direct Foreign Investment
DT	Dirección del Trabajo
FBA	Food Business Associates
FEPPS	Federación Estatal de la Pequeña Propiedad de Sinaloa
FIOACS	Federación Independiente de Obreros Agrícolas y Campesinos de Sinaloa
FOCVC	Federación de Obreros y Campesinos del Valle de Culiacán
FTC	Florida Tomato Committee
FTS	Federación de Trabajadores de Sinaloa
ISI	Import-Substitution Industrialization
JCCyA	Junta Central de Conciliación y Arbitraje
LNC	Liga Nacional Campesina

NTB	Non-tariff Barriers
PPS	Partido Popular Socialista, formerly Partido Popular
PRI	Partido Revolucionario Institucional
SAG	Secretaría de Agricultura
SARH	Secretaría de Agricultura y Recursos Hidráulicos
SNTAC	Sindicato Nacional de Trabajadores Agrícolas del Campo
SOCLyC	Sindicato de Obreros y Campesinos Legumbreros y Conexos
SOCSP	Sindicato de Obreros y Campesinos de San Pedro
SRA	Secretaría de Reforma Agraria
SRH	Secretaría de Recursos Hidráulicos
UAS	Universidad Autónoma de Sinaloa
UGOCM	Unión General de Obreros y Campesinos de México
UNAN	Unión Agrícola Nacional
UNPH	Unión Nacional de Productores de Hortalizas
USDA	United States Department of Agriculture
WMVDA	West Mexico Vegetable Distributors Association

PENETRATING THE INTERNATIONAL MARKET

INTRODUCTION

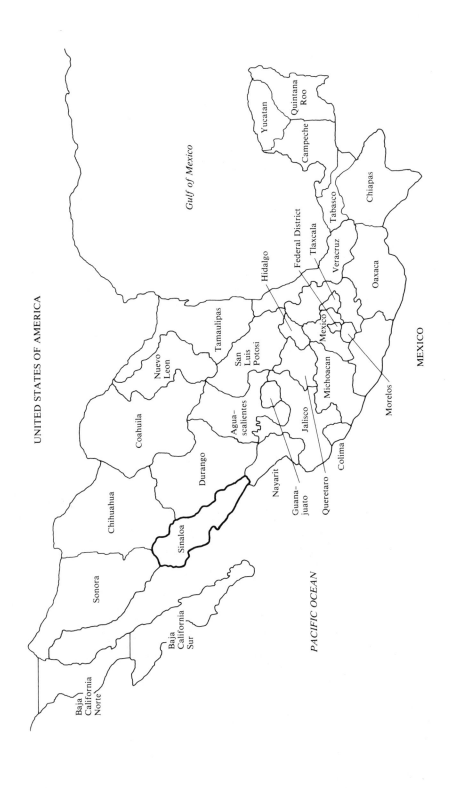

1

THE POLITICAL ECONOMY OF INTERNATIONAL COMPETITIVENESS: THEORY AND A FRAMEWORK FOR ANALYSIS

In 1979 the U.S. trade bureaucracy was holding one of its many hearings on allegations brought by U.S. entrepreneurs that were designed to impose nontariff trade barriers on competitive imports. In this particular case Florida vegetable growers were accusing their Mexican counterparts of "dumping" (selling below cost) their produce on the U.S. market. This was an important case for Mexico and is a typical problem faced by poor nations in their attempts to sell agricultural products to rich nations. Fresh vegetable exports were Mexico's fourth most important export, generating $400 million in 1979 and agriculture accounted for 23 percent of Third World exports.[1]

There are two contending approaches to explain why developing countries (the "South") face trade barriers from the "North"—dependencia theory and a modified version of free trade theory. Contemporary dependency theorists argue that Southern growers confront a pernicious tangle of obstacles. Foreign capital controls the most economically significant part of the industry—the processing and distribution networks. Furthermore, Northern farmers lobby for barriers to constrain Southern exports. Meanwhile, Southern governments unite in alliances with foreign capital and local industry in a way that limits the influence and welfare of the rural sector. And political stability in countries like Mexico often compels to the government to organize and control monopoly associations that represent the major sectors of the economy, including private capital. These arrangements, called "state corporatism" in the literature, constrain competitiveness.

Dependency theorists have relied on Steven Sanderson's work on Mexico's tomato export industry as important evidence for their case. Sanderson contends that the Mexican growers are really controlled by U.S. capital (Arizona distributors),[2] and that the trade conflict concerning Mexican tomatoes is one between competing domestic entrepreneurs in the United States: Arizona distributors and Florida growers (who had fought to limit imports since 1934).[3] But reports filed by the U.S. Customs Service about their investigation of the marketing of Mexican vegetables revealed that Mexicans in fact controlled the farms, and that grower-owned enterprises were carrying out a large portion of the importing and distributing of Mexican vegetables within the United States.[4] Since the export vegetable industry in Mexico had originated with U.S. capital and entrepreneurship, this Mexican participation meant that a major transformation had taken place: Southern domestic capital had replaced Northern foreign capital in a dynamic industry. Even more damaging to the dependency perspective, my research shows that these Mexican growers have achieved substantial, albeit delicately balanced, influence in Mexican national policymaking.

Not only had the Mexican growers wrestled control of much of the processing and distribution network, they had also built political alliances in the United States that gave them substantial leverage in Washington, D.C. Confronted by another attack by Florida growers in 1979, the U.S. executive branch sided with the Mexican defense and they won. One of the most prestigious Washington law firms, Arnold and Porter, represented them. Harvard Professor Hendrick S. Houthakker submitted an affadavit that blasted the prosecution's data analysis, declaring it was "no longer considered valid in the current theory and practice in the field of econometrics and statistics." The chief consultant to the U.S. Department of Agriculture on vegetable trade, Richard L. Simmons, constructed the first regression analysis ever used in a dumping case to support the defense. In addition, the president of the American Agricultural Economics Association, Richard A. King, testified in favor of the Mexican growers.[5]

The international political economy literature had not prepared me to expect such outcomes. Studies on North-South trade relations were overwhelmingly concerned that the rise of protectionism in the North bode ill for the South.[6] Analyses of Northern direct foreign investment (NDFI) in the South had come to recognize that the Southern state could influence the terms of that investment,[7] but private Southern capital was perceived to be relegated either to the nondynamic sectors of the economy,[8] or to subsectors ignored by NDFI and through which Southern entrepreneurs became important only in alliance with the "state bourgeoisie" (bureaucrats in the economic ministries and state-owned firms).[9]

The Mexican fresh winter vegetable case, moreover, is not unique. Recent studies have begun to demonstrate that Third World products continue to penetrate Northern markets, despite increased protection.[10] Southern DFI (SDFI) has begun to attract the attention of economists and management analysts. Although most SDFI is directed toward other Southern countries, many firms are looking northward to establish wholly owned subsidiaries or joint ventures to produce, process, market, or to raise capital.[11]

My criticisms of dependency theory are not, however, an endorsement of the political economy models implicit in even sophisticated models of free trade. The richest model of the interaction of trade, investment, and government intervention in imperfect commodity markets is the obsolescing bargain (a corollary of the product cycle). It predicts that an initial oligopoly controlled by foreign capital will eventually yield to local ownership as know-how is diffused internationally, Southern politicians see the advantages of seizing the rents of ownership and their bargaining skills improve. But this model cannot easily predict what happens after the initial shift in ownership of local production.[12] For example, can the new owners move successfully to own the foreign processing and distribution networks that use their commodities? This will depend on a combination of political incentives in the developing country and market opportunities. It will also require skillful trade diplomacy to avoid retaliation by Northern countries. This literature says little about how different types of political economic systems in the South influence these choices. (On this score the dependency literature is far more interesting.) It also fails to fit these sectors into the broader political patterns of international trade.

This book uses an analysis of the U.S.-Mexican trade for fresh winter vegetables to lay out a model for analyzing the evolution of international trade. It begins by showing how agricultural trade fits into the general political bargain governing world trade and investment. Then, it explains how the particular type of political economic order in a developing country—Mexico's system of state corporatism and private capitalism—shapes its competitive strategy in the world market. It demonstrates that the interplay of national and regional politics allows bargains under state corporatism that otherwise appear improbable. Finally, this study will show that the bargain struck at home shapes the political strategy used to open up foreign markets.

More specifically, the case study will examine the strategies of government, business, and labor. It will show that Mexican political elites considered the financial risks and regional political conflicts involved in the vegetable trade as too volatile. State ownership was neither politically nor economically attractive. Yet a major export business could deliver the highly prized rewards of foreign exchange earnings and numerous jobs. Therefore, the government gave support to private growers but refused to relinquish control. It therefore imposed corporatist associations on large and small growers as well as farm workers; these associations could restrict the strategic choices of all key economic actors to some extent. But the national government gave latitude to regional politicians regarding this industry in order to deflect some political controversies. And the national government conceded substantial latitude to the large growers in order to foster the export trade. This also led it to curb political protests by labor and small growers even while taking limited measures to assist them.

For their part the large growers needed the support of the government on three fronts. Government allocation of water resources, the government's ban on foreign ownership of critical farm lands, and the subordination of labor and small growers in corporatist peak associations permitted an effective oligopoly to emerge in the Culiacán region of Mexico. The corporatist framework then expedited the exercise of oligopolistic leadership (including taking some unilateral cuts in production) by Culiacán growers when bargaining with growers in the rest of Mexico concerning exports destined for the U.S. market. These same farmers then used their oligopolistic control of production to gain bargaining leverage with the more competitive financing, processing and distribution segments of the industry.

Yet private ownership also proved vital for Mexico's successes. Oligopolistic competition led to vigorous experimentation in securing new marketing outlets in the United States. Private ownership permitted the growers to be much more flexible in experimenting with foreign investment and marketing strategies than state enterprises. Innovative commercial tactics later blossomed into a broad web of transnational political alliances with interest groups in the United States who championed Mexican vegetable imports.

In short, this book is a tale of power politics within Mexico and between Mexico and the United States. Mexico's agrarian policies had very mixed effects on the weak, but forged a group of producers with the political and economic resources to claim a stake in a risky world market. It uses this story to show how a theory of the political economy of international trade can account both for an enduring management of key markets by all governments and for the ways in which domestic politics significantly shift competitive responses to such markets over time.

The balance of this chapter constructs a framework for the analysis of international competitiveness, rooted in understanding the political underpinnings of production and trade. A necessary preliminary step in developing such a framework is to interpret correctly the international regime within which production for the international market, and trade itself, occurs.* I shall first dispute the conventional understanding of the liberal trade regime in which the market supposedly determines trade patterns. In that view political intervention to alter trade patterns, as occurs in agriculture, is considered inconsistent with the requirements of growth. In contrast, I argue not only that there is a political basis for successful market penetration, but also that the conventional view cannot explain the coexistence of protection and a liberal trade regime. A focus not on comparative advantage but on the political bargain also permits prediction of when a product will, or will not, be protected

---

*Regimes are "social institutions around which actor expectations converge in a given area of international relations . . . [they] limit the discretion of their constituent units to decide and act on issues that fall within the regime's domain." John Gerard Ruggie, "International Regimes, Transactions, and Change," p. 380. Regimes consist of principles, norms, rules, and decision-making procedures. "Principles are beliefs of fact, causation, and rectitude. Norms are standards of behavior defined in terms of rights and obligations. Rules are specific prescriptions or proscriptions for action. Decision-making procedures are prevailing practices for making and implementing collective choice." Stephen D. Krasner, "Structural Causes and Regime Consequences," p. 186.

depending on a mixture of international, state and local variables. Thus, I shall present a new approach for linking local, national, and international politics in order to explain trade policies.

MANAGING TRADE IN AGRICULTURE: IMPLICATIONS FOR THE LIBERAL INTERNATIONAL ECONOMIC ORDER

The post-World War II international economic order is most often defined in terms of its liberalness. Whether because of hegemonic power or regime formation,[13] the description "liberal" is assumed to be of great analytic value because the advanced industrial countries accept that global welfare is enhanced by free exchange and strive for it. As Krasner notes, this search for global liberalism entails endorsing the principle that "the allocation of resources is determined by the endowments and preferences of individual actors who have the right to alienate their property according to their own estimations of their own best interests." This view is opposed to that which accepts "either the direct allocation of resources by political authorities, or indirect allocation by limiting the property rights of nonstate actors, including private corporations.[14]

In reality, however, both market and political allocation have been implicitly recognized by the post WWII trade regime. I shall describe this mixture as a regime based on "segmented liberalism." First I will examine the conventional liberal argument (and some of the revisions it has undergone) and its shortcomings in explaining the expanded scope of protection. Then I will elaborate my own model of segmented liberalism. Ruggie and Aggarwal have demonstrated that the international economic strategies of Northern countries may orchestrate both the market and the political allocation of resources in ways that contribute to liberal trade.[15] This book further develops their framework by sharpening the microeconomic analysis of the market and developing a fuller model of the impact of domestic politics. It then shows how to apply this model to the foreign economic strategies of the Southern nations and the organization of international commodity markets.

Conventional liberal analysts take the experiences of trade in manufactures and in the flow of investment capital to constitute the norm for understanding the foreign economic policy preferences of the North.

Liberalization in these two areas has been dramatic. With respect to trade, under the auspices of the General Agreement on Tariffs and Trade (GATT), tariffs have fallen to unprecedented lows. In the case of capital, it is relatively free to flow internationally through portfolio and direct investment, as well as loans.

But not all international economic transactions dominated by the North are governed by market-determined allocations. Transactions in which Northern political intervention continues to play an important role cover a wide range of products and factors of production: agriculture, strategic minerals, services, and labor. In fact, even in the case of manufactures, state intervention to protect domestic producers became commonplace in the 1970s. One study estimated that in 1982 nontariff barriers (NTBs) covered 34 percent of the U.S. market for manufacturers, 7 percent of Japan's, 10 percent of Canada's, 20 percent of West Germany's, and 32 percent of France's.[16]

Intervention by political authorities to guide these transactions is accepted by revisionists and legitimized because of alleged "special" circumstances. It is my contention that these "special" circumstances are not unique to these economic activities. Their absence in other international economic relations was rather a product of economic and political conditions at a particular time, the quarter century after World War II. My argument is that by examining the alleged exceptions we can learn more about the political nature of the international liberalization process. Agriculture is particularly suited for this purpose because the United States initially excluded it from the push for liberalization. Although the United States subsequently sought some degree of liberalization for agricultural trade, the Europeans then blocked major changes.[17] But although agriculture has its own dynamics, there is nothing inherent in agricultural trade that vitiates liberal theory. This case study of the political basis for agricultural trade therefore speaks to more general issues of the international trade regime.

The traditional argument about the special characteristics of agriculture which are said to preclude its liberalization rests on three points: (1) supply and demand are relatively inelastic, leading to instability in farmer incomes; (2) technological change has increased productivity, resulting in an excess commitment of resources (particularly farmers) to agriculture, and in surplus capacity;[18] (3) governments must respond with protection and subsidies to keep farmer incomes up because of the political weight of the farm sector.[19] Let us examine each item in turn to see what contribution it makes to the argument.

The question of inelasticities of supply and demand raises two issues: the implications of inelasticity for farmer incomes, and the response of Northern states to Southern calls for international commodity agreements to mitigate fluctuations in their export earnings. Agricultural economists who focus on the economic gains from trade reject the premise that inelasticity of supply and demand require keeping agriculture off the liberal agenda. They counter with three points: the inelasticities are not as large as believed in the 1950s and 1960s, the 1970s demonstrated the potential for exports to shift demand curves outward so that even in the face of inelastic demand total quantity demanded increased, and price instability can be moderated via futures markets and stocks.[20] Nevertheless, Northern governments continue to subsidize excess domestic production, guarantee farmers prices above what a free market would bring, and regulate imports to keep supply from increasing even more.

The three alleged special characteristics are assumed to render farmers inherently vulnerable because of the nature of their economic activity; consequently, they should be protected. Were these in fact the operating principles, we would expect to see Northern governments replicating their domestic farm policies internationally. But Northern governments have countered Southern attempts at managing agricultural trade by advocating the use of futures markets to stabilize prices and arguing that instability in national and farmer income stimulates development.[21] Although they did approve a financing scheme under the International Monetary Fund to counter short-run declines in primary export earnings, they did so only after years of debate and made funds available only under very stringent circumstances and conditions.[22]

As for the argument that agriculture requires protection because of excess commitment of resources and surplus capacity, this is neither inherent in agriculture nor unique to it. In the absence of support for staying in agriculture, and with opportunities for employment in the nonagricultural sectors of the Northern economies, resources (including farmers) could be expected to react to the surplus situation by exiting from agriculture. But farm policy gives them incentives to stay. If the key issue were transferring resources out of agriculture, then Northern agricultural policy should be designed to facilitate such shifts. Although adjustment has occurred, government policy has offset it and stimulated ever higher mountains of surplus butter.

Because economic arguments are inadequate to explain the failure to liberalize agriculture, we turn to political factors. Analyses of the dominant political coalitions in the United States and most of Western Europe demonstrate the key role played by agriculture. Gourevitch describes the coalitions as "built around a set of economic policies that combine Keynesian demand management, an open international economy, trade union autonomy in labor markets, private control of capital in both investment and management, and subsidies for agriculture."[23] These domestic political concerns are the motivating force behind the North's protectionist agricultural policies.

The agricultural case suggests that the potential impact of liberalization on domestic actors and their ability to influence sectoral policy are fundamental determinants of the scope of trade liberalization. The trade experiences of agricultural and strategic raw materials suggest two other conditions for rejecting liberalization of a particular international market. Studies of North-South trade, including Krasner's own earlier work, have demonstrated that the governments of the North will intervene in international markets when they perceive general foreign policy or national security interests at stake.[24] Analysis of trade in the contemporary period thus confronts a theoretical challenge: to develop an explanation of protection under a liberal trade regime that systematically accounts for protectionist outcomes in specified sectors.

Ruggie has taken the first step in constructing an alternative to the conventional liberal paradigm by demonstrating that postwar liberal regimes couple two principles which had previously been seen as inconsistent. These are the belief in an international division of labor based upon comparative advantage, and the need to "minimize socially disruptive domestic adjustment costs as well as any national economic and political vulnerabilities that might accrue from international functional differentiation." This coupling, which he calls "embedded liberalism," was a result of a "social reaction against market rationality" that occurred in the interwar period and altered the nature of liberalism.[25]

The concept of embedded liberalism forms the basis of my understanding of the liberal trade regime. But the implications of the concept for the structure of the regime remain underdeveloped. I build on Ruggie's approach to make an argument about the structure of the embedded liberal trade regime. My approach will account for change within the regime. It will also specify what would constitute a change from this regime to another.

My first focus is on the structure of the regime. Regime analysts have proceeded as if principles and norms of a regime produced a unicameral structure in which traded products that abide by the principles and norms either do or do not fit. One result of this model is that analysts become stymied when they observe protectionism under liberalism. Working within this framework, revisionist liberals (as compared with conventional liberals who reject the concept of liberal protectionism) must argue that liberal protection is anomalous, or perhaps a temporary phenomenon. Its purpose is seen as easing adjustment for the domestic producers of a particular product.[26]

Revisionist liberals, however, face a major problem: in some products (e.g., agricultural and textile), protection is neither predicated upon adjustment efforts by domestic producers, nor is it temporary. These protected products are thus recast as exceptions to the liberal trade regime. As I demonstrated in the case of agriculture, and as Ruggie has demonstrated with the concept of embedded liberalism, if we focus only on those products in which the market guides allocation, we will misinterpret the nature of trade relations within these industries as well as that of trade itself in the international economic order. It is only by examining how all the international trade relationships relate to the whole that we can understand both the whole and the pieces. This means recognizing that in the postwar period, trade in protected and unprotected products has followed the same principles, those of embedded liberalism.

We can avoid distorting our understanding of the nature of liberalism if we allow for a bicameral, or segmented, structure of the liberal trade regime. "Global Liberalism" (the phrase is Krasner's)[27] is actually "Segmented Liberalism": it is divided into a liberal segment, reliant primarily on market allocation, and an illiberal segment, more reliant on explicitly political interventions. These segments are complementary. Trade in products in which domestic costs are too high to allow for free play of the market (see below) is placed in the illiberal segment in order to allow for the market to guide trade in other products.

The distinction between the market and the politically guided segments is not determined geographically or by macroeconomic sector (e.g., agriculture, manufacturing).* Rather, it is determined by the interaction of economics and politics. Consequently, the size of the segments is constantly in flux as products are shifted from one segment to the other *depending upon the outcomes of domestic political battles over protection.* Which products will fall into which segment is a function both of the production characteristics and of the ability of those disadvantaged by trade to force accommodation by their governments. When the major players (the United States, E.E.C., and Japan) have basically complementary market positions, and/or the government authorities have the political leverage to block claims for protection, we find relatively open markets. Complementarity is particularly likely in products characterized by intra-industry specialization.[28] But even in these products state leaders may deem the political costs (including those related to security and/or foreign policy) of market allocation too high, and thus favor the more protectionist approach.

If my argument about segmented liberalism is to hold, I must distinguish between segmented liberalism and illiberalism. Adjustment is critical to the distinction between liberal and illiberal protection. Bargains are often struck in the domestic legislative and administrative process (as well as in international trade negotiations) that exchange protection in one product for liberalization in another. Liberal protection, therefore, is distinguished by its ability to pay-off interests that have the political power to block further liberalization. Illiberal protection, in turn, is that given to producers irrespective of their domestic political power in trade policy.

The concept of a liberal trade regime segmented by different political situations provides a first step toward understanding the political economy of international competitiveness. It helps explain the contrasting

---

*Lipson argues that there exists a potential for segmentation, but along geographic lines (North-South). Charles Lipson, "The transformation of trade: the sources and effects of regime change." My argument is that it already is segmented and along product lines which ignore geography, i.e., protectionism occurs in intra-North trade even within the manufacturing sector.

Northern behavior with respect to the international flow of two factors of production: regulation of labor but free movement of capital. In the case of labor, migration from poor to rich countries has certain economic gains which come from the equalization of labor costs and the inflow of capital to poor countries.[29] But the political externalities are great today (as opposed to the nineteenth century) because of the salience of the issue to members of political coalitions who fear a negative impact on their interests: organized labor (which fears job loss and depressed wages) and taxpayers (who fear expansion of social services to cover foreigners).[30] In contrast, Gilpin has demonstrated that economics as well as international and domestic politics have bolstered the free international movement of investment.[31]

By the same reasoning, the postwar liberalization in manufacturing was facilitated by the convergence of industrial destruction in Europe and Japan as a result of the war and the underdeveloped state of industry in the developing countries. Under these circumstances U.S. industry faced few competitors, European industry could develop in a complementary manner, and the United States could accept Japanese exports which Europeans refused.[32] As these conditions change we should expect to experience a shift toward more managed trade in manufacturing. Such a trend actually began as early as 1955 when the United States maneuvered to limit imports of Japanese textiles.[33] To paraphrase, "Liberal trade is the policy of the efficient."

This argument has great significance for our understanding of the international liberal order. It suggests that the market allocation side of embedded liberalism may be relevant only for particular products in which economic and political conditions combine to produce low adjustment costs in the North. The relatively open trade segment could find itself relevant to fewer and fewer categories of international transactions as the unique postwar environment gives way to a more integrated and competitive world economy. The areas in which market allocation principles maintain precedence may include most of the high value items and therefore allow analysts to demonstrate that most of the world's trade (in value) occurs under a liberal regime. But from the perspective of employment within the North and foreign trade from the South the world might appear increasingly protectionist.

In addition to helping clarify the nature of the contemporary trade regime, agriculture makes a contribution to the understanding of the potential effects of protection. Most liberals consider managed trade to be protecting outmoded production processes and thereby reducing the levels of trade. The agricultural case demonstrates that economic dynamism, both in terms of productivity and trade, is not dependent upon a liberal regime. Despite the exclusion of this sector from the liberalization process, productivity increases outstripped those in manufacturing,[34] while agricultural trade (including North-South) expanded rapidly as well: its value increased more than seven times between 1953 and 1975.[35]

I have argued that trade in the liberal international economic order is governed by the same principles whether markets are protected or free. I also argued that innovation and trade can occur within protected markets. In the next section I propose a framework of analysis that can help specify the manner in which economic and political variables interact to determine whether the opportunity to penetrate a Northern market exists and whether that opportunity will be seized.

A FRAMEWORK FOR ANALYSIS

Trade and production are analytically distinct, though often intimately interrelated. Both are influenced by the international and domestic political economies, but neither determines the other. If trade avenues are closed, production of a particular product might be rerouted toward the domestic market, depending upon the characteristics of the product and home market. Alternatively, an open international market for a particular product does not mean that a country will decide to allocate its scarce resources to that, rather than some other, product.

This assumption and the argument about the political nature of liberal trade combine to suggest a framework for analyzing the political economy of international trade from the perspective of Southern producers. Their ability to achieve international competitiveness depends upon the economic and political openness of the international market and their ability to produce at internationally competitive prices. These two situations, in turn, are the outcome of the interaction among three variables: the characteristics of the product in question, the structure of its international market, and the process by which productive resources are allocated domestically. My argument is that each of these variables, individually and in combination, creates opportunities for, while imposing certain limits on, penetration of international markets.

Product characteristics determine the basic incentives and risks for public and private actors in the market. These incentives determine the potential for competition (e.g., the ease of market entry) and strongly influence the pattern of local politics where everyday business considerations are unimpeded by considerations of realpolitick. But each commodity market's politics are played out in a broader system of political bargaining and state power. Therefore, I look for the degree to which local politics and product characteristics constrain, and are constrained by, the general political economic system of the country. This then provides a gauge for predicting the options in foreign economic strategy. The international trade arrangements for a market emerge from how two (or more) countries' set of feasible options intersect within an international trade regime that imposes a presumption of free trade.

Product Characteristics. The characteristics of a product influence its supply and demand. Some of these are inherent in the product itself, while others reflect the state of production technology at a particular time. Depending upon the nature of the product (service, manufactures, agricultural, or mineral) one or more of the following will create barriers to entry at various stages of production and marketing: geology, biology, and its production function. Each of these influences who produces as well as the speed with which the elasticity of supply affects output. For example, the biological characteristics of sugarcane require certain climatic conditions to thrive and its multiyear life span make it less responsive to short run price signals than a crop planted each season (such as soybeans). The product cycle model has demonstrated the importance of production functions in explaining the location of manufacturing production and patterns of trade.[36] Size of fixed costs also affects sensitivity of output to price fluctuations; for example, steel producers will react more slowly to shifts in demand than will textile firms. In addition, certain characteristics of the product will influence demand, chiefly through the degree of substitutability (e.g., cotton's competition with synthetic fibers makes it very price sensitive but the lack of a close substitute for petroleum gives it a low elasticity of demand) and whether it is an "inferior" good whose consumption declines as income rises.

In general, the characteristics of a product or of its production process influence product homogeneity via its substitutability and the levels of the barriers to entry. Of course, the pace and location of technological innovation are affected by state policy toward education, research subsidies, tax incentives, etc. Product characteristics help determine the level of competition in a market. In addition, markets with low barriers to entry are more likely to be regulated politically. The increased use of nontariff barriers by the North for manufactures that are well advanced in the product cycle would be an example. In addition, the characteristics of a product will influence the issues confronted in allocating scarce resources among competing uses. For example, a product which demands intensive use of a resource in great demand (such as water in arid zones or credit in poor countries) will more likely lead to a politicization of allocation.

Market Structures. The structure of the market—the second component of my model—will also influence both the product characteristics and the domestic allocation of resources. Markets that are competitive are more likely to produce technological innovations that can alter the production process or even the genetic make-up of a product as firms search for ways to stay ahead of the competition. In addition, the competitiveness of the market will influence the weight which market participants can utilize in the domestic political bargaining over allocation of a country's resources.

International market structure is defined in terms of its economic competitiveness (competitive, monopolistic, or oligopolistic) and political openness (free or managed access). The possibilities for import penetration in a market are consequently the result of both economic competitiveness and political openness.

The competitiveness of a market is especially influenced by "product homogeneity among suppliers . . . and the freedom of entry into the industry."[37] But even markets with domestic competition may at the same time regulate imports. In addition, there are cases in which countries that are not economically competitive are allocated market shares because the importing country perceives foreign policy concerns at stake.[38] Under such circumstances, the political openness of a market becomes important.

The degree of state intervention in a particular market varies according to the degree of mobilization of, and resources available to, those who find themselves at a disadvantage in it.* Public intervention in a market should be understood to result from its extension to incorporate new participants who threaten to upset the prevailing distribution of resources, and therefore benefits, in those markets. This challenge makes countries more sensitive to the international political economy. Although measures of this sensitivity are highly imperfect, most analysts agree that sensitivity to international markets has increased in both the North and South.[39]

As sensitivity to international markets increased states faced three choices: opt out of the game, change the rules of the game, or master a strategy for playing by the rules which offers greater benefit. Autarchy is not a particularly attractive alternative, a fact underlined by the opening of the socialist economies to the Western liberal economy in the 1970s. The option of altering the rules to favor a particular distribution of resources is open to few. In the last three hundred years only Britain and the United States have redesigned the rules of international economic interaction.[40]

Most players have had to operate within the existing structure, taking advantage of inherent possibilities,[41] or stretching the rules in their favor.[42] From the perspective of a state facing loss of market share to imports, it may follow one of two basic patterns. It could adjust to the changing distribution of competitive advantage either by altering domestic production to become more efficient or by protecting the old domestic economic structure from more efficient competitors.

Which of these broad strategies will guide adjustment decisions varies not only from country to country, but also by economic sector and even by industry within a sector. The literature typically points to four determinants of whether to seek competitiveness or protection: security of supply (especially for) raw materials markets, general foreign policy concerns, domestic politics (the chief determinant of Northern decisions to insulate the agricultural sector from the liberalization taking place in

---

*Lindbloom points out that even when we see conflict-free exchange, "It is possible only because the conflicts over who gets what have already been settled through a distribution of property rights in society. Was that distribution conflict free? Obviously not. Was it noncoercively achieved? Obviously not." Charles E. Lindbloom, *Politics and Markets*, p. 46.

manufacturing), and ideological conceptions about the desirability of a liberal international economy.[43]

From the perspective of the exporting state, attainment of international economic competitiveness may be insufficient. In the face of trade barriers against more efficient producers, exports must negotiate access. Success often requires explicit political bargaining to adopt technical formulas allowing for some continued market penetration. Odell and Yoffie have analyzed this process from the perspective of state to state negotiations and I follow their lead.[44] But their studies did not illuminate the domestic politics side of international bargaining. Because of the fundamental importance of domestic acceptance of such agreements I include domestic production politics in my analysis.

In addition, there are political and economic difficulties faced by entrepreneurs attempting to produce a product at internationally competitive prices. Entrepreneurs must not only be aware of those opportunities and desirous of seizing them, but must have access to the resources with which to formulate a response. Along with access comes the issue of the ability to organize a coherent response, particularly if barriers are low and oversupply a real danger. These concerns mean that analysis should be concerned not only with the competition among international firms, but also with the struggle over the organization of production at the national level in order to see how domestic resource allocation shapes international trade strategies.

Domestic Allocation. The third component of the framework for the analysis of international competitiveness, then, is the process by which productive resources are allocated domestically. International competitiveness requires a flexible domestic economic structure to respond to changes in the international economy. The openness of the national economy, however, has the potential of leading to political battles over the distribution of adjustment costs. If the economic and political costs of shifting from one product to another are acceptable to the state* and

---

*Understood as "a set of institutions (the civil and military bureaucracy—the state apparatus) and those who formally control them (the government)." Nora Hamilton, *The Limits of State Autonomy*, pp. 6–7. And operationalized as the decision makers central to the particular issue-area. Stephen D. Krasner, *Defending the National Interest*, pp. 10–13.

the dominant social forces, competition may be manifested in the form of individual entrepreneurs responding to market signals about the profitability of different crops. Alternatively, if the costs of such a switch are high (because of large fixed costs in the old crop, high barriers to entry for the new, ideology, national security, unemployment, etc.), competition for resources will occur by clashing claims on government rather than changes in the private marketplace.

While the question of the division of costs and benefits of adjustment confronts every country, the means by which it is settled varies considerably.[45] Of particular importance are the relationships between the representatives of the state and the different social groups relevant to the economic sector under competitive pressure. Much of the debate about the "ungovernability" of the advanced industrial societies and the political prerequisites for economic development in the newly industrializing countries (NICs) thus naturally focus on the means by which interest groups' demands are addressed.[46] This domestic structure is conditioned by both history and the ideological biases of the political elite.[47]

There are a number of studies on the domestic politics of international competitiveness. Most political economy analysts agree (but for an important dissent see Gourevitch),[48] that the structure of the domestic political economy is key to determining the range of policy tools state leaders can utilize to help direct the allocation and price of productive resources necessary for international competitiveness. Analysts then become very proprietary, arguing that the particular tool utilized in their case study holds the key to success. Among those identified are control over the allocation of credit, the exchange rate, the labor movement, or the character (size, skill, and independence) of the bureaucracy.[49]

What these studies demonstrate is that there is no one "tool" to carry out the domestic restructuring that may be necessary to attain, or maintain, international competitiveness. We can see this more clearly if we think of international competitiveness as the result of costs of production and of marketing, as well as the result of political negotiation over the openness of a market. Which factor matters most is the result of product characteristics, the structure of the international market, and the constraints of domestic political bargains—precisely the issues highlighted by my model.

The domestic allocation of resources influences international competitiveness directly via provision of necessary resources at competitive prices and also indirectly through its influence on market structure. Scarcity of resources means that some users will have access and others not. Users will be determined by the price mechanism and/or politics; in either case the allocation will contribute to the competitive situation in a particular market and to the demands for political regulation by those who may be losing competitiveness because they cannot use the resource in question.

My argument is that the degree of international competitiveness is the result of the manner in which the three components combine, as figure 1 shows schematically. This book uses the Mexican fresh winter vegetable case to illustrate the usefulness of this framework. There is a paucity of political economy literature analyzing efforts by Southern enterprises to compete internationally, integrate forward and, in the process, become multinational. The conclusion to the book incorporates analyses done by economists and management analysts and puts them in a comparative perspective to suggest the relevance and explanatory power of this political economy framework outside this particular case study.

A TRI-LEVEL ANALYSIS

Before analyzing the case study, it is necessary to confront a methodological issue. The "standard" international political economy analysis begins with the assumption that there are both international sources of domestic politics as well as domestic sources of international politics. Domestic politics is usually operationalized as state and interest groups confronting each other at the national level. Such an approach may be sufficient for analyzing macroeconomic policy where the number of local actors is sufficiently large to reduce them to "price takers." But in sectoral policy local actors become more important. Workers can influence policy more directly with their level of productivity, local entrepreneurs with their level of investment. Thus in sectoral analysis we need to include the preferences and bargaining power of local actors, as well as their ability to circumvent policy.

We can significantly increase the explanatory power of the proposed framework of analysis for international competitiveness if we conceive

A Framework for the Analysis of
International Competitiveness

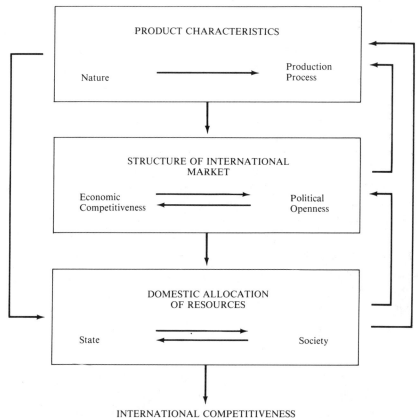

of the process of international market penetration as the result of the interaction of three levels of analysis: the international, the national, and the local. As in the case of the international and national focus for macroeconomic policy, in sectoral policy the three levels of analysis are interrelated; the challenge is to illuminate the relationship among the three.

The International Level. The international political economy plays a major role in Sinaloa's agricultural development, providing both opportunities and limits to growth and distribution. Since the late 1800s Sinaloan agriculture has been export oriented, with sugar, chickpeas, sesame, winter vegetables, and cotton finding their way to the United States, Canada, Cuba, Europe, and Japan. But the winter fresh fruit and vegetable agribusiness commodity system has been the dominant force,* accounting for over a third of the value of Sinaloa's agricultural production today.

Sinaloa's climate and geographical location just 600 miles south of the Arizona border made it a convenient site for production of winter fresh fruits and vegetables for the U.S. market (which began in 1906). In addition, the supply of cheap migrant labor in Mexico made production of a crop with high capital costs and great demand for labor, possible. The expansion of consumption of fresh vegetables in the U.S. market, the shift of California and Texas out of winter production for economic reasons, the exclusion of Cuba for political reasons, and freezes and rising production costs in Florida led to a constant expansion of Mexican production from the late 1950s until the late 1970s.

The international vegetable trade affects Sinaloa in a variety of ways. Most obviously, the export boom in winter vegetables has been the key to the economic growth experienced by the state. As a result of the success of the trade public and private investment increased, fueling development along the lines of staple theory and via forward/backward linkages.[50] In the process a social class, the farmworkers, has been dramatically fortified, while the growers utilized the trade to increase their own economic weight.

This international commodity system helps structure the context within which local actors interact by strengthening antagonistic social forces at the local level and heightening tensions among them. In addition, their position in the commodity system gives local actors the opportunity to make demands upon that system. Of course, local actors face constraints at the international level, too. Among the most important are that cost competitiveness must be maintained and supply guaranteed. Because the state's economy revolves around the winter vegetable trade Sinaloa also finds itself extremely vulnerable to changes which affect that international market. Such changes may be due to weather, a change in consumption or production patterns and, perhaps

---

*An agribusiness commodity system encompasses all the participants involved in the production, processing, and marketing of a single farm product." Ray A. Goldberg, *Agribusiness Management for Developing Countries—Latin America* (Cambridge, Mass.: Ballinger, 1974), p. 44. For an elaboration, see chapter 2.

most importantly, small changes in trade legislation in the consuming countries, in particular that of the United States.

The National Level. The Mexican state has also been an important actor in Sinaloa's development and its vegetable production. As in other late developing countries, the state in Mexico assumed a role as regulator of economic activity and social interaction. With respect to the agribusiness commodity system, policy decisions regarding the location and type of public investment affect entrepreneurs' decisions on private investment. Although production of winter vegetables for export predates construction of the transportation and irrigation networks that span Sinaloa, the boom in exports of the last quarter century would not have been possible without this massive social overhead capital investment by the state. In addition, by prohibiting direct foreign ownership of the Sinaloa vegetable lands (they fall within the fifty-kilometer distance from the coast where ownership is constitutionally limited to nationals) the state effectively made the presence of national producers an integral part of the international political economy of the winter vegetable trade. Finally, by stimulating the rural organization of the growers and legally supporting the ability of the farmer elite to control production and exports, the state laid the foundation for avoiding early tendencies to respond to price increases by oversupplying the market and thus depressing prices.

In terms of the local political economy, the Mexican state becomes a factor to consider not only because of the flow of resources it directs into Sinaloa, but also because of the role it plays in the ability of local groups to organize in defense of their self-defined interests. The Mexican state has been aptly characterized at the national level as authoritarian and corporatist.* The limited pluralism and directed participation char-

---

*An authoritarian regime is one with "limited, not responsible pluralism, without elaborate or guiding ideology (but with distinctive mentalities), without intensive nor extensive mobilization (except at some point in their development), and in which a leader (or occasionally a small group) exercises power within formally ill-defined limits, but actually quite predictable ones." Juan Linz, "Totalitarian and Authoritarian Regimes," in Fred I. Greenstein and Nelson W. Polsby, eds., *Handbook of Political Science* Vol. 3 (Reading, Mass.: Addison-Wesley, 1975), p. 264; under corporatism there are a "limited number of singular, compulsory, noncompetitive, hierarchically ordered and functionally differentiated categories, recognized or licensed (if not created) by the state and granted a deliberate representational monopoly within their

acteristic of this type of regime, combined with the capitalist nature of the Mexican state, suggest that the intervention of the state in Sinaloa would be in favor of the interests of the farmers who constitute the rural elite.* Nevertheless, the ideology of the Mexican revolution and the heritage of organic statism have given the state itself an interest to protect.† Consequently, the state has undertaken the critical function of regulating sociopolitical and economic interactions among the various social forces.

Of course, society is not totally responsive to state manipulation; the attempt by the state to channel demand articulation through established mechanisms cannot be assumed to be successful in all instances. One must, therefore, discern under what circumstances and with which issues the state is able effectively to play this role. In addition, one must ask what are the implications of success and failure of the state in this area for Sinaloa's vegetable production.

The state also has an indirect influence on the development process. As the state affects each of these political economies and as they interact with one another,‡ the state affects each of the other two indirectly. For example, the implications of state and society relations in Sinaloa go beyond the borders of Mexico to influence the international winter

---

respective categories in exchange for observing certain controls on their selection of leaders and articulation of demands and supports." Philippe C. Schmitter, "Still the Century of Corporatism?" *Review of Politics* (January 1974), 36:93–94. I elaborate on this in chapter 3.

*Farmers are considered to be producers in the private sector with more than five hectares. Although beneficiaries of the Agrarian Reform *(ejidatarios)* in these irrigated districts are very integrated into the market, their inability to mortgage their land to creditors (because they have usufruct and not property rights) means that it would be misleading to expect them to respond in the same way to market forces, since their access to credit is generally limited to inadequate public funds. I shall refer to them as *ejidatarios* or peasants.

†"'Organic' . . . refers to a normative vision of the political community in which the component parts of society harmoniously combine to enable the full development of man's potential. 'Statist' is used because of the assumption in this tradition that such harmony does not occur spontaneously in the process of historical evolution but rather requires power, rational choices and decisions, and occasional restructuring of civil society by political elites." Stepan, pp. 26–27, n. 58.

‡Obviously the implications of the three-level analysis I am using in the study are that the political economy of each level can only be understood as part of an interaction of all three levels. Thus there really is only one political economy. As long as this is understood I think it possible to revert to the fiction of separate political economies for the sake of clarity in stating the argument.

vegetable agribusiness commodity system, which in turn influences Sinaloa in its own right. The chief means through which this indirect effect is produced is by the Sinaloa rural elite (with the state as an ally) successfully demanding more of the surplus produced within that international commodity market. The state played a major role in the organization of the rural elite during the 1930s and subsidized it for a quarter of a century. Because of this effort by the state, which was interested in guaranteeing agricultural production and asserting control over political demand articulation, this organization was kept alive during the lean years of international trade. Consequently, when the export boom came, the Sinaloa growers were prepared to take advantage of it and, in fact, had been given the means through which to begin to dominate the trade.

Local Level. The third level of analysis is that of the local political economy. Economic growth based largely upon exports provides both the opportunities and the limits for the bargaining strength of local social forces. Thus, precisely because of the importance of foreign exchange and jobs, local actors essential to the production process acquire added bargaining power in the national arena. Successful attempts of the farmers to integrate forward, of labor to increase its wages and benefits, and of peasants to win land concessions have resulted in foreign capital moving out of direct participation in production to avoid land and labor confrontations and even giving way in the marketing phase as domestic capital moves into distribution.

Yet, Sinaloan demands cannot be so great or rigidly pursued to lead investors, retailers, or consumers to a search for new sources of supply. Like many commodity producers Sinaloa can command a premium as long as its quality, reliability, or transport cost advantages are great enough to have consumers content not to pay the cost to switch suppliers. But once they do, Sinaloa's economic importance for the national and international political economies would diminish, and along with it the negotiating power local forces built upon it. Moreover, Sinaloan interest groups can not push for changes that would challenge the state's right and ability to orient the national political economy.

The Sinaloa case nevertheless indicates that much negotiation as well as distribution can occur before either the economic or political limits are breeched. And so, despite the general characterization of the Mexican regime as authoritarian-corporatist, local social forces *are* able to bargain with the state over development and distribution policies. The extent and nature of this negotiation indicate that the state's response is not limited to the "ignore-coopt-repress the leaders" formulation emphasized by much of the literature,[51] but that an important part of the state's response in bargaining is the satisfying of some of the demands of workers and peasants.

This study thus emphasizes that the Mexican state and local social forces can and do modify the terms of interaction with the international market and capital. But the analysis also makes clear that the relatively independent action of each group vis-à-vis the international economy and/or the Mexican state depends upon a continuation of Sinaloa's particular pattern of development. A decline in growth stimulated by the export economy or a switch to other crops as the catalyst to Sinaloan and/or Mexican development will imply a shift in political and economic power which will affect all actors and consequently the alliance supporting winter vegetable production.

In summary, the framework of analysis tells us which variables are important in determining international competitiveness and how they relate to each other. These variables include characteristics of the product, the structure of the international market, and the domestic allocation of resources. The tri-level mode of analysis argues that in order to understand the relationship among the three variables in the framework it is necessary to add local actors and influences to the standard international political economy methodology which integrates international and national sources of politics.

This book uses the Mexican fresh winter vegetable case to illustrate the usefulness of this framework. The analysis in part 1 focuses on the opportunities which the international market presented Mexico (chapter 2) and the basis upon which the Mexican state and Mexican growers allied to address those opportunities (chapter 3). In part 2 the analysis turns to the competition for those resources necessary for production. I am particularly concerned with illuminating the economic and political processes through which scarce inputs are allocated to produce a crop at an internationally competitive price and in sufficient supply. Chapter 4 examines the distribution of water, chapter 5 analyzes access to farmland, and chapter 6 focuses on labor costs. Part 3 shifts to examine foreign challenges to Mexican international competitiveness. Chapter

7 analyses the process by which the state-grower alliance turned a U.S. industry located in Mexico into one controlled by Mexican capital. Chapter 8 examines the transnationalization of the alliance for Mexican competitiveness in order to defeat attempts by U.S. competitors to construct nontariff barriers to imports from Mexico. Chapter 9 demonstrates that variations in market characteristics and state-society relations, as captured by my model, produce different outcomes when comparing two other countries (Colombia and South Korea) in the international textile market.

This is a study at the juncture of domestic politics and international relations, as are many of the international political economy. It differs from others, however, in its insistence that the dynamics of local politics are not necessarily the same as that of national politics. Hence this study's tri-level analysis and its focus upon the abilities and limits of local groups to make both national and international politics and forces respond to some needs at the local level. The relevance of the Sinaloa case, of course, derives not from a wholesale transfer of the particulars of this case to another, but rather from the focus on institutional and structural factors of both the international and the domestic political economies which allow for effective inputs from the bottom up. The concluding chapter brings a comparative perspective to underline the power of such an analytic framework.

I

A MEXICAN STATE–GROWER ALLIANCE FOR PROFITS AND CONTROL

2

AGRIBUSINESS AND THE U.S.–MEXICO FRESH WINTER VEGETABLE TRADE

This chapter sets the international economic and political context for the analysis of the winter vegetable trade. Attention is focused on the intimate relationship among climate, economics, and politics in the creation of a structure of international trade between the two countries. It provides a political economy analysis which is sufficiently complex to allow us to appreciate the opportunities faced by Mexican growers, the domestic and international challenges to their ability to be internationally competitive, and the need for an alliance with the state to respond favorably to those opportunities and challenges.

The chapter is organized into three sections. In the first I investigate the agribusiness commodity system which developed to service the U.S. market. Of particular interest here is the evolution of the position of Mexican growers in that system. In the second and third sections I examine the political economy of the U.S.-Mexican market and the cost competitiveness of the two principal producers for that market, Sinaloa and Florida. Although the agribusiness commodity system for fresh winter vegetables is a truly international one—with the United States, Canada, Europe, and Japan as buyers and southern Europe, northern Africa, the Caribbean, Central America, and Mexico as producers—I focus on the U.S. fresh winter vegetable market because of its overwhelming importance to the development of the Mexican trade in vegetables. I then analyze the determinants of cost competitiveness in that market in order to understand the important fluctuations which have occurred on the supply side of the market.

AN AGRIBUSINESS COMMODITY SYSTEM—
FRESH WINTER VEGETABLES

Davis and Goldberg developed a model designed to illuminate the complexity and interaction of all the actors who participate in producing a particular crop and getting it to the consumers' tables. In their formulation,

An agribusiness commodity system encompasses all the participants involved in the production, processing, and marketing of a single farm product. Such a system includes farm suppliers, farmers, storage operators, processors, wholesalers, and retailers involved in a commodity flow from initial inputs to the final consumer. It also includes all the institutions which affect and coordinate the successive stages of a commodity flow such as the government, futures markets, and trade associations.[1]

For analysts interested in the interaction between domestic and international capital, as well as state intervention which influences that relationship, this concept provides an ideal starting place. Figure 2 presents a flow diagram of the Mexican side of the U.S. fresh winter vegetable agribusiness commodity system.* Each of the functions is distinguished for illustrative purposes, but the actual coordination and integration of each has evolved over time toward greater concentration.

Within this system coordination between levels was historically very loose. On the input side we find the number of private foreign and domestic firms as well as state-owned enterprises producing and marketing products. Production of crates is dominated by Mexican capital, although one transnational corporation (TNC) and one Mexican grower also have companies engaged in this activity.[2] Tractors are provided by six TNCs (Ford, Massey-Ferguson, Caterpillar, John Deere, International, and Komatsu), all of which operate in Culiacán through dealerships owned by the major Mexican growers. Fertilizer—except for potassium, which is imported—is provided by FERTIMEX, a state company. Seeds come overwhelmingly from six or seven independent agents in Arizona who sell a selection from a number of companies; although Mexicans also produce seed, they supply only 5 percent of demand.[3] These examples demonstrate a separation of tasks at this

---

*For a figure of the marketing system of the overall U.S. fruit and vegetable system, including all seasons and domestic production, see Ray A. Goldberg, *Agribusiness Management for Developing Countries–Latin America*, p. 44.

Mexico in the
U.S. Fresh Winter Vegetable Commodity System

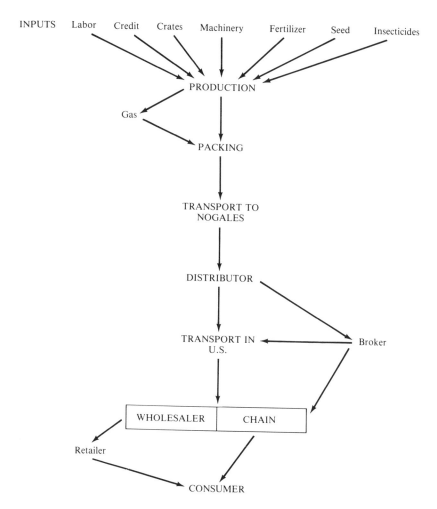

level of the agribusiness system except when we consider the Mexican growers who have integrated backward. No evidence was found that TNCs who provide inputs at this stage have ever integrated forward.

At the level of the producer, wholesaler, and retailer the perishability of the crops leads participants at each level to act on short-term criteria to maximize immediate returns. As the fresh fruit and vegetable system extended itself throughout the U.S. market, there was a tendency toward a large number of small units acting at each stage, in accordance with local market information.[4] Originally, immigrants from the Greek-American and Japanese-American communities, with ties to U.S. produce distributors, produced winter vegetables for export in northwest Mexico. Their success brought other U.S. entrepreneurs who provided capital for Mexican growers to plant these crops.

Vertical integration by foreigners, however, was difficult because Mexican law forbade foreigners from owning land along the coast (the prime vegetable-producing lands are located here). For those willing to trade in their citizenship these restrictions were irrelevant. For some entrepreneurs marrying off sons and daughters to Mexicans was more attractive.* Nevertheless, most foreigners attracted to the winter vegetable "deal" (as participants refer to it) were interested only in making a profit, not in leaving part of their families in Mexico. For them, contracting production was the answer.

While legislation guaranteed a role for Mexican landowners, Mexican capital was loath to invest in such a risky and expensive enterprise. The U.S. distributors became the principal source of capital to the industry.

At least two types of contractual arrangements developed between independent distributors and growers. The standard contract between the two entrepreneurs is one in which the distributor advances seasonal capital to the grower, which can cover everything from pre- to postharvest expenses. In return, the grower commits himself to sending all the produce to the distributor. A distributor can either market it under his own label or use a particular grower's label. The distributor then deducts a sales commission (which varies from 10 to 15 percent), rotates the capital back into Mexico, and, at the end of the season, the remaining funds are used to reimburse the distributor for his advances, with the grower receiving the remaining amount.[5] For those growers who do not need an infusion of working capital from a distributor but do value his marketing functions, another type of relationship can be worked out. In this case an understanding between grower and distributor

---

*For example, the father of the president of one of the larger Arizona distributors, James K. Wilson Co., married off one of his daughters to a local notable family, the Bon Bustamantes (see chapter 3). North American Congress on Latin America (NACLA), "Harvest of Anger," p. 15. The association has produced a formidable enterprise in the Mexican vegetable industry.

commits each to finance independently their respective operations on their side of the border. The grower agrees to send all export production to the distributor, who must liquidate all accounts within one week of receipt of shipment.[6]

The distributor's key role in financing and marketing led him to play the dominant role in the U.S.- Mexican winter vegetable market in its early stages of development. During this period, roughly from 1906 to the mid-1960s, an individual with drive and access to capital could move right to the top. One of the most successful distributors illustrates these possibilities well. Tooru Takahashi was a second-generation Japanese-American, son of a Los Angeles produce man. After World War II, he moved to Culiacán to fish for shark, its liver being valuable for producing vitamins. In Culiacán he met a Japanese-Mexican, Jorge Kondo, who shipped vegetables into Los Angeles. When synthetic vitamins dropped the bottom out of the shark liver market, Takahashi became a partner with Kondo. In 1959 Takahashi moved to Nogales, Arizona, and set up his distributorship, Kitty's Vegetable Distributors, Inc. His particular enterprise became one of the most successful in Nogales, and upon his death in 1982 his wife became president of the company.[7].

The industry's newspaper, *The Packer*, carries numerous stories quite similar to Takahashi's, although few are as successful. These experiences point up a variety of characteristics about distributorships which help explain subsequent developments that began to marginalize U.S.-owned companies from this stage of the commodity system. First is the importance of immigrants, both in the United States and Mexico. Greeks, Japanese, Germans, Italians, French, and others are intimately integrated into the industry. Second, we have the family nature of the enterprise. Again, on both sides of the border family members are found in most of the leadership positions of a company, and familial ties between distributor and grower are quite common.

A third and perhaps the most important characteristic of the distributing phase of the commodity system is the permeability of the distributing business. Barriers to entry are relatively low. The product is a service that can easily be offered in a warehouse with low overhead costs. The major requirements are time and access to capital. Time is crucial because the perishability of the crop means that sales prices often fluctuate dramatically in the same day,[8] and working hours begin early and end late. Long hours and the low barriers to entry probably

TABLE 2.1
Volatility of Distributorships (Nogales, Arizona)

Year[a]	Total	Closings	Openings
1970	46		
1971	51	10	5
1973	55		
1974	51	7	3
1977	47		4
1981		3	12
1982		3	14

SOURCE: *The Packer*, yearly supplement, "West Mexico Winter Vegetables."
NOTE: Figures for missing years and categories unavailable.
[a] Year for the beginning of the winter season.

explain the strength of family ties in the distributing phase of the industry: relatives work longer for less pay and benefits than others, and are less likely to use the experience they gain to set up their own competing companies.

Family enterprise is not the only type of distributor at the point of entry. Some agribusiness corporations, which may themselves be constructed around family ties,* and which have long been active in the U.S. produce system, set up shop in Nogales, Arizona, when Mexican exports to the United States boomed.

Two other enterprises at the port of entry also play important roles: the broker and the chain buyer. Independent brokers act as intermediaries between the wholesaler/retailer and the distributor. The chain buyer, in turn, is the retailer's direct representative.

Low barriers to entry and the possibility of high profits lead to high turnover rates in the distributing and brokerage phases (see table 2.1). Despite the volatility of the enterprise, there is a good deal of concentration at this level. In the mid-1970s, the industry newspaper reported that seven companies controlled over 50 percent of the produce moving through Nogales.[9]

Well aware of the profit potential, retailers have dramatically expanded space allocated to fresh produce both in the supermarket and at specialty shops. Whereas before the increased consumer interest in

* Deardorff-Jackson of Oxnard, Calif., is an example. NACLA, "Harvest of Anger," p. 16.

fresh produce a store allocated about 3 to 4 percent of total space to these products, today a "conservative estimate" is approximately 11 to 13 percent. In addition, variety has increased: in 1975 a produce department carried about 65 items, in 1980 this had risen to 135, and estimates are that today larger stores can carry over 250 items.[10] This response by the retailer benefits not only the consumer but the retailer as well. As one report notes:

> In 1980, the produce department had the highest average gross margin, approximately 31 percent among the major grocery store department categories[a] . . . While information on the net profit is scanty, industry spokesmen generally assume that produce is one of the highest, if not the highest, contributor to the net store profit. The industry seems to accept estimates of produce contribution to net store profit in the 25–30 percent range. One United Fresh Fruit and Vegetable Association study concluded that the share of store net profit accounted for by the produce department may be as high as 36.5 percent.[11]

The profit potential of the produce section and technological changes that allow retailers to identify consumer demands more closely[12] have encouraged retailers to shift costs and risks backward. One of the most comprehensive recent studies of the U.S. produce marketing system reports that "considerable" labor activities and warehouse space have been transferred from wholesale-retail areas to the less expensive labor and property areas of shipping points. In addition, retailers are increasingly calling for a wide variety of fruits and vegetables to be included in shipments, thereby putting the smaller distributor who works only a few types of vegetables at a disadvantage.[13]

If that analysis of the dynamics of the U.S. produce system is correct, Nogales distributors are doing very well in fighting off the pressure from the retail end. There is one very important structural characteristic of the Nogales import system which is fundamental to explaining the ability of these particular distributors to buck the national trend. Of the five major winter vegetables imported from Mexico, over 94 percent enters the U.S. market via Nogales.[14] This concentration of supply leads to a concentration of distributors in the area; in fact, over fifty distributors are located in a 15-mile radius. Under these circumstances the small distributor is not necessarily placed at a disadvantage vis-à-vis large distributors who work a variety of vegetables. Because the supermarket chains are increasingly giving their brokers a specific volume to fill, rather than letting them operate according to the situation at shipping point, small distributors can compete on the basis of price and quality. Under these conditions, the chain's broker/buyer visits a variety of distributors to fill his order.[15]

Even the case of technology does not support the view that a clear shift of power has occurred in favor of the chains. Interviews at the Nogales port of entry indicated that some technological change had negative consequences for distributors because of rigidities introduced into marketing. Apparently, chains are now setting two-week lead times on sales in order to program their computers at the retail site. This is disadvantageous to the distributor because the traditional means of confronting a sudden increase in supply was to convince a chain to run a sale on a particular item.

Despite the decreased ability of the chain to respond to the needs of the distributor (and the grower who sends him produce), there are at least two ways for the distributor to shift risk back to the retail end. First, there are the brokers affiliated with farmers' markets in large cities, working for smaller independent grocery stores and/or specialty shops, and the independent brokers who seek out buyers. They play a fundamental role in absorbing large fluctuations in supply.[16] Second, the two-week time lag can also be used against the chain. During one interview with a grower-owned distributor, I discovered that risk is still not a one-way street.

My host was interrupted by a phone call from his Mexican boss: he was displeased with the prices peppers were bringing. The distributor called an independent broker in Florida to ascertain the situation in the U.S. fields: bountiful. The grower was then informed and made the decision to plow under his maturing peppers in hopes that the market would increase prices for the next cycle of maturing plants. After this discussion, the distributor notified a buyer for a U.S. supermarket chain that he was unable to supply the quantity promised earlier for the store's upcoming sale. The buyer was left to scramble for alternative sources or face losses in the supermarket's already programmed sale.[17]

At the same time distributors are coming under increased cost pressure from retailers, they are facing the increasingly aggressive Mexican grower in search of larger profits. Chapter 7 examines the transformation of Mexican participation. For now let us just have a look at this group and their successes.

There are formally over two thousand vegetable growers in Mexico who produce for the U.S. market.[18] But that is a meaningless number, a fiction created by the Mexican rural elite to avoid land reform. For example, in the group of growers headed by René Carrillo Caraza, twenty-two individual growers are listed; of these thirteen are Carrillos, four are Barrazas, and five Carazas. Roberto Tarriba Rojo heads a group of thirteen, consisting of his wife, sons and daughters. As a U.S. customs investigator claims Tarriba Rojo explained it to him, "If he were in any other country, he would be considered to be the sole producer."[19] Although there are over four hundred tomato permits granted in the Culiacán region,[20] one knowledgeable source estimated that forty-three growers control those permits.[21]

Back in the 1950s a few growers were self-financing and had their own distributorships, but the vast majority were caught in a financial and commercially unequal relationship with U.S. distributorships. Since the early 1970s, that situation has undergone significant change. By 1979 Mexican growers had "significant" financial interests in at least half of the distributorships in Arizona which handled their produce.[22] Table 2.2 is a partial list of distributorships in Arizona in which a controlling interest is held by a Mexican grower. From this table it is clear that some Mexican growers are playing an increasingly important and independent role in the U.S. fresh winter vegetable agribusiness commodity system. The literature on the U.S.-Mexico vegetable relationship has ignored this outcome, some because they have not seen it,[23] while others who are aware of the complexity of transborder capital flows either find it difficult to perceive Southern capital extending into the domain of Northern capital[24] or are not interested in the question of power relations.[25] Before we can address this and other issues, we need to know more about the market.

THE U.S. FRESH WINTER VEGETABLE MARKET

The U.S. imports over sixteen different winter vegetables from Mexico, but the major fresh ones are tomatoes, cucumbers, peppers, eggplant, and squash (see table 2.3). The winter vegetable season is actually composed of three shorter cycles: fall (November–December), winter (January–March), and early spring (April–June). California and Texas are major suppliers (accounting for more than 10 percent) in the fall for

TABLE 2.2
U.S. Distributorships Controlled by Mexican Growers

Firm	Grower
Sigma Produce	Trifonas Strabrospulos
TriCar Sales	Daniel Cárdenas Izabal
Rene Produce Distributors, Inc.	Rene Carrillo Caraza
Frank's Distributing, Inc.	Frank Echavarria Rojo
Farmers Best	Roberto Tarriba Rojo
Bravo Distributing, Inc.	José Maria Gallardo
Omega Produce, Inc.	George Gotsis (a)
Melrose Produce Distributors	José U. López (b)
GAC Produce, Inc.	Canelos family (c)
LISA, Inc.	Lichter family (d)
Ta-De Distributing Co.	Tamayo brothers (e)
Sucasa Produce, Inc.	Three unnamed growers (f)
	Arturo & Ricardo Murillo Monge (g)
	Angel & Jorge Demetrio (h)
Rolit	Jorge & Enrique Rodarte (i)
San Rafael	Adolfo & Marco Antonio Clouthier (j)

SOURCES: U.S. Department of Commerce files and as noted:

(a) (d) (i) & (j): Confidential interviews with three distributors in Nogales, Arizona, 1983; George Gotsis is the son of a Culiacán grower.

(b) José U. López was president and Ascension U. Lopez the grower in Los Mochis, Sinaloa; they closed in 1981. *The Packer,* January 22, 1983, p. 9B.

(c) *The Packer.*

(e) Ta-De stands for Tamayo and Demerutis. In 1979 Charles and Robert Bennen owned half of the company's stock, and five Tamayo brothers owned the other half, part of which they acquired by buying out the Demerutis. U.S. Department of Commerce files.

(f) *The Packer,* January 22, 1983, p. 9B reports that this distributorship was created by three unnamed growers.

(g) *The Packer,* January 16, 1982; their unnamed firm closed in 1981–82.

(h) *The Packer,* January 22, 1983 p. 18B; their unnamed firm closed in 1979–80

tomatoes, peppers, and squash and again in the spring for cucumbers and squash. Florida is dominant in the fall and spring for all crops, with over 50 percent of supply for all vegetables except squash, of which its share is one-third (1974–1979 figures). Sinaloa, in turn, has been increasing its participation in the fall and spring quarters for all crops, and competes with Florida's share in the spring for tomatoes and eggplant. Florida and Sinaloa are unchallenged in the winter quarter.[26] Because climate allows only Florida and Sinaloa to supply the market over the course of these months and because of their dominance in the

TABLE 2.3
*U.S. Winter Vegetable Imports from Mexico
November 1982–May 1983*

Commodity	Value (U.S. $1,000)
Tomatoes	195,791
Cucumbers	50,229
Peppers	39,393
Squash	26,059
Asparagus	11,545
Eggplant	8,403
Lettuce	1,979
Brussels sprouts	1,554
Cabbage	546
Cauliflower	372
Okra	357
Corn on the cob	252
Endive	84
Broccoli	50
Chayote	23
Pumpkin	4
Other[a]	368

SOURCE: USDA, Foreign Agricultural Service, *U.S. Agricultural Imports*, Report 1, 07/08/83, pp. 003, 004.

[a] Includes broccoli, cauliflower, and okra entering under a different TSUS number as well as nonspecified.

fall and early spring, one can usefully refer to the entire period as the "winter season" and focus upon the Florida-Sinaloa interaction.

Let us now turn to investigating the demand and supply factors at work in the U.S. fresh winter vegetable market.

Demand. Demand for fresh winter vegetables in the United States is influenced by a variety of factors in addition to price. Changing lifestyles, and even the weather, have all contributed to the demand situation. Perhaps the most important influence is the increased awareness of the need for fresh, healthy foods in the diet, which has been greatly bolstered, perhaps even inspired, by major marketing campaigns.

In the late 1960s demand for fresh fruits and vegetables began its recovery after a long spell in which per capita consumption had declined.[27] During the 1973/74–1980/81 period this recovery intensified.

TABLE 2.4
Sinaloa's Share of Total Exports, 1981–82

Tomatoes[a]	94.9
Cucumbers	90.0
Bell peppers	97.5
Eggplant	98.7
Squash	66.1

SOURCE: UNHP, *XII Convención Anual*, 1982.
[a] Includes vine-ripe, mature green, cherry, and roma.

Consumption of all fresh vegetables in this period increased 8.7 percent per capita, while the rising popularity of salads stimulated consumption of tomatoes and green peppers, up 10 percent and 24 percent, respectively, in this period.[28]

Consumer advocates also began to demand that agricultural science and growers take taste and nutritional content into consideration. At times this interest has led to public outcry, in particular with respect to the "cardboard" tomato, against the production of U.S. growers and in favor of Mexican farmers who, due to the ability to use great amounts of labor, were able to allow the product to ripen on the vines (see chapter 8). As Mexican growers move increasingly toward harvesting green produce by machine, in an effort to reduce their labor costs (see chapters 6 and 7), the alliance between U.S. consumer groups and Mexican growers will probably weaken, although the former will still be solicitous of a sufficient winter supply from Mexico to keep retail prices down.

Supply Trends. As is evident from the preceding discussion, production of winter vegetables increased dramatically to keep up with demand. Despite the increasing size of the market, not all producers gained, or gained equitably. The last two decades can be usefully divided into three periods, each distinguished by the identity of the dominant winter supplier: the early 1960s, 1968–1973, and 1974–1983.

In the early part of the 1960s U.S. demand for fresh winter vegetables was met by production in two regions of the United States, Florida and California, and imports from two countries, Cuba and Mexico.[29] But politics intervened to upset the structure of the industry. In 1962, after a few years of increasing tension, all U.S. trade with Cuba was embargoed, thereby effectively eliminating the island from the U.S. winter vegetable market. Two years later, the U.S. terminated the Bracero Program with Mexico, under which Mexican workers served as a low-wage labor supply for U.S. industry. With the end of the program California tomato growers abandoned the risky winter production in favor of other higher value, less risky, and less labor-intensive crops.[30] By 1966, therefore, Mexico and Florida split demand between themselves.

Production of winter vegetables in Florida, however, began a decline in 1966–67 which lasted through 1973–74. Hurt by high labor costs, increasing land costs due to real estate development, and unusually adverse weather, production of winter vegetables stagnated or declined (depending upon the crop) throughout the 1968–73 period (see tables 2.5 and 2.6). As the only other source during the winter season, Mexico gained dramatically from Florida's inability to meet the ever increasing demand. Imports from Mexico dominated the Western markets and began to make inroads into Eastern ones.

About 1974 trends started to change. Mexican growers began to suffer from rising costs, of labor in particular, and an overvalued currency. At the same time, Florida producers began to reap the benefits of mechanization and better cultural practices. Severe cold weather in Florida during 1976–1977 and 1977–1978 gave Mexican growers a temporary reprieve, but could not keep Florida producers from regaining all that they had previously lost to import competition by the end of the decade.

The behavior of the supply side of the market in the last fifteen years suggests that although total supply has increased dramatically, Florida and Mexico are locked in a competitive struggle, rather than a complementary relationship. In the next section the effect of climate and costs of production are analyzed in both Florida and Mexico. Investigation of these factors will contribute to our understanding of the competitive supply trends.

THE DYNAMICS OF INTERNATIONAL COMPETITION

Climate and Weather. Climate has determined that Florida and Sinaloa are the optimal locations in the United States and Mexico for producing the winter vegetables which the U.S. market demands. In the long run climate may also contribute to further shifts in the location of produc-

TABLE 2.5

U.S. Winter Vegetable Market, Supply from Florida and Mexico,
November–May (bushels)

Season	Tomatoes[a]		Cucumbers		Peppers		Squash		Eggplant	
	F	M	F	M	F	M	F	M	F	M
62/63	20617	9807	3405	266	4071	480	1052	25	800	104
63/64	22395	9929	3751	282	4401	369	924	42	850	95
64/65	22131	10690	3699	572	4345	567	988	108	953	137
65/66	21510	13052	3669	762	4475	807	992	104	906	173
66/67	22401	14028	3469	1211	5171	885	984	239	966	202
67/68	21248	13123	3696	978	5593	772	1158	156	724	270
68/69	17706	17790	2778	1897	5030	1318	1093	386	731	502
69/70	13139	23152	2784	2344	2914	2202	808	547	532	711
70/71	16515	20706	2442	3446	3821	3928	943	532	708	735
71/72	18697	20699	3231	2988	4800	3160	1041	608	794	871
72/73	18798	26228	3130	3244	5716	3835	1126	617	763	1218
73/74	19676	21125	2916	3289	5521	4402	1124	683	896	1044
74/75	23348	18707	3645	2052	7007	2790	1427	608	1203	835
75/76	24380	21125	4061	3404	6320	2997	1406	800	1191	994
76/77	20737	25302	3970	3910	6279	3792	1700	996	1224	1037
77/78	24180	31026	4018	4632	7976	5956	1536	1459	1291	1289
78/79	28990	22765	4226	4718	7188	5213	1810	2353	1294	1215
	(1,000 cwt)									
79/80	11623	4651								
80/81	11608	1959								
81/82	12658	4712								

SOURCE: Robert S. Firch, "Florida and Mexico in Competition in the Fresh Winter Vegetable Market," unpublished, 1980, pp. 2–3. What I list here as Mexican is listed in this report as total U.S. imports, but 99.4 percent of total U.S. imports in 1982–83 were from Mexico, and we can assume similar proportions for the other years. USDA, FAS Report 1, July 8, 1983, p. 001.

[a] 1,000 30 lb. cartons.

tion, from Florida to the Caribbean and/or Sinaloa to the Yucatan. In the short run, weather is often the conclusive factor in determining which region will supply the U.S. winter market in a particular season. Three weather conditions are fundamental to understanding the evolution of competition between Florida and Sinaloa: freezes, rains, and heat.

Freezing temperatures are the Achilles heel for the Florida producers. Although south Florida has the best winter climate in the state for

TABLE 2.6
U.S. Winter Vegetable Market, Relative Shares, Florida and Mexico

Season	Tomatoes		Cucumbers		Peppers		Squash		Eggplant	
	F	S	F	S	F	S	F	S	F	S
1962/63	67.8	32.2	98.1	1.9	89.5	10.5	97.7	2.3	88.5	11.5
1963/64	69.3	30.7	93.0	7.0	92.3	7.7	95.7	4.3	89.9	10.1
1964/65	67.4	32.6	86.6	13.4	88.5	11.5	90.1	9.9	87.4	12.6
1965/66	62.2	37.8	82.8	17.2	84.7	15.3	90.5	9.5	84.0	16.0
1966/67	61.5	38.5	74.3	26.7	85.4	14.6	80.5	19.5	82.7	17.3
1967/68	61.8	38.2	79.1	20.9	87.9	12.1	88.1	11.9	72.8	27.2
1968/69	49.9	50.1	59.4	40.6	79.2	20.8	73.9	26.1	59.3	40.7
1969/70	36.2	63.8	54.3	45.7	57.0	43.0	59.6	40.4	42.8	57.2
1970/71	44.4	55.6	41.5	58.5	49.3	50.7	63.9	36.1	49.1	50.9
1971/72	47.5	52.5	52.0	48.0	60.3	39.7	63.1	36.9	47.8	52.2
1972/73	41.7	58.3	49.1	50.9	59.8	40.2	64.6	35.4	38.5	61.5
1973/74	48.2	51.8	47.0	53.0	55.6	44.4	62.2	37.8	46.2	53.8
1974/75	55.5	45.5	64.0	36.0	71.5	28.5	70.1	29.9	59.0	41.0
1975/76	53.6	46.4	54.4	45.6	67.8	32.2	63.7	36.3	54.5	45.5
1976/77	45.0	55.0	50.4	49.6	62.3	37.7	63.1	36.9	54.1	45.9
1977/78	43.8	56.2	46.5	53.5	57.2	42.8	51.3	48.7	50.0	50.0
1978/79	56.0	44.0	47.2	52.8	60.0	40.0	43.5	56.5	51.6	48.4
1979/80	71.4	28.6								
1980/81	85.6	14.4								
1981/82	72.9	27.1								

SOURCE: Calculated from Table 2.5.

producing vegetables, it suffers a minor freeze every other season on average and seems prone to a devastating freeze at least once a decade. Culiacán, the chief producing region in Sinaloa, has no recorded history of freezes, and its winter production limits the ability of US. growers to offset losses due to weather via higher prices.

With this climatic characteristic one might wonder why the Florida producers do not shift their production to balmier climes. In fact, in the 1950s they did invest in winter production in Cuba and were quite successful until Castro's rise to power pushed them out.[32] They continue to be faced with climatic disadvantage in their competition with Sinaloa and thus need to keep searching for a Caribbean or Central American alternative.

Sinaloa production is also affected by the weather, as untimely rains, cloudy conditions and extreme variations in temperature (from a high of 91° to a low of 54°) affect yields, quality, and harvest dates.[33] In fact, U.S. growers can take heart from a recent change in weather patterns affecting Culiacán: untimely rains (October–December and some in January) the past six years have significantly damaged plants, in some cases prevented quick replanting of the area, and contributed significantly to the recent decline in Mexican exports. Were such a precipitation schedule to be more than temporary, Culiacán's climatic advantage could be upset. Another climatic factor which initially decreases Culiacán's advantage is heat, as the fall harvest must be planted in late summer when temperatures are often over 100°.

Sinaloa's climatic vulnerability can be lessened through changes in cultural practices and technology. Containerized transplants are now extensively utilized, and among their benefits are sturdier young plants better able to resist disease stimulated by early heavy moisture.[34] In addition, the research center financed by growers and the state (Centro de Investigaciones Agrícolas del Pacífico Norte, CIAPAN) is making progress toward a hybrid tomato with increased resistance to heat.[35] Nevertheless, the weather can still strike a significant blow against Mexican production. For example, the effect of the drastic devaluations of 1982, which should have given Sinaloa producers an important advantage over Florida during the 1982–83 season, was largely offset by the rains of fall and January. Despite "substantially" increased plantings for 1982–83, by May Mexican exports to the United States were up by only an average of 13 percent over 1980–81 for five vegetables, with peppers off by 25 percent.[36]

In this latest case the weather worked to Florida's advantage in offsetting the full impact of Mexican devaluation upon the U.S. winter vegetable market. But it can also work in the opposite direction. After the 1976 Mexican devaluation, a tremendous freeze hit Florida in January 1977 and increased the Mexican presence over what it would have been solely on the basis of the new exchange rate.

Cost Competitiveness. The cost of producing and marketing a crop is one of the fundamental determinants of competitive advantage at a particular point in time. An examination of the evolution of costs of production in both Florida and Sinaloa over the past two decades provides insight into the shifts in competitive edge and provides a basis for speculation about future trends. No studies appear to have undertaken cost comparison between Florida and Sinaloa squash production, so unfortunately this vegetable will have to be omitted from the following discussion.

Tables 2.7–2.10 illustrate the trends in cost of production, which, not surprisingly, correspond quite well to the evolution of market shares between the two regions over the period. In 1967–68 costs of production, f.o.b. shipping points, were equal between the two regions for tomatoes; in this situation transportation from shipping point to consuming markets would tend to determine geographical distribution of markets.* For the other three major winter vegetables Mexican costs were significantly above Florida's. But note that Mexican growers face certain costs which their U.S. counterparts do not. In the tables these are denominated "export costs" and include transportation to Nogales, Arizona (the U.S. shipping point), Mexican (nonincome) taxes, and the U.S. tariff.

These costs peculiar to Mexico are significant, accounting for one-quarter to one-half of total cost. Given that transport costs to Nogales, Mexico are unavoidable and Mexican taxes are extremely small,* the key item of interest is the U.S. tariff. The relative weight of the tariff has declined as prices and the costs of other inputs rose, while the tariff level remained the same.[37] It does, however, still play a crucial role in the winter vegetable market. Elimination of this tariff is not sufficient to give Mexico a cost competitive advantage in two cases (cucumber and peppers in 1967–68), but in all others its effect would be either to increase Mexico's advantage or to shift it from a disadvantaged position to an even one. These price changes would all occur at f.o.b. shipping points but would reverberate to the consuming terminal market. In fact, a study by the U.S. Department of Agriculture noted that the elimination of the U.S. tariff in the 1973–74 season would have given Mexican growers a cost advantage in all U.S. markets except those of south Florida.[38]

Let us return to the actual market situation, in which U.S. tariffs are

---

*Other factors may affect the destination of a shipment of produce: quality and price differences, imperfect price information, and weekly supply fluctuations. Richard L. Simmons et al., *Mexican Competition for the U.S. Fresh Winter Vegetable Market*, 1976, p. 39.

*1978–79 Mexican taxes on these vegetables range from 2 to 13 cents USCY, while U.S. import taxes range from 38 to 135 cents USCY.

TABLE 2.7
*Tomatoes: Total Production Costs
(dollars per 30 lb. carton or equivalent)*

Commodity and Cost Item	1967/68	1970/71	1973/74	1978/79
Florida				
Mature green, staked				
(winter crop)				
producing	—	—	2.65	2.85
marketing	—	—	2.35	2.74
Total	—	—	5.00	5.59
Mature green, ground				
(winter crop)				
producing	0.94	1.05	2.59	2.82
marketing	1.02	1.40	2.20	2.92
Total	1.96	2.45	4.79	5.72
Mature green, staked				
(spring crop)				
producing	—	—	—	2.26
marketing	—	—	—	2.68
Total	—	—	—	4.94
Mexico				
Vine-ripe				
producing	0.31	0.32	0.94	1.25
marketing	0.82	0.86	2.33	3.14
export cost	0.82	0.84	1.25	1.36
Total	1.95	2.02	4.52	5.75
Without tariff	1.56	[a]	3.96	5.19

SOURCE: C. John Fliginger et al., *Supplying U.S. Markets with Fresh Winter Produce: Capabilities of U.S. and Mexican Production Areas*, 1971 supplement, USDA, Economic Research Service, p. 18; R. L. Simmons et al., *Mexican Competition for the U.S. Fresh Winter Vegetable Market*, Agricultural Economic Report 348, USDA, Economic Research Service (1976), p. 21; and Zepp and Simmons, pp. 42, 25; note this later study includes sales commissions as an export cost for Mexico, despite the fact that Florida growers also pay sales commissions; therefore, I include it in marketing costs for both.

NOTES: F.o.b. shipping point for Mexico: Nogales, Arizona; for Florida: the packinghouse.

Producing costs include the preharvesting costs of land rent, machine services, labor, fertilizer, pesticides, other purchased inputs, administrative costs, and interest on operating capital; marketing costs include picking, hauling, packing and marketing labor, machinery, pallets, cartons, other purchased supplies, administrative costs, and sales commissions; export costs include transport to Nogales, crossing charges and fees, U.S. tariff, and Mexican taxes (nonincome type).

[a] Fliginger et al. does not provide a tariff figure for 1970–71. The U.S. import tax varies by seasons within the year, becoming greater as U.S. production increases. The amount of the tax itself has not varied during the 1967–1979 period; therefore, the variation in the tariff figures for the different years suggests that they have been weighted by volume exported under the different tariff stipulations. For our purposes, it does not seem necessary to go back to 1970–71 and reconstruct export volume.

TABLE 2.8
Winter Cucumbers: Total Production Costs for Selected Seasons
(dollars per bushel)

Commodity and Cost Item	1967/68	1970/71	1973/74	1978/79
Florida				
producing	0.82	0.89	2.68	3.53
marketing	1.99	2.48	2.66	3.38
Total	2.81	3.37	5.34	6.91
Sinaloa				
producing	1.06	0.87	1.58	1.99
marketing	1.72	1.74	2.00	2.91
export costs	2.23	2.26	2.54	2.47
Total	5.01	4.87	6.12	7.37
Without tariff	3.71	a	4.72	6.05

SOURCE: See table 2.7.
NOTE: See table 2.7.

charged. The tables indicate that in 1967–68 Florida had a cost advantage in all crops except tomatoes, where costs were even. Within three years Mexico gained the advantage in tomatoes and drew even in eggplant. Mexico consolidated its gains in the two most important crops, tomatoes and cucumbers, and although Florida regained it in eggplant, its margin was only half that of 1967–68. By 1978–79, how-

TABLE 2.9
Eggplant: Total Production Costs for Selected Seasons
(dollars per bushel)

Commodity and Cost Item	1967/68	1970/71	1973/74	1978/79
Florida				
producing	0.77	0.80	1.87	2.76
marketing	1.18	1.58	1.33	1.84
Total	1.95	2.38	3.20	4.60
Mexico				
producing	0.31	0.33	0.72	1.23
marketing	1.14	1.15	1.59	2.23
export costs	0.86	0.90	1.09	1.39
Total	2.31	2.38	3.40	4.85
Without tariff	1.98	a	3.04	4.47

SOURCE: See table 2.7.
NOTE: See table 2.7.

TABLE 2.10

Bell Peppers: Total Production Costs for Selected Seasons
(dollars per bushel)

Commodity and Cost Item	1967/68	1970/71	1973/74	1978/79
Florida				
producing	0.95	1.01	2.16	2.98
marketing	1.69	2.11	2.21	2.83
Total	2.64	3.12	4.37	5.81
Mexico				
producing	1.30	0.74	0.94	1.79
marketing	1.53	1.56	1.76	3.04
export costs	1.45	1.46	1.31	1.67
Total	4.28	3.76	4.01	6.50
Without tariff	3.55	a	3.31	5.80

SOURCE: See table 2.7.
NOTE: See table 2.7.

ever, Florida had a cost advantage in all crops, thereby bettering its position vis à vis Mexico at the start of this cycle.

If we focus on tomatoes we can gain insight into this evolution of cost advantages. Sinaloa had a cost advantage in 1970–71 of $0.43, which declined to $0.27 and became a $0.03 disadvantage with respect to the most popular Florida cultivation practice, mature green on the ground.*

---

*Tomatoes are distinguished into two general categories, mature green and vine-ripe. Vine-ripe tomatoes are ones that are allowed to begin their ripening stage on the vine; they are picked after turning a pinkish color (sometimes they are called "pinks"). Many people believe that vine-ripe tomatoes are both more flavorful and nutritious because of their longer exposure to the sun. Another advantage to the grower is that staked tomato yields are three times those of tomato bushes lying on the ground. These advantages, however, have their negative aspects. Picking tomato plants daily requires much labor, tomatoes already into their ripening process are more easily damaged by handling, and their shelf life is short. The latter is a key reason why vine-ripes demand a lower price from the retailer.

A mature green tomato, in contrast, is harvested after it has matured but not yet begun to ripen; it is then subjected to ethylene gas to bring out the red coloring, and it slowly begins to ripen. It has a number of characteristics which make it attractive to both grower and retailer. First, it saves labor. When grown on the ground, the hardness of the green tomato makes it possible for it to be harvested by machine. Even when grown on stakes and hand harvested, labor costs are minimized by the ability to pick all the fruit of varying maturities, allowing harvesting every three days, rather than daily. In addition, the hard tomatoes are more resistant in the handling process and have a shelf life of at least a week longer than vine-ripes.

Table 2.7 also indicates that while in the earlier two periods Sinaloa had a cost advantage in both producing and marketing, by 1973–74 it had lost it in marketing and seen it decline in producing. Costs in the latter increased 147 percent in Florida and 300 percent in Mexico between 1970–71 and 1973–74; i.e., Sinaloa's costs rose twice as fast as Florida's. Between 1973–74 and 1978–79, although rates diminished, Sinaloan costs rose by three and a half times Florida's: 9 percent to 33 percent.

A variety of factors contribute to Sinaloa's progressive loss of its competitive advantage over Florida in all crops,* but the chief ones are rising labor costs and tomato yield advances far below Florida's. Wages constitute the single most important factor in input prices in both Mexico's and Florida's vegetable production. Although wage rates are significantly lower in Sinaloa than in Florida (about one-fifth in 1978), the rate of increase of Mexican wages doubled that of Florida from 1967–68 to 1973–74. The devaluation of the peso in 1976 broke the pattern of ever-increasing Mexican real wages, but by 1978–79 the predevaluation rate had been equaled.[39] As chapter 6 demonstrates, wage increases in Sinaloa, Mexico, continued to outpace their U.S. counterparts.

Let's take a closer look at the responses by Florida and Sinaloa producers to the problem of the increasing cost of producing winter vegetables. First I will examine Florida's successful response and then turn to Sinaloa's failure to respond sufficiently (at least to 1982).

Florida growers adopted a variety of means to decrease their costs, most revolving around technological changes. Technological change in Florida manifested itself in three ways. One was increased use of the mechanical harvester and varieties of tomatoes which were resistant to damage under conditions of mechanized harvesting.[40]

A second important innovation was the introduction of staked production and the shift in production zones from the southern end to the southwest coast and the west central portion of the state to take advantage of the new technology which required certain types of soils. In 1966–67 some 25 percent of Florida's area was staked, and by 1979 it accounted for more than two-thirds of the acreage planted. With the

---

*Fertilizer, machinery, pesticides, cartons, and transportation; but increases in wages outdistanced increases in these other input prices, and labor is responsible for 40 to 50 percent of input prices in both regions.

use of staked technology larger yields are achieved at a reduced average cost because of the use of higher-yielding varieties and different production practices.[41]

The third technological change favorable to growers was the introduction of plastic mulch. This thin film of plastic over the fields keeps the soil warm and moist and increases the efficiency of fertilizer as well as weed and disease control. Because most of Florida's soil is sandy, plastic mulch technology contributes another benefit to the growers: excess rains no longer wash away the chemical inputs in the soil.[42] Technological change helped Florida regain cost competitiveness by reducing their costs through increased yields: between 1974–75 and 1977–78 tomato yields rose 65 percent in Florida but only 27 percent in Sinaloa.

Complementing these technological transformations was state policy. Florida growers were benefited at the end of the 1970s by a macroeconomic policy of the U.S. government which set minimum wages at declining real levels.[43] Although one cannot attribute this state policy to Florida growers, analysis of international cost competitiveness is not complete without it.

In contrast to the Florida situation, there was much less technological innovation in the Sinaloa fields from the early 1960s up to 1982. There are two major reasons for this difference: international cost competitiveness and the ability of Sinaloa growers to lower their wage bill significantly either through their own efforts or as a result of the state's macroeconomic policies. Over the last twenty-five years Sinaloa growers have adopted six strategies with respect to their costs of production.

First, technological change played a fundamental role in Sinaloa's recovery from the disastrous period of 1959–1961 (although chapter 7 suggests that regulation of supply was also necessary). At that time Sinaloa growers shifted from ground to stake culture to take advantage of their relative advantage in labor costs. This successful switch gave Sinaloa producers a cost advantage over Florida until at least 1973–74, thereby diminishing concerns over costs of production. Although Sinaloa lost cost competitiveness in 1973–74, the devaluation of the peso and the tremendous freeze which hit Florida in 1976 masked the loss of competitiveness until late 1979. In reaction to their dramatic loss of market share from 1978–79 to 1982 Sinaloa growers began to speed up the adoption of new technology, this time manifested in the increase in area planted for mature green production; a few growers have already set up gassing facilities in Culiacán, and one distributor has done so in Nogales. It is estimated that in 1980–81, 15 percent of Sinaloa production was mature green, whereas a decade earlier there was virtually no mature green production.[44] This change in production technology reduces cost not through increased yields, but rather through decreasing the labor force and thus reducing labor costs.

Although technological transformation of production in Sinaloa lags behind that in Florida, Sinaloa growers were by no means stagnant in their efforts to increase yields, a second strategy. These efforts depended upon more intensive use of existing technologies rather than innovation. Sinaloa producers changed cultural practices to include greenhouse growing for starting seedlings, thereby producing larger, healthier, and more disease-resistant plants. In addition, Sinaloa growers are now spacing their plants closer together and making more use of fertilizer. In other crops Sinaloa has done better (peppers 127 percent, eggplant 175 percent, and cucumbers 280 percent increases) than Florida where yields were relatively stable for peppers, slightly increased for cucumbers, and dramatically up for eggplant.[45]

Other labor-saving efforts have been undertaken. Mechanization is a third strategy in the Sinaloan growers' arsenal and appears to be the most important arena in which advances have recently been made: two growers have patented machines which speed up a variety of tasks in both the preharvest and harvest stages. The most successful of these machines saves up to one-third of the labor previously utilized in these tasks and is even being marketed in the U.S.; the first U.S. client was, ironically, a Florida grower.[46] These labor-saving trends, however, may be stopped if the administration of President Miguel de la Madrid is successful in keeping wages low to stimulate export-oriented industries.

Two other strategies to decrease the wage bill relate to unionization of the farm labor force (see chapter 6). Contracts were signed with the government's less aggressive union in an effort to expel an independent union which was successfully wringing concessions from growers. In addition, some growers have begun to shift production to nonunionized areas. Here grower concerns coincide with state interest in developing previously marginal areas to incorporate their farmers into the national life. Under the program "Desarrollo Productivo en Apoyo a los Distritos de Temporal" (Productive Development in Support of Rain-fed Districts, DEPRODIT), the state provides infrastructural investment, ejidatarios provide their land and labor, and growers contribute their knowledge and some working capital. Because ejidatarios are partners in the business effort, they provide their labor outside of the parameters of the labor legislation. The grower, in turn, receives 20 percent to 50 percent of the profit depending upon his participation in sharing costs, and does not have to deal with wages, benefits, or labor agitation. By 1982 twelve growers had associated with ejidatarios to produce vegetables for the export market.[47]

Sinaloa growers have also undertaken a sixth measure to help offset the rising costs which have eliminated their cost advantage over Florida production. Since the mid-1950s Culiacán tomato producers have regulated supply to the export market in an effort to raise prices, and by the 1970s these regulations had been extended to the major winter vegetable export crops. (See chapter 7, which also discusses policies to make the domestic market a profitable place to send the supply which is not exported.)

Despite this picture of more advanced production in Florida and Mexico's progressive loss of competitive advantage, Florida producers continue to be squeezed. While some growers have turned large profits as Mexico's participation in the U.S. market has declined, producers in certain regions are at best earning marginal returns. In 1980–81 producers of ground tomatoes in Dade County did not quite break even; this followed upon an average of only 2.5 percent return from 1976 to 1980. Similarly, producers of staked tomatoes in the Immokalee-Lee area lost almost 10 percent in 1980–81, after having made a modest 7 percent return over the previous five seasons. It is easy to argue that these producers should not be in the market. Elimination of these producers implies that Florida should not be producing from mid-December through April; only spring production in the Manatee-Ruskin area appears to be seriously competitive with average returns of 15 percent over the earlier period and 19 percent in 1980–81.[48]

Why do Floridians continue to produce? They gamble on an ability to capitalize on higher prices as a result of tighter supplies as Mexico drops out of the market. Squash and cucumbers provide an example of what can occur in such a situation: net returns to these Florida growers ranged from 32 percent to 65 percent in 1980–81.[49]

At this point the reality of competitive advantage is quite evident.

Florida is competitive in the winter because of the U.S. tariff, the technological lag in Sinaloa, and certain macroeconomic policies in Mexico which fueled inflation and an overvalued exchange rate over the past decade. Sinaloa growers are addressing the technology problem, and the Mexican state is coming to grips with the latter circumstances; to the extent they are remedied, Mexico will once again gain the competitive edge which climate and factor endowments indicate should be theirs.

State Policies. The U.S. government has much less direct effect upon production that its Mexican counterpart. Nevertheless, some U.S. policies stand out when the relationship between state and grower is examined. These are (a) state recognition of grower collusion to manipulate supply to the domestic market via marketing orders, (b) immigration policy and its effect upon the rural labor force, and (c) tariff and other trade policies.

The supply of tomatoes coming out of Florida in the winter season is subject to a federal marketing order under the auspices of the Agricultural Marketing Agreement Act of 1937. These orders are "regulatory programs issued and supervised by the secretary of agriculture that legally obligate commodity handlers (that is, first buyers) to abide by certain specified trade practices and restrictions on sales. Requests for orders are usually initiated by the producers, although the secretary, too, has that power."[50] The tomato marketing order applies to imports as well, although foreign producers have little influence over the order. In 1968 Florida growers utilized this order to keep smaller-sized Mexican tomatoes off the U.S. market. This maneuver resulted in the first "tomato war," which was not resolved until seven years later when U.S. distributors of Mexican tomatoes utilized the courts to force the Secretary of Agriculture to modify use of the order (see chapter 8). Still, the USDA ranks the tomato order as moderately powerful because it continues to subject imports to minimum grade and size restrictions.[51]

Immigration policy is another major arena where state policy directly affects winter vegetable production. We have already seen that termination of the Bracero program in 1964 pushed California out of winter tomato production and contributed to the cost crunch which plagued Florida growers for a decade. Despite official policy, illegal migrants from Mexico and the Caribbean continue to find their way to the Florida vegetable fields. If the U.S. government is successful in either stemming the flow or raising its costs to the growers through employer sanctions, U.S. immigration policy will once again hasten the day of the final demise of winter vegetable production in the United States.

United States tariff policy is also fundamental in maintaining a particular supply structure in winter vegetables even when Mexican growers have their costs under control. In this respect one must note the protectionist stance of the U.S. government. Such an accusation may sound erroneous, considering the refusal of the legislative and executive branches to construct the nontariff barriers sought by Florida growers (see chapter 8). Any contradiction between these two positions is resolved if we understand that the U.S. government is attempting to make Florida and Sinaloa production complementary in order to diminish tensions between the two countries. But the inefficiency of Florida production determines that the relationship between the two producing regions will be inherently competitive.

A number of trade policies in different arenas can be utilized by the U.S. government to influence imports of winter vegetables from Mexico. Florida growers and their allies try to use all of them against Mexican imports, but have only been marginally successful. Chapter 8 examines trade conflicts in detail, so here we will only note the three arenas in which trade policy has been played out. The legislative branch has been the scene of efforts to put more of the burdens inherent in a perishable commodity market upon Mexican producers. In addition, the executive branch has been pressured to utilize discretionary powers to alter the competitive structure of the fresh winter vegetable industry in favor of U.S. producers. Finally, the judicial branch has become a last resort for these growers in their attempts to overcome their failures with the executive branch.

The Mexican state is more of a factor in agricultural production than its counterpart to the north. Its revolutionary heritage gave it a legitimate role in guiding the economy and society in harmonious interchange. The stability of the Mexican system is partly attributable to the Mexican elite's construction of an interventionist state (see chapter 3). State intervention in the agricultural economy, therefore, is merely an extension of this overall characteristic of modern Mexico. Chief among agricultural policies is the regulation of land tenure, and indirectly of production, through agrarian reform. In subsequent chapters I examine state support of growers' organizational efforts (chapter 3), irrigation policy (chapter 4), land tenure policy (chapter 5), and labor policy (chapter 6) for their influence upon the evolution of Mexico's winter vegetable production.

Subsidies are another important element of state policy which affects the winter vegetable industry through internally oriented policies. Many agricultural inputs have historically been subsidized, whether as a general agricultural policy or as one specifically directed toward export production. Under the weight of the economic crisis commencing in 1982, Mexico revised its subsidy policies. As those perceived as inefficient and unnecessary are eliminated (for example, irrigation fees), the cost of production in Mexico will rise. They will be counterbalanced by other subsidies, such as the pricing of domestic energy. An empirical study of the actual impact of each revision is needed before evaluation of the overall impact of internally oriented subsidy policy is possible.

A final major policy of the Mexican government which significantly influences the U.S.-Mexico winter vegetable interaction is monetary policy, specifically the exchange rate. The earlier discussion about costs of production in Mexico referred to the recent disadvantage which Mexico's overvalued currency bestowed upon Sinaloa's growers, but it is worth stressing in this section that although exchange rate policy is not made with winter vegetables in mind, the analyst must consider its effects. In the medium run, an undervalued exchange rate will contribute to Mexican growers' international competitiveness, but its actual weight will depend upon other state policies, particularly those related to labor costs.

In summary, an examination of the U.S. fresh winter vegetable market suggests that climatic and economic factors give Mexican producers an advantage over U.S. producers, but that politics intervened to significantly diminish that advantage. If one were to consider only climate, Florida should not produce in winter because other regions are better suited by nature for producing in this season. This conclusion is reinforced by expanding the analysis to include the economics of production. Given that even after a decade of technological innovation in Florida's tomato fields labor costs continue to be the major cost factor, U.S. producers cannot compete with Mexican producers. Were production carried out solely on the basis of efficiency, Mexican producers would be competing with Caribbean area producers for the U.S. market. But politics is an intimate part of the trade relationship, both shaping economic forces and limiting their impact.

With this overview of the political economy of the U.S.-Mexican fresh winter vegetable trade in mind, we can turn to an analysis of the terms on which state and grower in Mexico have allied to penetrate the international market.

3

THE STATE–GROWER ALLIANCE: CONVERGENT AND DIVERGENT INTERESTS

One of the arguments of this book is that an alliance between the Mexican state and Mexican vegetable growers facilitated production at internationally competitive prices and significantly influenced the terms upon which Mexican growers would participate in the agribusiness commodity system. In this chapter I analyze the development of that alliance, paying particular attention to distinguishing between their convergent and divergent interest. By discovering the common and conflicting goals of state and grower, chapter 3 contributes to the context for parts 2 and 3 in which I examine the alliance's ability to deal with challenges from the domestic and international political economies (which affect each of their particular interests differently), keep the alliance intact, and strengthen Mexican participation in this international market.

This chapter has two sections. In the first I examine Mexican state interests which affect the production and trade of vegetables. The Mexican state has a number of interests, some generic to its state of development and others peculiar to its history.[1] Two are most relevant to this case study. Maintenance of an authoritarian version of corporatism is actively sought because it facilitates both policymaking and political control. In addition, agriculture is expected to contribute to a development strategy of import-situation industrialization (ISI). The second section provides an analysis of the development of the state-grower alliance by focusing on farmer associations and their domination by vegetable growers.

An Authoritarian-Corporatist System. Mexico's political elite is distinguishable from the economic elite.[2] The president leads the elite during a nonrenewable six-year term, and, because of the characteristics of the authoritarian political system, he has wide latitude to formulate policy. Although the preferences of the political elite tend to give the country's political economy direction, this elite needs to create alliances with societal groups in order to implement policy. I have argued elsewhere that each of these social forces has general interest which must be met, but the manner in which they are is dependent upon the incumbent president.[3]

The ruling coalition includes all politically important social groups, but the distribution of influence within the coalition varies over time. Because Mexico's political economy is capitalist, the state has had to incorporate the long-term interests of capital. In very specific terms, this task means that the bourgeoisie will form part of the political alliance which supports the Mexican state. Foreign capital also plays an important, although perhaps indirect, role in the political alliance.

This capitalist nature of the Mexican economy, however, provides only very broad insight into the Mexican political process. As Hirschman has noted, a crisis in the process of economic development can be met in a variety of ways without violating the limits of a capitalist economy.[4] Therefore, the capitalist nature of the economic processes does not determine which policies the state utilizes to further accumulation. Rather it is the political alliances and elite choices which design socioeconomic policies.

Through the leadership of the national labor and peasant unions, these two classes form part of the ruling coalition. The stability of Mexico's politics (every president since 1934 has achieved office via the ballot box and served out his entire term) is fundamentally dependent upon the participation of those two classes in the ruling coalition. Although labor and peasants may have fewer material benefits to show for their participation than capital, those material gains combined with the rhetorical and ideological benefits they receive have kept them in the coalition to date.

The elite coalition has been extraordinarily stable since 1934, when the last president who had been able to maintain his leadership position after his tenure was overthrown (Plutarco Elías Calles). Some key bargains struck among the leaders of the major groups insure that all will continue to perceive their interest in remaining within the coalition. Two domestic political bargains are of particular interest. The first involves support for the system even in the face of short-run losses, because of a guarantee of compensation in the long run. The second involves joining an alliance for growth to produce the benefits that will allow peaceful distribution from an expanding pie.[5]

The state utilized an authoritarian variant of a corporatist system of interest representation to structure the political system. This system is formalized in the official party (Partido Revolucionario Institucional, PRI) but is also present in other state-society relations where the party is marginal, e.g., in relations with businessmen and in the special commissions created to deal with national problems.[6]

Corporatism represents a potentially powerful interest intermediation system through which to structure interest group participation to mitigate conflict. As an ideal-type definition we should not expect any corporatist system to meet all of the criteria noted earlier. In addition, no state-society relationship is ever structured around just corporatist mechanisms.[7] Actually, the structural heterogeneity of an interest intermediation system may allow one group to "form competitive subsystems seeking to influence and/or control only segmented policy arenas, each with a distinctive pluralist, corporatist or syndicalist mode."[8] As the major comparative study of corporatism in Latin America notes, it should be seen as a "series of traits that may be present or absent to varying degrees."[9]

The cross-regional use of the concept now makes it possible to derive three coordinates of corporatism: nature of the political regime it serves (democratic-authoitarian); nature of the corporatist system of interest intermediation itself (state-societal);* and scope (how many sectors and

---

*The distinction between the two is related to whether the characteristics of corporatism described above are the result of state elite manipulation or arise autonomously from forces in civil society. Philippe C. Schmitter, "Still the Century of Corporatism?" p. 99. Further elaboration has been made of the state variant by whether the corporatist structures incorporate or exclude the popular sectors. Guillermo O'Donnell, "Corporatism and the Question of the State."

actors it covers). Facilitation of policy making under corporatism occurs with any of the variants, although in very different ways and with very different socioeconomic implications.

By stressing bargaining over form rather than policy output, perceptions of winners and losers on those issues which fall within the scope of corporatist politics are significantly decreased. Consequently, the possibility of formulating and implementing particular policies perceived as necessary for a country's economic strategy, but costly to one group, is heightened.[10] In the societal version the ability of social forces to become autonomous participants in the bargaining process arises from control over the resources which their particular socioeconomic position grants them. The result is that labor (and peasants, if any) is not systematically discriminated against, and finds important benefits forthcoming from the process. In the state version, corporatist structures serve to weaken dissent by limiting the organizational resources, ability to mobilize, and access to decision-makers of the dissenters. Given the capitalist nature of the political economy, labor and peasants find their bargaining positions systematically weakened. The result has been that these social groups benefit in direct correlation with the state elite's perceptions that such benefits serve their needs, and not necessarily those of these sectors.

Corporatism, then, appears to offer a mechanism which may help mitigate the domestic tensions arising from the political economy of international competitiveness. If we accept corporatism as a strategy chosen by the state and the dominant social forces rather than as a cultural institution with a life of its own,[11] we need to investigate the political dynamics which give those corporatist structures their continued viability. Our understanding of the policymaking facilitation characteristics of corporatism requires analysis of how competing interests are compensated under corporatism. In fact, I will argue in this book that the success of the authoritarian variant of corporatism in structuring and channeling demands which affect international competitiveness depends heavily upon the existence of noncorporatist channels of interest representation at the subnational (local) level. These "safety valves" relieve the frustrations of those who lose too often (peasants) or are not accustomed to losing (growers) at the national level.

Bringing the discussion to the case at hand, this book will demonstrate that corporatist structures helped the state maintain the viability of the

Mexican vegetable export industry in the face of changes in both the international and local political economies. The Mexican case also demonstrates that corporatism is not a guarantee of international competitiveness. In an authoritarian polity what the state chooses to do with the increased capacity for policymaking which the corporatist structure provides is heavily influenced by factors outside the system of interest intermediation. As I have shown elsewhere, if the state leaders choose inefficient strategies, international competitiveness will be unattainable.[12] As exporters everywhere have frequently found, what the state often gives in specific incentives, it more than takes back in macroeconomic policy, particularly that concerning the exchange rate.[13]

Despite major economic failures, the authoritarian-corporatist system has been quite effective in maintaining political stability. A brief review of the past half century demonstrates this and helps set the national context for our agricultural case study.[14]

From 1934 to 1938 President Lázaro Cárdenas emphasized nationalism and distribution of economic resources. Labor and peasants found their influence within the ruling coalition at its height. But Cárdenas maintained control over the ability of both classes to press for continued economic redistribution in their favor. Beginning in 1938 the president perceived that the ruling coalition was reaching the limits of its tolerance for populist politics. He reined in labor and peasants and oversaw the transition to a moderate emphasis within the coalition.

In this transition small-scale Mexican manufacturers for the domestic market also found their influence waning in the 1940s, as heavy industry and foreign capital began to dominate the import-substitution development strategy; they were given protection, but the dynamic sectors of the economy were increasingly out of their hands. The urban middle classes also found their democratic aspirations increasingly marginalized. These shifts were not frictionless: there were major strikes in the late 1940s and 1950s, land invasions in the late 1950s, and serious electoral attempts in 1940 and 1952 to create a new ruling coalition. The dominant coalition met the challenge through electoral fraud, repression, cooptation, and the distribution of some benefits. Once political control was consolidated, the alliance among industrialists, finance capitalists, farmers, direct foreign investors, and fiscal conservatives in the bureaucracy ushered in a new stage of import-substitution industrialization. Known as "stabilizing development" it emphasized wage restraint, increased transfers from the agricultural to the industrial sector, and a close watch over state expenditures.

By 1970 economic growth under an import-substituting model was beginning to show stress, particularly in agriculture. Partly as a result of the economic situation but also because of the authoritarian nature of the political system, cohesion in the ruling coalition deteriorated. Of special concern was the alienation of the middle class. Middle-class representatives had attempted to reform the PRI, but Carlos Madrazo's expulsion from the party's presidency dashed their hopes. Their children took up the cause of reform through university strikes in 1965 and 1968, the latter brutally suppressed by military force. President Luis Echeverría (1970–1976) sought to stabilize the coalition by overseeing a shift in influence back to small-scale national capital, labor, and peasants in support of a new effort to further import substitution, broader distribution of the fruits of economic growth, and some electoral reform. His failure aggravated the economic situation while alienating entrepreneurs and the middle class. The result was massive flight, devaluation, political unrest, and the adoption of the IMF stabilization program in 1976.

President José López Portillo (1976–1982) began his term by attempting to construct a fiscally conservative coalition which would support efforts to increase Mexico's industrial competitiveness in world markets. Legalization of the Communist and other parties was also offered as an incentive for dissidents to direct their energies into an arena controlled by the state (the electoral). But with the new inflows of foreign exchange via petroleum exports ($3.6 billion and $10.1 billion in 1979 and 1980, respectively) and foreign debt (it reached $85 billion, almost tripling from 1976), the economy pushed into a historically high rate of expansion. Every social group benefited as the state sought to buy its way out of the economic and political problems which had plagued it for the past decade.

Unfortunately, this program had placed the Mexican economy in complete dependence on two international markets over which the Mexican state had no influence. These markets began to turn against Mexico (financial in 1980, energy in 1981), but the state was reluctant to slow the economic growth which both brought it renewed domestic legitimacy after the 1975 crisis and seemed to promise increased national autonomy in the international sphere. It was not until energy clients and holders of the national currency significantly reacted (the first suspended purchases in the summer of 1981, while the second dumped pesos in February 1982) that the state was forced to act. Nevertheless, in July 1982 a new Mexican president was to be elected and the political elite did not want the official party to face the electorate under conditions of austerity. Stop-gap measures were enacted (a devaluation followed by wage increases and rumored central bank intervention to limit the fall) until the elections. After that came unprecedented devaluations, currency controls, bank nationalization, another IMF program, and an international debt restructuring. Through it all, the Mexican authoritarian-corporatist system showed little sign of being unable to cope with the domestic side of stabilization.

State Interests and Agriculture. Mexican agriculture experienced high growth during 1948–1965 (output tripled[15]) and has since slowed dramatically. Production of basic foodstuffs (corn, beans, rice, and wheat) suffered most while livestock and its associated forage crops experienced a second Green Revolution.[16] Population growth and public policy designed to expand urban consumption at cheap prices resulted in demand significantly outstripping Mexican supply. By the end of the 1970s imports of basic foodstuffs and oilseeds for animal consumption had become major, reaching a peak of 30 percent of domestic production in 1980.[17] As a result, much of the policy debate in Mexico centers on the competition (often mistakenly perceived as zero-sum) among basic foodstuffs, crops for animal consumption, and export crops. Most investigators have found that, in general, state policy has clearly favored the livestock sector.[18]

Despite what appears to be evidence in support of the primacy of the livestock sector over export production (a dramatic increase in the area devoted to the former and a significant decline in that of export production), I think the decision is not as clear-cut. The decline in area dedicated to export crops has been greatly affected by a fall in the demand for cotton (which had been Mexico's chief export for over a decade) and the dramatic increase in yields for fresh winter vegetables, which allowed output to soar at the same time land use declined.[19] This study will demonstrate that the state has a continued interest in export production and will, in a zero-sum situation such as drought, channel resources to these crops even at the expense of crops for animal feed.

What are the state's interests in export crops? Basically they are twofold: foreign exchange and employment. The ISI development strategy inevitably runs up against a foreign exchange bottleneck as the industrial sector's use of imported inputs exceeds its capacity to produce internationally competitive products. Agricultural exports help pay for those necessary inputs. Fresh vegetables just missed leading the list of Mexican agricultural exports, generating U.S. $400 million in 1984.[20]

The state also has an important interest in rural employment generation. Since one of Mexico's chief comparative advantages vis-à-vis the industrialized countries' agriculture is its level of wages, Mexican agricultural exports are labor intensive. Sinaloa's vegetable production employs about 200,000 seasonal workers[21] who, despite poor working conditions in the fields, would be hard pressed to find replacement jobs in an economy in which 55 percent of the population was unemployed or underemployed even before the current economic crisis.[22] The employment factor is one element which is usually absent in discussions about export crops, except with respect to labor exploitation. Table 6.1 presents figures on employment for a variety of domestically oriented and export-oriented crops. These figures actually understate the work force per hectare for the export producers because they are the basis for an agreement between Sinaloa private farmers and the Social Security Institute (Instituto Mexicano de Seguro Social, IMSS) for the farmers' contribution to IMSS; IMSS has complained that the export producers actually employ many more people.[23] These employment requirements for a variety of representative crops range from a low of 6 to a high of 14 workers per hectare among domestically oriented crops and a low of 15 to a high of 143 among export crops, clearly demonstrating the employment advantages of production for export over that for the domestic market.

In sum, the state will confront agriculture with both economic and political goals. In the case of export agriculture, Sinaloa's vegetable producers become attractive candidates for helping achieve state goals. In the next part of this chapter we examine why, and under what terms, those growers find it profitable to ally with the state.

STATE AND LOCAL INTERESTS IN ORGANIZATION

During the last years of the 1920s, Juan José Villa began to meet with other small farmers in the "El Limoncito" section of the Culiacán region to discuss common problems and ideas relating to their livelihood.[24] Throughout the Culiacán Valley small producers began to share experiences, mostly those related to the export crops of fresh winter vegetables and chick-peas. Production and commercialization were difficult in those days: vegetables were produced with U.S. credit, and shipment meant taking truckloads through the cold winter Sonoran desert via unpaved roads to the U.S. border at Nogales, Arizona. Chick-peas presented similar problems. Those with credit, storage facilities, and marketing contacts in New York and Spain reaped the lion's share of the profits, and the businessmen were rarely farmers.

Generally speaking, these informal meetings were not attended by the larger farmers. For example, in the Limoncito group Jorge Almada never attended, although his younger brother was an important, albeit occasional member. Don Jorge owned the nearby Navolato sugar mill and most of the irrigated land on the Limoncito side of the river and was son-in-law to General Plutarco Elías Calles, ex-president and then current strongman of Mexico. The Podestá, another of the rich farming families in the area, did not join either, and only one of the Greek families that dominated production of fresh vegetables for export was to be found among the group which laid the basis for the organization of the Sinaloan rural elite.

In the early thirties, however, the conjunction of various forces outside these small groups, indeed outside the state, was to throw these farmers into the center of Mexico's agricultural development and the controversies surrounding it. With the world depression the agriculture of northwest Mexico, the most productive and cash crop oriented in the country, suffered dramatically.[25] At the same time there was a shift in national agrarian policy as General Calles was becoming more outspoken in his views of the ejido not as a pillar of Mexican agriculture but as a transitional stage toward private small farms. In this scheme, public policy was to help farmers produce efficiently (be they large or small) and help ejidatarios develop the mentality and skills to allow them to become small farmers.[26] In addition, it is quite possible that Calles wished to establish a counterpart in agricultural politics to that of the pro-ejido forces; certainly none existed at this time. The incipient national political party, created in the wake of Obregón's assassination and at this time actually just a conglomeration of regional political bosses, searched for key constituent support for its candidates;* in Sinaloa,

*This led to some strange alliances. For example, President Cárdenas, the most radical Mexican president, found himself relying upon the support of the pro-Catholic

because agriculture was the mainstay of the state's economy, the support of this sector became coveted.

Melessio Angulo, one of the Limoncito farmers, was a close friend of Manuel Paéz, confidante of Calles and an ex-governor of the state. Through Don Melessio the group came into close contact with Paéz. Sometime around 1930–1931 the ex-governor and the Limoncito group came to believe that by working cooperatively they could eliminate the middlemen. Paéz's close ties to Calles boded well for the success of the project. A proposal for legislation to organize farmers and promote the modernization of agriculture through cooperative efforts was presented to Calles. He agreed with the merits of the project (increased efficiency of the private sector being the pillar of his agricultural program) and sent it to the Ministry of Agriculture and Development. On August 27, 1932, President Pascual Ortiz Rubio signed legislation based on the Limoncito proposal, giving it standing in the country as a whole, not only in Sinaloa.[27]

The Calles-controlled government chose to follow a corporatist path in organizing the producers, thus indicating the importance of considerations other than productivity.[*] The two federal statutes governing the structure and functioning of the producer organizations were manifestly corporatist in nature: they were licensed by the state, limited in number, singular, hierarchically ordered, functionally differentiated, subject to official recognition, and given a representational monopoly. The only characteristic missing for the legislation to constitute a perfect case of Schmitter's classic definition of corporatism, compulsory membership, was promulgated by the state government five years later.

Chapter 1 of the 1932 legislation provided the economic justification for the state's intervention in this area: producer organizations would contribute to the modernization of the country's agriculture. Through these organizations farmers are to provide support for infrastructure

---

cacique Saturnino Cedillo in San Luis Potosí. Alicia Hernández Chávez, *La mecánica cardenista*, vol. 16, *Historia de la Revolución Mexicana* (Mexico: El Colegio de México, 1979), p. 38. Porfirio Rubio was also a key ally in a province of Hidalgo state. See Frans J. Schyrer, *The Rancheros of Pisaflores* (Toronto: University of Toronto Press, 1980), pp. 92–95.

[*]The pervasiveness of the corporatist ideology among the revolutionary elite is illustrated by the fact that Calles' arch rival in the mid-1930s, Cárdenas, utilized the same type of system of interest representation to organize the other major social force in the Mexican countryside at that time, the *ejidatarios*.

projects (both public and private), cut out middlemen, and generally make their needs known to the various branches of government. Chapters 2 and 3 set up local, state, and national organizations with each association at the lower level obligated to belong to the next higher one. The local associations were also to be organized in accord with their members' production of particular crops. Chapter 4 established that the Ministry of Agriculture and Development will authorize the "creation, organization, and function" of each association. Thus each association must register with and report their activities to the Ministry.

In 1934 amendments were made that defined terms and specified administrative tasks. Three additions were most significant. In terms of financing, Article 21 required that membership fees be set by the assemblies of each association. Article 22 determined that 50 percent of these funds would be sent to the state organizations, which in turn would keep 30 percent for their expenses and send the remaining 20 percent on to the national federation.[28] Economic stability for each level of association was thus tied to general prosperity in agriculture and the benevolence of local farmers in taxing themselves.

Another important addition lay in Article 24, which established the basis for dissolution of an association; among the conditions was the judgment of the agricultural ministry that the association was not living up to the precepts of the law. One of the new requirements called for the immediate withdrawal of recognition from those associations which became involved in political or religious affairs* (Article 55). Finally, Articles 28 and 42 prohibited the creation of more than one association at each local or state level, respectively.

Despite the formal prohibition of political behavior, farmers were inevitably politicized as the political elite maneuvered to seek support for public policy. For example, the leaders of the national federation created by the 1932 legislation, the Federación Mexicana de Organizaciones Agrícolas, have always been appointed by the Mexican president, and the farmers themselves recognize that its purpose is to demonstrate farmer support for the president's policies, not to be the national voice of private producer interests.[29]

The gap between formal goals and reality also applies in the opposite

---

*The Cristero civil war brought state-church relations to a crisis in 1926–1929 and again in 1934–1939.

direction, from the bottom up. Despite the elaborate mechanisms constructed to insure the political elite's domination of the organizations, and their success for over twenty years, since the 1950s state and local organizations in Sinaloa have spoken for the farmers against efforts by the political elite to determine unilaterally the specifics of agricultural development in Sinaloa.

For an understanding of the evolution of the political role and autonomy of these farmer organizations, we now turn to the analysis of the state confederation of farmer associations.

THE STATE CONFEDERATION

Governor General Macario Gaxiola promulgated Decree No. 26 on November 19, 1932, laying the functional basis for the creation of local producer organizations within the state. On November 22 vegetable farmers from the Culiacán area established the first association, the Associación de Productores del Río Culiacán. Three days later vegetable producers from the Fuerte, Sinaloa, Elota, and Mocorito River basins (in this last area the export-oriented chick-pea producers joined their vegetable counterparts) created four more associations.[30] These five organizations of export producers formed a statewide institution, the Confederación de Asociaciones Agrícolas del Estado de Sinaloa (CAADES) on November 28.

From the very beginning it was clear the organizations had not been created solely for the benefit of the export producers. After constituting CAADES the leaders of these farmers set up a provisionary executive council to serve until the first meeting of the General Assembly, to be held within a month. The day before the scheduled meeting of the General Assembly the provisional executive council met with the chief of the Ministry of the Interior* for the state of Sinaloa. The representative of the state government added two new members to it. These two farmers came from the circle of large commercial farmers,[31] the same ones who had virtually ignored the informal meetings of small farmers out of which the associations grew.

Government intervention in CAADES at this point suggests two key

---

*Secretaría de Gobernación. This Ministry has as its main function responsibility for political affairs.

elements of the role the organization would play. The state had provided that public funds for agricultural development be channeled through these organizations. Inclusion of small and large farmers meant that there was an alliance for production taking place in which large farmers who were interested in commercial agriculture, rather than merely social power and prestige, would be welcome despite the emphasis upon the small farmer ideal prevalent at that time. But another element is political: the political elite (which included the larger farmers) appeared determined to guarantee that the organization of the smaller farmers would not allow them to constitute a pressure group which could question the distribution of power in Sinaloa.

In 1933 General Gaxiola stepped down from the governor's chair, and Calles' confidante Paéz took office once again. The intimate link among CAADES, Governor Paéz and Calles seemed to promise a rosy future for Sinaloa's private farm sector. But national politics came over the horizon to upset the balance of forces in Sinaloa and threaten the viability of CAADES.

Tension between *cardenista* and *callista* factions reached a point where the two groups fired in a session of the national Chamber of Deputies, resulting in the death of two deputies and the wounding of two others. The gun battle was used as a justification by the left wing in the Chamber to expel seventeen *callista* deputies. Among those expelled was the Sinaloa deputy Carlos Careaga. The day after Calles returned to Mexico City after a brief self-exile at his Sinaloan retreat El Tambor, the Senate reacted by expelling five *callistas*, among them Cristóbal Bon Bustamante of Sinaloa. Two days later the left wing in the Senate became a catalyst in the Senate's dissolution of power in four states, thereby throwing *callista* governors out of office; among these was Sinaloa Governor Paéz.[32]

The national purge of *callistas* had a profound effect on Sinaloan politics and thus upon the chief organization of the rural elite in the state. The new strongman in Sinaloan affairs became Colonel Rodolfo T. Loaiza. Loaiza at the time was a federal deputy and sought to run affairs in Sinaloa through a pact with two other colonels, Gabriel Leyva Velázquez and Alfredo Delgado.

But the *Pacto de Coroneles* did not last long. With the fall of Paéz, Loaiza put Leyva Velázquez in the governor's chair. The latter, however, quickly fell under the influence of Miguel Gaxiola, a rival of Loaiza.

Leyva Velázquez was removed from office, and someone with no political ties in the state, Guillermo Vidales, was brought from Mexico City to watch over Loaiza's domain while he consolidated his power in Sinaloa. In 1937 the other colonel remaining in the pact, Delgado, became governor as Loaiza moved to the Senate. During Delgado's reign control over CAADES was strengthened and institutionalized as the *cardenistas* manuvered to eliminate the *callista* flavor of CAADES and make it serve their own needs.

Governor Delgado first installed his brother-in-law, Rafael G. Ibarra, as president of the confederation.[33] Ibarra served three terms, from 1937 to 1941, roughly coinciding with Delgado's governorship. Shortly after taking office in 1937 the governor moved to formally restructure CAADES and the local association.[34] Local associations were now legally compelled to form part of the state confederation (Article 12a); fiscal incentives were provided to serve as a carrot, but the need for government recognition constituted the stick. Article 37 also gave the governor a representative on CAADES' executive council which, combined with his influence in the selection of CAADES' president, would allow any governor to dominate CAADES.

But there were also economic reasons for state intervention. Agricultural production in the private sector had fallen dramatically, affected by both the Calles-Cárdenas dispute and by the depression. The new legislation sought to stimulate production by joining ejido and private producers in organizations to watch over and influence the common agricultural environment they faced (Article 10) and by subsidizing their expenses.

The idea that ejidatarios and private farmers had an interest in working together was consistent with the orientation of Cárdenas' perception of the future of Mexico. It required, nevertheless, the submission of the private farm sector to the agrarian reform. The Sinaloa rural elite did not accept this proposition, and virtual civil war broke out in Sinaloa after 1937. In addition, the associations were never successful in supporting the interests of both ejidatarios and small farmers, because they could not operate as effective spokesmen for producers as long as the governor controlled them and because their independence from outside political control was accomplished by the elite of the *neo-latifundistas* (private farmers using subterfuge to exceed legal limits on land ownership) who controlled production of export crops. Thus the organizations served these interests and not those of the small farmers or ejidatarios.

The plan to finance the agricultural sector had two aspects. The subsidy was equivalent to the state taxes collected under the rubric of agricultural health programs, but it was to be returned to the agricultural sector through the CAADES-local association network. All producers contributed, but only members of an association reaped the benefits. A farmer expelled from an association also lost the opportunity to benefit from the subsidy. Thus there were fiscal incentives for farmers to join local associations, for the local association to form part of the state confederation,* and for both to abide by the rules.

The second element in the efforts to finance the agricultural sector relates to the composition of the local associations themselves. The 1937 state law raised the number of members for a local association to thirty (federal legislation stipulated ten) who could demonstrate the financial capacity to administer the association (Article 7). The organizations still faced a serious financial constraint. In order to guarantee the economic viability of the local associations, a minimum working capital of 10,000 pesos was to be collected from the membership (Article 14). Under these conditions it is no surprise that the local associations continued to represent the rural elite.[35]

Another method to confront the financial crisis of Sinaloa's agriculture was to give the association and CAADES the legal ability to become credit subjects for any or all aspects of agricultural production and marketing. A state bank was also established, the Banco de Sinaloa, S.A., whose funds were to be derived from stock which farmers were obligated to purchase through their local associations (each crop was taxed a certain percentage of its value) and whose sphere of activity was to be agriculture, broadly defined.

In sum, the state gave the members of these organizations the ability to determine the use and distribution of funds which were raised by the fiscal power of the state from society at large. Despite the subsequent evolution of state-farmer organizations, this transfer of functions from the state to the rural elite was not altered.

---

*In this case there was also a legal obligation.

Restructuring of the financial basis of CAADES, however, had relatively little influence upon its ability to perform the economic aspects of its mandate through the 1940s and mid-1950s. Three elements contributed to this failure. First, the economic infrastructure which only massive public investment could provide was just beginning to appear in Sinaloa. Although the presidential decree establishing the first irrigation district in the state dated from 1940, the dam for the district was not completed until 1948. It took over a decade to bring the second major dam into operation. The international highway which connected Sinaloa with both the United States to the north and Guadalajara and Mexico City to the south was not completely paved until 1952; before that time the highway to Nogales, Arizona, was intransitable any time it rained. The railroad running north to south through Sinaloa was in decay; in perhaps the most significant action of the organized farmers in this period, they put up 10 percent of the total cost of revitalizing the railroad when President Miguel Alemán bought it from its U.S. owners in 1951.[36] Finally, the Chihuahua-Pacífico railroad, which connects Sinaloa with eastern Mexico and the Texas border, was not completed until 1961.

A second factor that helps explain CAADES' failures was the political environment within which the organization was caught. After the 1937 state legislation the governor was a more active participant in the executive committee and utilized that influence to bring the confederation to support his political and economic policies. In addition, because agriculture was the economic basis of the state's economy, aspirants to the governorship sought to win political support of the farmers' chief organization. The disproportionate concern for politics over economics factionalized the organization with dire implications for its continued existence.

The weight of the organized farm sector in state politics reached its peak in the 1940 gubernatorial elections. In this election Loaiza decided to take over the governorship directly and assumed he would be the official party's candidate. But the Partido de la Revolución Mexicana's (PRM) presidential candidate General Manuel Avila Camacho sought to install his own men in the state governorships; thus Loaiza's identification as a *cardenista* now worked against him, even though he had been an early supporter of Avila Camacho's candidacy within the PRM.[37] The PRM's candidate became Guillermo Liera.

Nevertheless, Loaiza did not renounce his desire for the governorship.

Running on the ticket of the political party he utilized to consolidate power in Sinaloa, the Acción Revolucionaria Sinaloense, Loaiza entered the race while making sure his party supported Avila Camacho for the presidency. The elections in Sinaloa were hard fought among the three candidates (the third, General Ramón F. Iturbe, ran with the party which backed General Juan Andreu Almazán for the presidency). The Loaiza organization and the support of CAADES (led by the brother-in-law of the other colonel in the Pact) proved too much for Avila Camacho's candidate, and Loaiza took the disputed election.* In order to keep peace with the new president, however, Loaiza ceded the posts of federal deputy and senator to the *avilamachistas* and retained control of the state.[38]

CAADES' support of Loaiza brought forth calls for the independence of the confederation. After losing the election, Liera warned about the factionalization of CAADES as it became involved in politics outside of the agricultural sector and called for the complete reorganization and independence of the organization. He also suggested that the relationship between the confederation and the federal and state governments should be clearly delineated.[39] Within a decade Liera's comments would seem prophetic.

A third element contributing to the rural elite's failure to provide an impetus for agricultural growth in Sinaloa at this time was the Depression: because the North Pacific had more of a cash crop agriculture than the rest of the country, the world economic crisis had the greatest impact in this region.[40] By 1940 total hectares (has.) harvested in Sinaloa had fallen 21.2 percent below the 1930 total. In addition, communications were hardest hit in the North Pacific: in 1940 the value of railroads and roads had fallen in real terms, 70.3 percent in the country, 86.7 percent in the region, and an incredible 92.4 percent in Sinaloa (see table 3.1).

The fourth factor in the weakness of the private sector's agricultural production was the arrival of agrarian reform. The North Pacific region had been relatively isolated from early agrarian policies: in 1930 it had the lowest percent of land belonging to ejidos, 7 percent. By 1940, the end of Cárdenas' presidency, the region had the second highest share of ejidal land, 52 percent; thereafter it declined to the second lowest,

---

*This is the only case of which I am aware that the official party in Mexico has recognized electoral defeat in a gubernatorial campaign.

TABLE 3.1
Changes in Sinaloan Agriculture 1930–1940
(1940 prices)

	1930	1940	% Change 1930–1940	% Total 1940
Number	14,675	10,857	—	—
Non-ejidal	14,644	10,416	−28.9	95.9
Ejidal	31	441	1,322.6	4.1
Total Has Possessed[a]	2,808,627	3,100,684	10.6	—
Non-ejidal	2,668,489	2,080,995	−22.0	67.1
Ejidal	140,138	1,019,739	627.7	32.9
Total Has Harvested	208,293	164,060	−21.2	—
Non-ejidal	201,254	87,612	−56.5	53.4
Ejidal	7,039	76,448	986.1	46.6
Value of:				
Land	57,356,599	67,401,925	17.5	—
Non-ejidal	55,487,521	30,289,453	−45.4	44.9
Ejidal	1,869,078	37,112,472	1,885.6	55.1
Construction	5,153,372	4,111,328	−20.2	—
Non-ejidal	5,123,914	1,197,037	−76.6	29.1
Ejidal	29,458	2,914,291	97.9	70.9
Hydraulic Works	10,322,641	4,841,267	−53.1	—
Non-ejidal	10,311,667	1,332,136	−87.1	27.5
Ejidal	10,974	3,509,131	318.8	72.5
Machinery, Tools, etc.	5,731,592	7,651,618	33.5	—
Non-ejidal	5,709,332	2,323,936	−59.3	30.4
Ejidal	22,260	5,327,682	238.3	69.6
Agri. Production	31,321,580	22,242,270	−29.0	—
Non-ejidal	31,032,545	9,787,766	−68.5	44.0
Ejidal	289,035	12,454,504	42.1	56.0
Railroads & Roads				
Mexico	29,062,396	8,641,916	−70.3	—
North Pacific	2,288,739	306,078	−86.7	
Sinaloa	1,929,959	147,000	−92.4	

Source: *1940 Censo Agrícola, Ganadero y Forestal;* 1930 prices were computed to their 1940 value using the wholesale price indices in Nacional Financiera, S.A., *Statistics on the Mexican Economy* (Mexico: Nacional Financiera, S.A., 1977), p. 218.
[a] Includes all types of land, not just farmland

43 percent in 1960.[41] The net effect of this rapid social evolution in the region was the frightening of the private sector, with its concomitant reduction of private capital stock in agriculture, and production fell throughout the decade.

Nowhere is the magnitude of this revolution better illustrated than in Sinaloa. At the beginning of the decade the state was among the lowest in the region on indicators of ejidal share of agriculture. By the end of the decade the state ranked highest on all but one indicator, value of agricultural production, in which Nayarit barely edged it out; however, Nayarit began with ejidal production five times greater than Sinaloa's. Table 3.2 illustrates the magnitude of the change in Sinaloa's ejidal-private property relations.

The agrarian tensions broke out in 1937 in a virtual civil war in the state and lasted a decade, while the federal government never intervened militarily. In an ironic twist, even as Governor Loaiza (1940–1944) downplayed the attacks upon the ejidatarios, he himself was gunned down by the most notorious of the white guards at the service of some private farmers. Peace was finally restored in the mid-1940s when the central government sent General Pablo E. Macias Valenzuela to take over the governorship and restore order.

Macias was able to bring the agrarian conflict to an end as land distribution diminished. The central government sought to keep Sinaloa politics quiet by installing a poet from outside the political wars as governor when Macias' tenure ended. But the politically naive governor, Enrique Pérez Arce, allowed Leopoldo Sánchez Celis to return to Sinaloa after Macias had driven him out. Sánchez Celis had formed part of the Loaiza machine and quickly consolidated his control over the state legislature.* A conflict between the governor and Sánchez Celis ensued, and in 1953 the latter carried the state legislature to declare Pérez Arce unfit to continue as governor due to illness, an accusation not without foundation as Pérez Arce died shortly thereafter.[42]

---

*Sánchez Celis, governor from 1962 to 1968, noted in a 1981 interview with this author that he presented the president with a list of about five names and that the president chose the next governor from that list. Certainly his influence extends, at least in a negative fashion, to the national level: while governor he was one of the key elements in forcing the downfall in 1965 of PRI President Carlos Madrazo. See Rodrigo Ai Camp, *Mexican Political Biographies* (Tucson: University of Arizona Press, 1976), p. 294.

TABLE 3.2
Value of Agricultural Production 1930–1970
(thousands)

	Current Prices	1950 Pesos	Real Increase Over Previous Decade	Relative Share of Value
1930				
Non-ejidal	25,000			99.1
Ejidal	233			0.9
Total	25,233	94,942		100.0
1940				
Non-ejidal	9,788			44.0
Ejidal	12,455			56.0
Total	22,243	67,241	−29.0	100.0
1950				
Non-ejidal > 5 has	134,766			58.8
Non-ejidal ≤ 5 has	3,860			1.7
Ejidal	90,653			39.5
Total	229,279	229,279	+240.1	100.0
1960				
Non-ejidal > 5 has	457,544			61.6
Non-ejidal ≤ 5 has	7,839			1.1
Ejidal	277,346			37.3
Total	742,729	354,837	+54.8	100.0
1970				
Private Farms > 5 has	932,665			47.3
Private Farms ≤ 5 has	4,094			0.2
Ejidal and Comuni-				52.5
dades Agrarias	1,036,664			
Total	1,973,423	743,931	+109.7	100.0

SOURCE: *Censo Agrícola, Ganadera y Ejidal* for respective years.
NOTE: The 1930 and 1940 census did not separate the private sector farms by the five-hectare division. From 1930 to 1960 the census agglomerated "comunidades agrarias" under the private sector, in 1970 they fell under the ejido sector.

The fall of Pérez Arce created new controversy over the identity of the interim governor which split CAADES wide apart. From Mexico City ex-governor of Sinaloa, ex-president of the Culiacán farmers' association, and presently a federal deputy, General Macario Gaxiola attempted to mobilize CAADES behind his candidate for governor,

Antonio Amézquita. Although Amézquita had been one of the founding fathers of CAADES and its third president, the confederation was so factionalized that he could not gather the support of the institution. Thus the Amézquita faction resorted to creating a parallel organization which would support their candidate in the name of the Sinaloa farmers.

Amézquita failed in his bid to become interim governor. Rigoberto Aguilar Pico, son of an ex-governor of the state and intimate friend of the federal minister of interior (Gobernación) became acting governor.[43] During Aguilar Pico's term various factors led to his reforms of CAADES' statutes, which helped give the confederation de facto autonomy from state control. The extreme factionalization which threatened the continued existence of CAADES as an umbrella organization for the private farm sector also raised threats for cooperative agricultural development efforts among farmers themselves and between farmers and government. Given that the state's economy was based on agriculture, it was not totally incomprehensible that Aguilar Pico, a man from outside the political wars of Sinaloa, would decide that agricultural development was more important than political control.

Within a year of taking office Agiular Pico issued a decree which gave the confederation "autonomy" from the government (the governor eliminated his direct representation on the CAADES board).[44] CAADES was still not completely formally autonomous because government recognition remained a prerequisite for the legal existence of the confederation. Therefore the basic corporatist orientation of the legislation governing the farmer organizations remained, and the government could theoretically still utilize the stick of withdrawing recognition in order to control CAADES and the local associations.*

Another factor *enabled* CAADES to stay relatively free of factional politics; without this key element Aguilar Pico's decree would have remained just one more hollow law. Growers themselves began to perceive that they did not need to participate directly in politics in order that their interests be respected. As the development of Mexico, not just Sinaloa, progressed quite spectacularly from the 1940s until 1970, the national bourgeoisie found that it did not need to play a direct role

---

*Chapter 5 illustrates that the cost of using this instrument has proven too high for it to be a viable tactic. The bias in agricultural development toward the rural elite further undermines the ability and desire of the state to use this ultimate weapon.

in politics; its general interests were being taken care of through the economy's need for capitalist production, the government's consequent fear of encroaching too much on the capitalists' economic interests, and the constantly growing economic pie which allowed all to gain. In Sinaloa development took off only in the 1950s, and therefore the realization of the farmers that they could concentrate on making money rather than politics dates from that decade. The slowing of agricultural growth, which began to be serious in the late sixties, changed the reality of the political economy within which the rural elite operates and thus forced modifications in past strategies.*

In the 1970s the economic pie was no longer expanding at the same rate and the authoritarian-corporatist system was experiencing great domestic strife. President Luis Echeverría utilized campesino mobilization as one means of confronting the challenges, and the export producers of Sinaloa were one of his chief targets. The rural elite assessed that they were being forced into the role of scapegoat in order that the political system could maintain the all-important allegiance of the campesino. This perception of the change in Mexican politics and the everyday reality of land invasions convinced the organized farmers of the need for direct and sustained political action.

Chapter 4 analyzes in depth the particulars of the political reactivation of the rural elite during the land tenure crisis of 1975–1976. Here we focus our analysis after a temporary resolution of the confrontation was achieved when José López Portillo took office in December 1976. López Portillo's emphasis was on production, not redistribution, a shift in goals which the farmers welcomed wholeheartedly. But caution was still the byword for the farmers, especially when the new president appointed Salomón Faz Sánchez head of the National Confederation of Agricultural Property Owners (Confederación Nacional de la Pequeña Propiedad Agrícola); Faz Sánchez had aspired to the secretary generalship of the national peasant union, CNC.[45] The loyalties of Faz Sánchez become further suspect to the growers in 1978 when he called for the return to Mexican politics of their archenemy, former President Echeverría.[46]

---

*The chapters on land tenure disputes (5) and farm labor strikes (6) illustrate that the land and labor conflicts of the 1950s were resolved with relatively little political mobilization of the farmers, certainly when compared with that which took place in the 1970s.

TABLE 3.3
*Presidents of the Confederación de Asociaciones
Agrícolas del Estado de Sinaloa (CAADES)*

Period	Presidents
1933–1934	Eduardo R. Arnold
1935	Manuel Paéz
1935–1936	Antonio Amézquita
1937	Rafael G. Ibarra
1938–1939	Rafael G. Ibarra
1940–1941	Rafael G. Ibarra
1942	José Mariano Romero
1945	Enrique Riveros
1946–1951	Enrique Riveros
1952	Carlos A. Careaga
1953–1955	Venancio Hernández
1956–1957	Fortunado Alvarez
1961–1964	Luis Gaxiola Clouthier
1965	Miguel Leyson
1965–1967	Alfredo Careaga Cebreros
1968	Raúl Batíz Echavarría
1968–1970	Manuel Flores Rodríguez
1971–1972	Manuel Flores Rodríguez
1973–1974	Manuel Tarriba Rojo
1975–1976	Lauro Díaz Castro
1977–1978	Lauro Díaz Castro
1979–1980	Emilio Gastelum Angulo

SOURCE: CAADES, *Analysis*, 1:1 and other numbers.

In an effort to formally institutionalize their participation in national politics in a manner which would guarantee control over their representative, a movement was launched within CAADES to demand that the official party, PRI (of which they are members via the popular sector channel), allow them to elect a federal deputy. The sentiment within CAADES was unanimous that its two-term president, Lauro Díaz Castro, who had "brilliantly" guided them through the four-year confrontation with Echeverría, would be that representative.

The personalism which permeates Mexican politics[47] and most likely a desire on the part of PRI to avoid formally institutionalizing farmers' political participation in national politics undermined the efforts of the

Sinaloa farmers. They got a deputy, but one chosen in Mexico City: José Carlos de Saracho, a major export producer who was also president of the National Union of Horticultural Producers and personal friend of the Minister of Agriculture.[48] A perhaps more important failure for growers came in 1982. Governor Antonio Toledo Corro sought to return to the old practice of placing his man in the CAADES presidency. Though some members initially tried to fight this reassertion of direct governmental influence, the Confederation eventually conceded.[49]

The governor's success with respect to CAADES does not necessarily imply a loss of control by CAADES members and a return to the external political influence of the past. First, the governor himself is a *neo-latifundista* whose interests may well coincide with those of CAADES members; at no time in the past when the governor controlled CAADES was he himself a member of the rural elite. Thus past gubernatorial influence may be qualitatively different from that which is currently taking place. A second indicator that historical trends may not have reversed is the fact that CAADES is already mobilized in defense of its own interests as its members define them.* Should the new CAADES president prove unsatisfactory to members, they may have the political experience to oust him.

A LOCAL PRODUCERS ASSOCIATION

Few local associations were created in the wake of the 1932 federal legislation. The 1937 state legislation called for the creation of nine local associations. Only six seem to have been in existence in 1943: the Río Fuerte Norte, Río Fuerte Sur, Río Sinaloa, Río Mocorito, Río Culiacán, and Río Elota associations.[50] Perhaps for this reason the 1954 decree granting CAADES autonomy also lowered membership requirements for local associations from thirty to twenty and eliminated the 10,000-peso working capital stipulation.[51] Although this move had the effect of opening up membership to more farmers, it still did not challenge control by the export producers. This will become clear in the following analysis of the strongest local association in Sinaloa.

The Culiacán vegetable producer association was the first created in

---

* After this was written I returned to Culiacán and a local newspaper reporter told me that growers were successfully battling the governor's attempts to control their organizations. Interview with Antonio Quevedo.

the country, and its members played a leading role in the creation of CAADES. Chick-pea producers, also export oriented, soon followed suit, and when the effect of the 1930 agricultural tariff changes in the United States reached Sinaloa,* sesame producers also organized themselves. In 1935, just as the populists were taking control of national and state politics, the organizational infrastructure of the private farm sector was reoriented to stress the participation of all farmers. The Associación de Productores de Legumbres del Río Culiacán (vegetables), the Asociación de Productores de Garbanzo del Río Culiacán (chick-peas), and the Asociación de Productores de Ajonjolí del Río Culiacán (sesame) fused themselves into the Asociación Agrícola de la Región del Río Culiacán. In 1937, one month after the expansion of functions given to the local associations by state legislation, the Asociación Agrícola became the Asociación de Agricultores del Río Culiacán, AARC.[52]

In reality, these Culiacán associations appear to have been the formalization of the Limoncito group which had been meeting irregularly for years before the 1932 federal legislation. The first formal meetings of the association were attended by twenty to thirty farmers.[53] Despite the progressive institutionalization of the group, the same problems with infrastructure, although apparently not politics,† which inhibited CAADES' development similarly limited AARC's influence on the area's agricultural production for quite some time.

Government legislation encouraged effective control of the activities of the Culiacán association by the local elite of private producers. The 1937 state law, in addition to the aforementioned working capital requirements, also allowed the associations to determine membership requirements. AARC's statutes recognize two types of members: affiliated and active.[54] All private farmers are automatically affiliated because their production is taxed for the aforementioned state subsidy to the local association. Affiliate status allows use of all association facilities and programs, but for many reasons (e.g., lack of awareness of

---

*The relevant change consisted of raising the tariff on processed oilseed products, thereby stimulating the importation of sesame seeds from Sonora and Sinaloa, just south of the border.

†In contrast to the politicization of CAADES, local associations lived relatively peaceful lives. Because control of state and national organizations could be achieved by direct intervention, presidents and governors tended to ignore local associations. Nevertheless, for the first twenty years the governor and the president of CAADES decided who would hold the local presidencies. Interview with Francisco Campaña.

programs, transportation problems, etc.) few farmers who are not active members utilize its resources.[55]

Only active members, however, may vote on association matters, including election of officers and use of the state subsidy. Formal requirements for active membership are not strict: if one is not Mexican, official permission to farm is required; one must be involved in production (by ownership, renting, or sharecropping) within the association's jurisdiction; and one must be registered on the tax rolls. Three factors limit active membership. Although the association's statutes do not mention it, in practice an application for active membership must be accompanied by letters from two active members attesting to the moral uprightness of the applicant and recommending him/her for membership; the application specifically warns those who would recommend the applicant to guard the interests of the association. This procedure screens potential members making it easier to maintain elite control (see below for an important example). In addition, it increases the effort necessary to become an active member. Perhaps most important is the third cause: most small farmers prefer not to become involved in the association. One possible explanation for this reluctance is the perception that the problems of the rural elite are not those of the family or subsistence farmer. The most vivid indication of this attitude is that only about half of the private producers participated in the meetings to protest the land occupations of 1975–1976.[56]

Membership, therefore, is highly representative of the larger farmers and the family corporations constructed to circumvent the land reform laws. Although from 1964 to 1966 the association suffered a net loss of 326 members (because they failed to provide all the information required by the statutes), the trend has been upward ever since. In 1967 there were 645 active members, in 1969 there were 800, and for 1978 AARC listed 1,451 active members of a total of more than 5,500 farmers in its jurisdiction.[57] The association does not make public the acreage held by its members, collectively or individually, but one statistic suggests the elite nature of this membership: 1,594 farmers, or 28.7 percent of private producers, hold at least 66.9 percent of the land in private hands.[58] According to informed sources, it would be "logical" to assume that AARC's 1,451 members come overwhelmingly from this stratum.

Even this figure exaggerates the number of farmers represented because it counts each member in a family corporation farm. The fact that these are in many cases fictitious distinctions is supported by the difficulties AARC encounters in reaching a quorum even for elections. In its thirty-three year history to 1980, AARC had never had a quorum the first time out (51 percent is needed). Informed sources report that this problem arises because approximately 40 percent of the active members are wives and children (often minors) whose "proprietorship" is used to circumvent agrarian reform legislation.[59]

Within this elite is found an even more select group: those who have held the presidency of AARC. Up to the early sixties the president of AARC was actually chosen by the governor and the president of CAADES. With the decreased intervention by the governor in CAADES affairs in the mid 1950s, AARC's weight in the Confederation has increased: although it is only one of nine local associations, from 1960 to 1980 five of the eight different CAADES presidents have been AARC presidents.

The presidency of AARC has revolved around a select group of families. Seven of the first eight presidencies (1937–1954) came from two lineages: two from the Romeros and five from the Gastelum-Gaxiola-Clouthier clan (who would also hold four of the next thirteen presidencies, 1954–1980). Although beginning in 1955 AARC presidents hailed from families other than the two already mentioned, they were still part of the socioeconomic elite of the Culiacán region.

Until 1979 every president was a horticultural producer. Although over thirty crops are produced in the valley, horticultural production is by far the most lucrative and the most oligopolistic: the over 400 tomato permits are said to be controlled by at most 43[60] and at the least 10[61] growers. Acceptance of the domination of these growers over the organization appears to have been a prerequisite for attaining voting rights in AARC. In the early 1960s private sector grain producers mobilized behind a candidate for AARC's presidency but were not allowed to cast votes in the organization they were taxed to support.[62] Grain producers did get the vote later but have never again attempted to force a presidential candidate on the vegetable producers, whom they outnumber.

In addition, most presidents were descendants of those who had been early leaders of the rural elite. Atilano Bon Bustamante (1957–1958) is the son of Cristóbal Bon Bustamante, *callista* senator expelled from congress in 1935; Atilano was also president of the Cattlemen's Union

TABLE 3.4

*Presidents of the Asociación de Agricultores del Río
Culiacán (AARC)*

Period	Presidents
1937–1939	Emilio Gastélum Gaxiola
1940	General Macario Gaxiola
1941–1943	Marciano Romero
1944	Benito Anchondo Dozal
1945	Alberto Gaxiola
1946–1948	Ramón Gastélum Sánchez
1949–1951	Santiago Gaxiola Gándara
1952–1954	Benjamín Romero Ochoa
1955–1956	J. Enrique Rodarte T.
1957–1958	Atilano Bon Bustamante
1959–1960	Hector R. González
1961–1962	Luis Gaxiola Clouthier
1963–1964	Alfredo Careaga Cebreros
1965–1966	Raúl Batíz Echavarría
1967–1968	Roberto Tamayo Muller
1969–1970	Manuel J. Clouthier
1971–1972	Manuel Tarriba Rojo
1973–1974	Jorge Bon Bustamante
1975–1976	Emilio Gastélum Augulo
1977–1978	Emilio Gastélum Angulo
1979–1980	Severo Gutiérrez Beltrán

SOURCE: AARC, *Boletín Agrícola*, "Texto documental de la AARC," circa 1972 and other numbers.

(Unión Ganadera) in 1966. Atilano's son Jorge was AARC president in 1973–1974. Alfredo Careaga Cebreros (1963–1964) is the nephew of Carlos A. Careaga, *callista* deputy also expelled from congress in 1935 and later president of CAADES (1952–1955); Alfredo himself became CAADES president in 1965. Raúl Bátiz Echeverría (1965–1966) is the son of Rafael Bátiz Paredes, secretary of CAADES in the first executive council (1933).

A final distinction separating the upper echelon of the rural elite from the middle class farmer is social. Until 1979 AARC presidents had all been members of Culiacán's most select social club, El Casino de Culiacán. When the elite's supply of candidates for the presidency was exhausted, it was forced to look elsewhere and chose Severo Gutierrez

Beltrán, a grain farmer who had worked closely with previous administrations.[63] It is still much too early to tell if Gutierrez Beltrán's presidency foretells the weakening of the control of export producers in AARC or whether it is just a trough until the third generation of Culiacán vegetable producers is able to step into the place of their fathers and grandfathers.

Three factors are important in understanding the evolution and present influence of the Culiacán association. The first is related to the history of CAADES: with the defactionalization of the state confederation, AARC also found that its president could devote more time to association affairs. The reorganization of the association's statutes in 1955, one year after Governor Aguilar Pico granted CAADES autonomy, reflected this new sense of responsibility within AARC. In addition, the economic infrastructure projects in Sinaloa (dams, roads, etc.), sponsored by the federal government, proved a catalyst for the agricultural development of the state and thus contributed to the strengthening of the growers' organizations.

Perhaps most crucial in explaining the expansion of AARC's functions in defense of its members' interests is the tremendous success of fresh fruit and vegetable exports beginning in the fifties. In 1952–1953, Culiacán tomato producers exported 65,000 tons for the first time, and in 1976, 240,000 tons were exported.[64] The early financial importance of export production in the local association is clearly reflected in the balance sheet: in 1960 and 1961 fees on tomato exports constituted 80 percent of AARC's income.[65]

With the increase in income, AARC began to provide services to its members. In 1957 the association established its monthly bulletin to inform members not only of actions taken by AARC but also of government programs for private farmers (e.g., how to obtain certificates of immunity from agrarian reform[66]) and to create class consciousness with articles on the importance of the private agricultural sector for economic progress.[67] In response to labor strikes the association also began administering a tax on horticultural producers to finance construction of housing for their farm labor supervisors and to support publicity campaigns, as well as legal and illegal tactics to control their workers. Also in the late fifties AARC bought pickup trucks so that the army could patrol the valley's roads, ostensibly to protect against theft of payrolls, but with a side benefit of maintaining a police presence to discourage labor agitation. In 1963 AARC created departments to monitor agricultural statistics and land tenure problems. The association is also heavily involved in warehouse construction and establishing cooperatives for supplying agricultural inputs and marketing the harvest.

The variety of subjects treated in AARC's 1977–1978 annual report illustrates the scope of the organization's interests:

I. General
  1. Membership 2. Security and Vigilance in the Fields 3. Regulatory Committee of Horticultural Products of Sinaloa for the National Market 4. Tertiary Roads 5. Agricultural Sanitation 6. Defense of Agricultural Exports to the United States
II. Various
  1. State and Federal Taxes 2. Social Welfare of Farm Laborers 3. Drought Conditions and Programs
III. Services To Members
  1. Marketing Pools 2. Warehouses 3. Petroleum and Gas 4. Hardware Shop 5. Agricultural Inputs in General 6. Import Permits 7. Use of the Association's Bulldozer 8. Economic Studies 9. Services to the Farm Labor Community
IV. Outlook of Agricultural Situation in the Valley
  1. Grains 2. Horticulture
V. Land Tenure Problems
VI. Financial Situation of the Association[68]

In sum, AARC is recognized by official channels to be the only representative of private farmers' interests in the Culiacán area. As such, publically financed aid to this portion of the agricultural sector is channeled through the association. In addition, the association has the power to tax the vegetable exports of nonmembers. The association thus derives much of its institutional strength because the state has given it effective control over some state fiscal functions. But the membership structure of AARC results in articulation of the interests of the elite growers. The family and subsistence farmers, therefore, lack direct access to policymakers.

PRODUCER ORGANIZATIONS AND AUTONOMOUS MOBILIZATION

This chapter has analyzed the establishment and transformation of producer organizations in Sinaloa. These organizations were based on an initial bargain with state control over demand articulation in return for a resource and organizational monopoly. The growers' experiences with these corporatist organizations demonstrates that under certain circumstances the subjects of state corporatism can gain control over their organizations. Three questions arise from such a discovery: how did such a transformation come about, why did the state tolerate it, and what are the implications for the state-grower alliance?

The ability to make their organizations respond to the defense of growers' interests, even where they define them in ways that conflict with state interests, is taken to constitute autonomy. A combination of three factors contributed to the increased autonomy of producer organizations. These were (a) the designation as interim governor of someone who drew his political power from his relationship with the central government at a time when CAADES was in shambles; (b) the consolidation of control over state politics in the hands of a regional strongman; and (c) a constantly expanding economic pie, to which vegetable exports contributed greatly.

The independence of CAADES came about at a moment when the political system in Sinaloa (and Mexico) was maturing. In the twenty-year period from 1934 to 1954 the state saw ten governors: one was deposed by the federal government, two by forces within the state, and a fourth was assassinated. The state has since continued to face serious political problems, especially in 1957–1959 and 1975–1976, but these were ultimately resolved within the institutionalized channels; a few more campesinos and farmers would die violently, but no governor would fall either through presidential order or assassin's bullet.

But why did the state continue to grant these now very autonomous organizations the representational and distributional benefits common to state-controlled organizations? The answer lies in the importance of the corporatist structure for policymaking in Mexico and the alternative means at the state's disposal for bringing the growers into line on important issues.

With respect to the corporatist system itself, as I argued in the first chapter, one of its chief attractions lies in bringing the state and relevant societal groups together to present the image of social harmony, or at least civility, in the allocation of resources and benefits. To have one of the major local actors absent would seriously undermine the process, perhaps leading various sectors to question their own participation. As we shall see in chapter 4, when the rural elite threatened to disrupt the process of corporatist bargaining, the state did mobilize an alternative organization. Once conflict between the private sector and the state reached this point, however, both sides seemed unwilling to risk the destruction of the corporatist system and compromised.

We thus come to the question of how convergent and divergent interests influence the ability of the state-grower alliance to confront domestic and foreign challenges to production and trade of fresh winter vegetables.

II

DOMESTIC CHALLENGES TO PRODUCTION

4

COMPETITION FOR WATER

Water is fundamental to the production of any crop. Its distribution among both producers and crops thus becomes one of the primary concerns in Mexico's arid northwest. Here most agricultural production takes place in irrigation districts built and operated by the state. The political economy of water distribution consequently serves as an appropriate issue with which to begin analysis of how the state-grower alliance ensures the international competitiveness of Mexican vegetables, as well as the implications of the alliance for other producers and Mexican consumers.

This chapter is divided into three sections. First, we examine the fundamental importance of irrigation in Sinaloa's agriculture. Next, production in Irrigation District No. 10 is analyzed in terms of both crop distribution and the relative contributions of ejidatarios and farmers. A concluding section analyzes the relation among water politics, corporatism, and the state-grower alliance.

IRRIGATION AND SINALOAN AGRICULTURE

The beginnings of modern capitalist agriculture in Sinaloa date from the onset of the Porfirian peace and prosperity (1876–1910). Among the Mexican entrepreneurs who began to invest in agriculture to service the needs of a growing internal and external market were many of the elite of Sinaloa. In some instances the concentration of land allowed industrious owners to undertake large capital investments and use their land for production, and not just social prestige.

The Almada family is one which invested heavily in their landholdings.[1] This hacienda was quite extensive and was situated along the banks of the Culiacán River. The Almadas were foresighted capitalists who ran their businesses well, invested heavily, and provided for their workers. Aside from a desire to integrate their enterprises vertically, the Almadas sought to diversify the region's economy and so pushed for the industrialization of the area. After introducing hemp to the region, the Almadas created a hemp factory on the northern outskirts of Culiacán. Directly across the highway the family built a brewery. To avoid paying someone to process the cane produced in their sugar cane fields, they built sugar mills at El Dorado and Navolato. The search for increased agricultural production from their holdings led the Almadas to construct rudimentary irrigation works on the Culiacán River; by 1928 the Compañía Azucarera Almada, S.A.,was irrigating 6,000 hectares on the left bank of the river.[2]

Another Culiacán family, the Redos, was involved in early irrigation projects. In 1908 the government of President Porfirio Díaz created the Loan Fund for Irrigation Works and the Development of Agriculture. Although this effort failed miserably, Diego Redo, ex-governor of Sinaloa, obtained a loan which enabled him to irrigate 10,000 hectares with water from the San Lorenco River.[3]

Domestic capital was not the only one attracted by Sinaloa's agricultural potential. Toward the end of the last century, U.S. entrepreneurs and utopian socialists became aware of the agricultural potential of this arid state with eleven major rivers cutting across it. Some of these, such as the Sinaloa Land Company, S.A., associated themselves with Mexican hacendados.[4] Others, such as the Credit Founcier of Sinaloa and the United Sugar Company, went it alone. The influence of these latter two foreign ventures proved the greatest. Credit Founcier created a socialist colony which undertook to irrigate parts of the Fuerte Valley (northern Sinaloa) in the 1870s. At the turn of the century a U.S. entrepreneur, Benjamin F. Johnston, began buying out the members of the Credit Founcier. By 1910 Johnston had accumulated the assets of the socialists and bought out the small sugar mills of the area, in the process creating his United Sugar Company. With this monopoly he built a booming town (Los Mochis) around his lands and turned the area into one of Mexico's chief sugarcane-producing areas.[5]

Despite these early efforts by private individuals, by the 1930s little of Sinaloa's hydraulic resources had been harnessed. In the 1930s Mexican agricultural policy shifted to emphasize development of large-scale irrigation districts. Because of its hydrologic uniqueness (a long thin state crossed by eleven rivers) the Ministry of Hydraulic Resources focused upon Sinaloa: from 1941 to 1970 the state received 22.3 percent of the total public investment in irrigation as compared with the next most favored state (Tamaulipas), which received only 10.4 percent.[6] As a result of this attention, acreage harvested expanded rapidly. In the 1940s the increase was at an average annual rate of 8.3 percent; in the 1950s it slowed somewhat to 3.7 percent, only to accelerate again in the 1960s to 7.1 percent and continue to increase to 7.2 percent from 1970 to 1975. By 1974–75, 700,000 irrigated hectares were planted (compared with only 260,000 hectares in rain-fed regions), and their production represented 94.66 percent of the value of agricultural production in Sinaloa.[7]

Public investment in infrastructure in the state's irrigated districts helped to make Sinaloan producers, whether private farmers or ejidatarios, responsive to the market. A market orientation, however, does not necessarily mean that export crops will predominate. Export crops may not be profitable: cotton, at one time a major crop in the state, lost its attractiveness as a result of large price fluctuations in the international market after the mid-1950s. Alternatively, there could be high economic or political barriers to entry: production of winter vegetables has been tightly controlled since the early 1960s to avoid depressing prices on the international market (see chapter 7).

With these constraints on production for export, producers have turned increasingly toward the domestic market. Here producers have encountered guaranteed prices for staples which have been kept purposely low as one component in the transfer of resources from agriculture to industry (via low food prices for workers and low prices for raw materials). The logical response for the farmer has been to shift toward the higher-value industrial and feed crops, when possible. Table 4.1 illustrates some of this shift in crop production.

In terms of specific crops, from 1939 through 1960 corn was the principal crop produced in Sinaloa, but its relative share in terms of area was declining: 42.7 percent in 1939; 41.5 percent in 1950, and 35.0 percent in 1960. Finally, in 1966 corn fell behind sorghum, a crop introduced in 1960, 13.8 percent to 17.3 percent. From 1971 to 1978 corn's share also fell behind safflower and soybean. In irrigation districts corn

TABLE 4.1
Share of Harvested Area, Sinaloa

| Period[a] | Crops (Percent of Total Harvest) | | |
	Industrial and Feed	Staples	Export[b]
1940	5.9	77.8	8.1[c]
1963	24.3	41.1	15
1965	31.2	38.6	15
1970	44.9	33.5	10
1977	57.5	33.9	10

SOURCE: *1940 Censo Agrícola, Ganadera y Forestal* and Báldemar Rubio et al., "Algunas conclusiones sobre la evolución del padrón de cultivos en Sinaloa," manuscript, p. 3.

[a] 1940: all crops; other years consider only the 12 principal crops. Industrial and feed: sorghum, safflower, soya, sugarcane, sesame, and rice; staples: wheat, beans, and corn; and export: cotton, tomatoes, and chick-peas.

[b] These figures actually overrepresent the share of area producing for the export market because not all of the production is exported, e.g., half of the winter vegetables in the state are not exported. Leonidas P. Bill Emerson, Jr., *Preview of Mexico's Vegetable Production for Export, 1980*, p. 26.

[c] Private sector only; figures approximate; unspecified 8.2 percent hectares were 46.6 percent of total cultivated land, but one can safely assume that ejidal production patterns did not differ significantly in their orientation toward commercial crops.

was never high on the list (in 1965 CAADES recommended expelling it completely from these areas);[8] it occupied ninth place among twelve principal crops in the 1963–1978 period.[9]

The structure of production also demonstrates an inefficient use of irrigation. Mexico is reported to be the only country in the world in which wheat is grown in irrigation districts.[10] In addition, sorghum hybrids were developed for rain-fed areas and do well with little water. But in Sinaloa and other parts of the country they are produced in irrigation districts because their yields increase with more water. This increment in sorghum production, however, comes at the expense of displaced crops which are less drought-resistant than sorghum and cannot be grown in rain-fed regions.[11] The state's interest in meat for the middle class and bread for the urban working class lead it to favor this pattern of production.

An important difference exists between the ejidal and private sectors' production in Sinaloa's irrigation districts. Primarily because of difficulties in receiving credit (their land, upon which they have usufruct, cannot be mortgaged, so private banks are reluctant to meet their needs), ejidatarios tend to produce crops requiring lower investments but also having a lower price. In the 1974–75 season the ejido sector was responsible for 58.2 percent of the area planted in Sinaloa's irrigation districts, yet its average income represented only 23.7 percent that of the private sector.[12] We can analyze this difference better at the local level.

IRRIGATION DISTRICT NO. 10

Sinaloa's irrigation infrastructure comprises five irrigation districts: Valle del Carrizo and Numbers 75 (Fuerte Basin), 74 (Guamúchil Valley), 63 (Guasave *municipio*), and 10 (Culiacán Valley). Irrigation District No. 10 (basically the irrigated area around the capital of the state, Culiacán) comprises 227,602 hectares, which are divided into three systems: Culiacán irrigates 103,751 hectares, Humaya 94,281 hectares, and San Lorenzo 24,570 hectares. Within the first two systems there are 14,903 ejidatarios with 110,042 hectares or 73 percent of the users with 49 percent of total surface area.* This leaves 5,546 private-property owners with 112,560 hectares, or 27 percent of the users with 51 percent of total irrigated area. Ejidatarios average 7.4 hectares, while private-property owners average 20.3 hectares.[13] Of course, these figures concerning land tenure must be augmented with other estimates, difficult to present accurately, if one is to have a clear impression of the tenure situation in the district. Table 4.2 stratifies private property by size, revealing great disparity in holdings as well as significant concentration.

If one adds to this picture the number of hectares controlled through other family members and third parties (*prestanombres*) in a maneuver to circumvent the agrarian laws, the concentration would further increase. For example, the Cristantes and Canelos families each has more than 1,000 hectares registered in different family members' names, while one source estimates that in addition to the 400 hectares registered under the Clouthier family, they control another 4,900 through *prestanombres*.[14]

The renting of ejido lands (illegal under Mexican law) also contributes to the concentration of landed wealth. For obvious reasons it is impossible to determine the exact magnitude of this practice, but most observers recognize it as a problem: the Centro de Investigaciones Agrar-

---

* Data for the third system could not be located; 1978 figures.

TABLE 4.2
*Distribution of Private Property,
Irrigation District No. 10*

Has. Per Individual	Irrigators	% of Irrigators	Total Has.	Average	% Total
less than 5	1,305	23.5	3,889.8	3.1	3.5
5–10	1,342	24.2	11,589.4	8.6	10.3
10–20	1,305	23.5	21,855.7	16.7	19.4
20–50	1,148	20.7	39,463.4	34.4	35.1
50–100	437	7.9	34,433.8	78.8	30.6
over 100	9	0.2	1,328.31	147.6	1.2

SOURCE: SARH, "Padrón de usuarios, Distrito de Riego No. 10, concentrado," Culiacán, Sinaloa.

ias reported 30 percent of the ejido land in the district rented in 1957;[15] *Proceso* reported that 31 percent of the lands watered by the Sanalona Dam (Culiacán system) were rented before 1976; and in the same time period *Proceso* found that 80 percent of the lands of the López Mateos Dam (Humaya system) were farmed illegally.[16] Finally, the president of CAADES claimed that statewide 50 percent of the ejido lands in the irrigation district were rented in the early 1970s.[17]

The structure of production in the district constitutes another important element in analyzing this area. The most important crops, by area cultivated and value, for the 1976–77 season appear in table 4.3. Four of the thirteen crops (tomato, chile for export, cucumber, and chick-peas) are exported-oriented products, one (sorghum) is for animal consumption, and the other eight are primarily for domestic human consumption (including soybeans, which are consumed by both animals and humans).

District No. 10 ranks first in the nation in value of agricultural production.[18] Nationally, Sinaloa in 1978 was the leading producer of fresh vegetables, safflower, rice, and soybeans, the second ranking producer of wheat and chick-peas, the fourth-ranking producer of cotton and sugar-cane, and the fifth-ranking producer of sorghum;[19] this district is the major factor in that production.

The value of production is skewed in favor of the private sector; for example, even though ejidatarios planted more area than private farmers (137,385 to 104,875 hectares, respectively), the value of the private sector's production more than doubled that of ejidal production (3.8 million pesos to 1.8 million pesos, respectively). These differences in

TABLE 4.3
Structure of Production, Irrigation District No. 10, 1976–1977

Crop	Has. Cultivated	Crop	Value of Production (Thousands of Pesos)
Safflower	72,984	Tomatoes	1,209,289
Soybean	57,758	Soybean	588,096
Sorghum	47,384	Sorghum	480,428
Rice	33,508	Rice	384,240
Sugarcane	30,578	Sugarcane	380,119
Beans	18,070	Safflower	332,558
Wheat	16,795	Chile for export	221,029
Tomatoes	8,449	Cucumbers	164,180
Corn	6,897	Chick-peas	120,889
Chick-peas	6,758	Wheat	79,133

SOURCE: SARH, "Producción y valor de los cultivos del ciclo agrícola: 1976–1977," Culiacán. In the 1977–1978 and 1978–1979 seasons drought procedures led to acreage limitations so the production in these later years is not representative of the structure of production when the district operates as intended.

income are related to the production of fruits and vegetables for export and basic foodstuffs. The private sector (and only a relatively small number within that sector) planted 15,699 hectares of fruits and vegetables in contrast to the ejidal area of 2,900 hectares, whereas the latter sector cultivated 47,085 hectares of corn, beans, wheat, and rice compared with the 20,709 hectares of the private farmers.[20]

Differing crop requirements as to amount and timing of irrigation, along with distinct commercial values, create a situation which often leads to conflicts among water users. Given that production of fruits and vegetables is overwhelmingly concentrated in the private sector, these conflicts usually break down along ejidatario–private property lines; nevertheless, disputes within each sector also exist. As we shall see below, the distribution of water in Irrigation District No. 10 follows the pattern described elsewhere in the Republic[21] or, in the words of ejidatarios, "the private growers never lack water."

THE DISTRIBUTION OF WATER

In 1953, after a disastrous harvest in the country's irrigation districts, a presidential decree created Directive Committees (Comité Directivo Agrícola, CDA) to manage each district; their raison d'être was the "rational" planning of production and use of resources. Nevertheless, the institutions were not immediately organized; in 1959 Sinaloa farmers protested the delay.[22]

The Directive Committee formally integrates the various public and private groups responsible for production into the official decision-making body of the district. In addition to creating a channel for inputs by these groups, the CDA structure also provides a mechanism for the dissemination of its decisions: each representative is responsible for informing his constituency. The Directive Committee's existence thus allows federal officials to insist that it is the users themselves who run the district.[23] But rather than constituting a local organization designed to administer the district, as in parts of Spain,[24] the CDA is better understood as the formal arena where national and local interests are played out under the watchful eye of the state.

Membership in the CDA changes over time to reflect the increased complexity of development programs in Mexico. In 1965 the Directive Committee consisted of six members:[25]

Executive: Ministry of Hydraulic Resources
Secretary: Ministry of Agriculture
Representatives: Farmers
                Ejidatarios
                Banco Nacional de Crédito Agrícola (agricultural bank)
                Banco Nacional de Crédito Ejidal (ejido bank)

By 1977 the two government banks became one, and five more memberships had been added:[26]

Ministry of Agrarian Reform
Agricultural Insurance Group of Sinaloa
Ministry of Industry and Commerce
Private banks
Farmers of District No. 74

The following year another five representatives were incorporated, bringing the total to fifteen:[27]

State government
Productora Nacional de Semilla (national seed manufacturer)
Comisión Nacional para la Subsistencia Popular (agency for food subsidy)
Nacional Financiera, S.A. (state development bank)
Another member from the Ministry of Hydraulic Resources

A few characteristics of the committee are worth mentioning. Irrigators make up three votes out of the fifteen total; one other vote, that of the private banks, is nongovernmental. Thus the federal government controls ten votes, with a single additional vote accruing to the state government. In terms of the leverage of irrigators in guiding CDA policy toward their interests, it appears that unless they form alliances with governmental agencies, their voices will be overwhelmed. Unfortunately, votes are never recorded, and members refused to discuss them.

The representativeness of the users of the CDA also requires note. Article 67 of the Federal Water Code stipulates that the representatives of the producers should be divided proportionally according to total number of producers in the district. Since District No. 10 has 14,903 ejidatarios and 5,546 farmers,* the ejido sector should have at least two votes to the private sector's one. However, the Directive Committee actually has two votes for the private sector and one for the ejidatarios.†

The communication between the CDA and irrigators also calls into question its representativeness. The CDA published a bulletin but only 500 copies were published per issue for over 20,000 irrigators, and half of the copies were appropriated by bureaucrats both within and outside the state. Furthermore, little space was dedicated to airing user complaints, and in 1978 publication was suspended.[28] Consequently little information about CDA meetings reaches the producers, a circumstance which leads to the discovery of new charges when water bills are paid and much ill feeling.

State control over the committee is attributable to three factors: the overwhelming presence of the federal government, technological expertise, and national policy. In setting water rates the SARH presents the basic data for calculations,‡ although the local farmer association also presents its data. Perhaps the most important function of the CDA is

---

*Unfortunately, as I indicated above, these figures are only for the Culiacán and Humaya systems. Nevertheless, the small size of the San Lorenzo system (24,570 has., or not quite 10 percent of the total district area) means it cannot drastically affect the basic tenure distribution in the district.

†The CDA for district No. 10 is also the same for District No. 74, which is quite small (20,290 hectares in 1977). Only the Water Schedule (explained below) is decided by district; all other decisions cover both districts.

‡The Ministry of Hydraulic Resources was combined with that of Agriculture, becoming the Secretaría de Agricultura y Recursos Hidráulicos, SARH.

the setting of the Water Schedule, a program regulating the area planted by hectare and crop. But in arriving at an "optimal mixture" the CDA is dependent upon SARH data on the amount of water stored in the dams and the water each crop needs. Farmers are not always in agreement with these figures.[29] Other factors considered to some degree are: the market for each crop; a crop's profitability; the type of soil; soil infestations and plagues in the area; export demand; local demand; preference of producers for particular crops; and coordination with national agricultural planning.[30] The secrecy surrounding the actual functioning of the CDA once again hampers investigations: no informant claimed to know the weight assigned to each of the above factors.

The integration with national policy places formal constraints on the actions of the CDA. The CDA formula is subject to modifications by the Regional Agriculture, Livestock and Forestry Committee, which requires that the district plan conform to state plans. From there the plan is forwarded to an interministerial commission constituted by representatives from the Agriculture and Agrarian Reform Ministries, which gives final approval to the district program, certifying that it conforms to the national plan.[31] The Federal Water Code and the Federal Agrarian Reform Law provide other constraints. For example, the range of fines is set by the water code[32] and administered by the water ministry; the CDA has nothing to do with fines or police action.

Given the dependence of the region's agriculture on irrigation, an examination of how water is actually distributed during drought periods will give us insight into the functioning of the state-grower alliance.

Each of the systems in District No. 10 has a master list of those lots with water rights, the *padrón de usuarios*. Everyone in the register has rights to water, regardless of the date of entry. The SARH has the right to modify the register when new lands are opened, when private property is expropriated in favor of ejidos, or in the rare event that it is necessary to expel an irrigator. When private property is divided by inheritance or sale, however, the entry in the register continues to be for the original lot, but now with subaccounts. In time of water restriction, it is the original lot which has water rights. If a 100 hectare lot is divided into five 20 hectare lots and the CDA authorizes water for 20 hectares per user, the five subaccounts must decide how to divide the 20 hectares, rather than each receiving 20 hectares worth of water. Despite this legal stipulation, reality is often different.[33]

Once the Ministry determines a water shortage condition exists, Article 60 of the Water Code stipulates that the volume of water will be divided by the number of users to determine the amount corresponding to each. In accordance with the water demands of the particular crop, the number of hectares each irrigator can plant is determined by the CDA in the Water Schedule. If these procedures were followed, they would conform with Article 27 of the same code which gives preference to ejidatarios in such circumstances; thus if the limit is 20 hectares, the ejidatario (whose legal limit is 10 irrigated hectares, although the average in the district is only 7.4 hectares) can plant his entire lot while the private owner with over 20 hectares must plant the rest of his plot with crops which do not need irrigation or allow it to lie fallow. As we shall see, neither the spirit not the letter of the law is always followed.

Complaints about water distribution flourish in periods of drought. The basic complaint is that vegetable producers secure the water they need to irrigate their normal area while ejidatarios are forced to cut back on their production or to cultivate corn and hope it can survive without irrigation. In 1978 in a particular section of the district some ejidos lost most of the corn because it was too dry; many ejidatarios did not plant rice because the water was not available until a month after the optimal planting period, but, according to the canal keeper in charge, one vegetable producer was able to plant his 800 hectares. [34]

When the CDA distributes the authorized surface area per crop to the private and ejidal sectors, each representative assumes the responsibility of allocating the authorization among his sector. Until the 1976–1977 season the CDA administered this process, but the complaints by irrigators became too bothersome, so the Directive Committee transferred this responsibility to the sectoral representatives.[35] Without a change in the power relations within ejidos, however, this decentralization merely affords the ejido elite (often referred to as "caciques ejidales")[36] one more opportunity to benefit at the expense of the rest of the sector, rather than providing for democratic local control. For example, the water code provides for regrouping (*compactos*) of water rights when efficiency so requires;[37] thus in water shortage periods when an ejidatario is authorized to plant only a fraction of his lot, SARH will request that the ejidatarios plant cooperatively in complete lots. In one ejido in which I interviewed, the community's leader and a few ejidatarios claimed the ejido planted rice in groups; yet a number of ejidatarios located at the extreme of the ejido were unaware of the opportunity to plant.

Surveillance of the allocated area is the responsibility of the ejido's leaders (*comisariado ejidal*) and SARH. The former gives the ejido's leaders permission for an individual to plant a portion of the area allocated to the ejido; when the ejidatario, through the official bank which finances his production, pays the water bill for his crop, SARH checks his surface area against the total authorized for the ejido. The private property owner, except in the case of fruits and vegetables, is checked against the total for his sector when he pays for his water. Fruit and vegetable growers are regulated by the local producers' organization (in Culiacán, AARC), which in turn is allocated a certain area by the national producers' union (Unión Nacional de Productores de Hortalizas, UNPH; see chapter 7).

Given the numerous violations of the Water Code in the actual distribution of water, questions arise concerning the ejido sector's participation in the CDA. The basic question centers on the independence of the ejido vote on the CDA. This representative is always appointed by the state organ of the CNC, the Liga de Comunidades Agrarias. Two other campesino organizations in the district (Confederación Campesina Independiente (CCI) and Consejo Agrario Mexicano (CAM) have a voice but no vote on the committee. The delegate of the Unión General de Obreros y Campesinos Mexicanos (UGOCM) resigned in 1979, complaining that the CDA was at the service of the "*latifundistas* disguised as small property owners . . . which is why the programs which are presented in committee meetings are previously analyzed by the farmers, which is also why 90% of the times the program favors them."[38]

There is evidence to support such a view. In the thirteen years of minutes examined, only once was a committee appointed to look into complaints by ejidatarios about vegetable producers' water usage. The minutes gave no indication that the Liga representative brought the matter up for discussion; rather it was the fact that the press had begun to report such complaints that seemed to persuade the CDA to move on the matter.[39] In addition, neither the charges made by the UGOCM nor their representative's resignation were reported in the press.

Despite the bias of the CDA, one would err in assuming that ejidatarios are completely subjugated by their corporatist representation on the CDA. Certainly the ejidatarios' organization in the CNC and their dependence upon the official bank and official agronomists make protest difficult; investigation of CDA records demonstrates the passivity of the CNC representative. But as Ronfeldt discovered in Atencingo,[40] and as this book confirms, ejidatarios gain a measure of success in achieving some of their local goals as long as they remain within the limits set by the central government. In irrigation districts this means basically not blocking canals in protest of water distribution: ejidatarios interviewed could only recall one such action, and when the army arrived to patrol the canal, the action ceased. But there is some maneuverability around crop areas and bureaucratic red tape. This leeway is not attained through the corporatist link with the Liga, but rather through clientelism.[41] For example, one patron intervened before the CDA to increase by 2,000 hectares the area of rice to be watered by the flow of the San Lorenzo River.[42]

Centralized agricultural development plans take little notice of the needs of local producers, especially in the case of ejidatarios. In the interests of political stability some mechanism to allow them to influence the plans is necessary to insure a slight degree of social mobility and thus less incentive for recourse to political participation.[43] With respect to ejidatarios it must be done in such a manner as to make clear that the disagreement over the particulars of a policy does not imply that the sector disagrees with general development policies. Since the CNC is designed to express passive and blanket ejido support of the political regime, it would be dangerous to allow the CNC to become involved in modifications of policy.

Thus patrons become the channel through which requests for specific modifications are made. The result is a separation of tasks (one which most likely evolved through experience rather than as a deliberate state policy): CNC leaders continue to provide the unquestioning support at the level of national politics that the system requires, while local groups of ejidatarios find some response to their immediate economic needs.

Most small farmers find themselves in a similar position to that of ejidatarios: with respect to the operation of the district they are uninformed, have little voice, and are put on the defensive when confronted with a water shortage problem or new programs to which they must contribute. The private sector representative to the CDA is appointed by AARC, which, as we saw in chapter 3, is dominated by the large farmers. When the interests of the family and subsistence farmer (71.2%

of private farmers) coincide with those of the rural elite (such as on water fees), they benefit when AARC is successful. But when their interests diverge (as in drought periods), family and subsistence farmers find few means to place their interests on the CDA agenda. Since AARC leaders do not need their allegiance, either to maintain control of the organization or to bargain with the state, these farmers cannot circumvent the corporatist system via patron-client networks. Consequently, family and subsistence farmers are actually in a worse position for defending their interests than are ejidatarios.

Culiacán's rural elite find themselves in a much better position. They have a vote, and, though their ability to form voting alliances with some government agencies on the CDA over particular issues was impossible to ascertain given the secrecy of voting records, the fact that Mexican development has disproportionately benefited an agricultural and industrial elite[44] suggests that one can assume they have powerful allies within the government. In addition, they have access to resources which allows them to bargain with the state on a technical and therefore less politically sensitive basis. Thus when a Hydraulic Resources study called for raising the water fees,* AARC countered with its own technical experts, resulting in a smaller increase in fees than that sought by the Ministry.[45]

The economic strength of this group also allows them to bribe the gatekeepers and plant more than the area authorized. One indication of this is found in the official statistics of SARH and AARC: the former reported 8,449 hectares of tomatoes in 1976–1977[46] while the latter reported an additional 624 hectares.[47] Given that SARH figures are based on water fees while AARC figures are based on market statistics, the latter most likely represent the area actually cultivated.

But the most telling indication of the ability of the growers to defend their production for export successfully is the distribution of water in drought periods. The year 1976–1977 was such a period and the state, through the CDA, initially determined that there was sufficient water to allow each producer to irrigate 20 hectares. The UNPH's market

---

*Ejidatarios are exempt from water fees, although they do pay maintenance fees. The various payments by users fall far short of covering the costs of operating the districts, leading to an enormous subsidy by the state.

analysis, however, indicated that the production of 14,615 hectares for the 437 tomato growers of the AARC would allow Mexico to meet international demand. The UNHP allocated permits for the full area, averaging 33.3 hectares per tomato grower, to AARC. The Culiacán association requested that the CDA authorize water for the full area, to be distributed in the normal fashion (AARC would parcel them out to the tomato growers).

The state confronted a dilemma at this point. To allow the tomato growers more than 20 hectares would violate Article 60 of the Water Code. But if each tomato grower planted only 20 hectares the country would lose both foreign exchange and employment. These would be costly sacrifices at any time for Mexico because of the shortcomings of the ISI development strategy, but at this moment of economic crisis (1976) the state could ill afford foregoing the benefits of export production. The decision was made (CDA minutes contain no indication of who proposed it) to allow *permutas* of water rights—an individual could transfer his water rights to another lot in the same sector.[48] According to interviews with personnel from SARH, the intent was to allow non-tomato growers to coproduce with tomato growers and therefore partake of the profits of the most remunerative crop in the state. But, according to the same sources, the tomato growers were reluctant to do so and instead bought the water rights—an action which should be illegal since under Mexican law water belongs to the nation and cannot be sold (the irrigation fee in a district covers the cost of distribution).

A number of people benefited from this resolution. Although the resultant distribution of benefits from tomato production was less than that sought by the state, sellers of such water rights presumably received a larger profit from selling the water than from using it to produce their normal crop. Mexican vegetable producers were able to meet international demand and employ their labor force, which met state interests. And tomato growers retained control over their lucrative crop, even though their profit was lower than would have been the case if they had been able to acquire the requisite water directly from the state.

The constraints on ejidatario and family farmers, as well as the interest of the state in foreign exchange and employment generation lead to a situation in which the crops which require most water are the ones whose production expands in time of drought. Tomatoes serve as

TABLE 4.4

Irrigation and Production

Product	Waterings Required	1976–77 Has. Planted	1977–78 Has. Planted	Percent Change
Total		318,280	242,260	− 24
Basic Foodstuffs				
Corn	3.5	6,897	3,869	− 44
Beans	1.3	18,070	13,999	− 23
Rice	11.1	33,508	29,153	− 13
Wheat	5.0	16,795	19,576	+ 17
Safflower	1.7	74,580	73,981	− 01
Soybeans	5.5	57,758	4,368	− 92
Vegetables		14,519	18,749	+ 29
Tomatoes[a]	9.2	6,747	8,095	+ 20

SOURCE: SARH, "Producción y valor de los cultivos del ciclo agrícola," Distrito de Riego No. 10; SARH, "Cuotas de Servicio."

[a] Does not include tomatoes for industrial use *(tomate industrial)* in the domestic market.

an example: they require approximately three times as much water as corn, yet in 1978, another drought year, corn dried up in the fields while tomato growers maneuvered to acquire a disproportionate share of the scarce water. Table 4.4 provides a vivid picture of this trade-off.

WATER AND THE STATE-GROWER ALLIANCE

The international market makes its impact felt upon the politics of irrigation through its fluctuating demand for winter vegetables. This demand can be strongest at precisely the time when the producing area is suffering from water shortage. Competition between these export-oriented crops and those for the domestic market ensues. The Mexican state plays a fundamental role in the distribution of water, both via provision of the infrastructure and the decision as to which crops receive water. The state uses the CDA to structure the relationships among various social forces present in the district in such a manner as to increase its mediative capacity. Because the federal government controls two-thirds of the votes, the state is able to use the committee to support the state-grower alliance's ability to respond to the international market.

Despite general agreement on the need to produce vegetables for export, divergence of interests between state and grower does arise in water politics. In this particular case, growers were successful in convincing the state to accept grower preferences. As we saw, the state wished to produce all the tomatoes the export market could bear. Although the state made an initial attempt to spread the benefits of tomato exports in hard times, when the tomato growers maneuvered to buy the water rights of other farmers illegally, the SARH ignored the situation. As a result, corn for subsistence withered and died while tomato producers were given an opportunity to increase their earnings over the previous year. In addition, the economic strength of the export producers allows them to circumvent the Water Schedule allocations by greasing the palms of canal keepers.

As chapter 3 noted, AARC, created by the state and maintaining an official monopoly over the representation of farmers in the area, is definitely corporatist in structure. I argued in that chapter that growers had gained control over the organization and were using it to defend their interests as they defined them. In this chapter that analysis is reinforced by the cases of water prices and tomato production. Here AARC advocated policies which competed with the government's and succeeded in modifying state policy. Such an outcome cannot be accounted for if one adheres to the authoritarian-corporatist model with its controlled demand-making structure. This chapter suggests, therefore, that within the Mexican political system there exists a subsystem of competitive interest representation between the agricultural elite and the state.

Ejidatarios also find some room to moderate their weakness in the corporatist system by recourse to a clientelist subsystem of interest representation. The state is able to accommodate this divergence because patron-client relationships contribute to political stability at the local level without linking local issues to the broader distribution of power in the country's political economy. In addition, patrons powerful enough to carry weight outside the ejido are few, and clientelism remains the basis of power for corrupt ejido leaders.

Although long-term national plans seek to increase both export and basic foodstuffs,[49] scarce resources in the short run may pit one goal against the other; it all depends upon the demand from the international market. If demand increases, the Mexican state-grower alliance will see to it that Mexican supply increases. The costs of meeting that demand will be shifted to producers and consumers of other crops. This includes cutting back on feed grain production, which analysts have believed serves as the guide to the pattern of agricultural production in Mexico. This analysis suggests that although the area dedicated to export crops has significantly diminished, their impact on the country's agriculture remains significant.

5

ACCESS TO LAND

Production of vegetables for export is carried out by a small number of growers in the best lands of the Culiacán irrigation district. The combination of the state's agrarian reform and irrigation programs make land tenure in the district particularly contentious. The district's Directive Committee had no jurisdiction on this matter. But because land reform has fundamental political significance for peasant identification with the modern Mexican state, the president plays a direct role in resolving these questions when they arise in areas with high visibility. This chapter, therefore, provides us with another opportunity to examine the ability of the state-grower alliance to resolve crucial production issues in favor of the vegetable producer.

The chapter is organized in two sections. The first provides the descriptive elements of two cases of land tenure disputes. In the second section, we turn to the analysis of the strategies of the rural elite, campesinos, and state. The heterogeneity of each group as well as their actions are analyzed from a perspective comparing the two different periods.

TWO CHALLENGES

Campesinos on the Offensive (1958–1959). On February 5, 1958, UGOCM Secretary General Jacinto López and a group of followers peacefully occupied the lands of the foreign-owned Cananea *latifundio* in northern Sonora. Five days later 3,500 members of the UGOCM's Culiacán affiliate, the Federación de Obreros y Campesinos del Valle de Culiacán (FOCVC), invaded 20,000 hectares of vegetable lands in the Culiacán Valley. The land invasions in Culiacán lasted four days and ended only when the president sent his personal envoy to the area to negotiate a settlement. The settlement consisted of a pledge to provide the invaders with land in a soon-to-be-opened section of the irrigation district and to set up a commission to study the illegal concentration of land.[1]

This first phase of the land conflict drew to a close with all sides apparently satisfied. The government had terminated this illegal manifestation of discontent. The UGOCM received a commitment that lands would be distributed. The rural elite seemed to have made out well also, as none of the vegetable farms which had been the physical focus of the occupations was expropriated. Nevertheless, both local actors knew that the days to come required constant vigilance to safeguard the fulfillment of the agreement reached.

Statewide 4,000 Sinaloan members of the UGOCM and 3,000 CNC members were requesting land.[2] On March 9, 4,000 hectares from the "El Venadillo" section south of Culiacán were promised to 200 UGOCMistas and 200 CNCistas.[3] Although these lands had not previously been cultivated, they were to be included in the San Lorenzo section of Irrigation District No. 10; however, the dam which would provide a guaranteed supply of water to these lands was still in the planning stages while the Humaya dam in the other new section of the district was near completion.* Consequently these campesinos received what at that time was marginal land within the irrigation district. The land distributed was divided equally between the UGOCM and the CNC as an inducement to CNC members to remain loyal in the face of UGOCM militancy and rewards. CNC members actually fared better than UGOCMistas in early April when 484 UGOCMistas and 578 CNCistas were promised land in the "Las Bocas" area of the San Lorenzo section.[4]

Success, though partial, stimulated the UGOCM leaders to push forward. Joaquin Salgado, secretary general of the FOCVC, traveled to Mexico City to obtain credit for the new ejidatarios of "El Venadillo" and announced that 20,000 hectares belonging to the Costa Rica sugar mill controlled by the national development bank (Nacional Financiera)

---

*Until the San Lorenzo dam was completed in 1981, however, these lands were irrigated only if water from the other sections of the district were left over after meeting the needs of those lands.

would be turned over to UGOCM campesinos.[5] A brigade of Agrarian Department surveyors was reported to have come from Mexico City to survey 145 ejidos to be created in the state for the UGOCMistas, 75 in the Culiacán Valley alone.[6] In May reports circulated that President Ruíz Cortines would expropriate 28,000 hectares which would also benefit the UGOCM; since, however, the UGOCM claimed to require at least 50,000 hectares for its members, problems were expected to continue.[7] Also in May the UGOCM raised the issue of "foreign"* ownership of coastal lands and asked for an investigation by the commission set up as part of the agreement to abandon the lands occupied in February.

The spectre of renewed land invasions remained on the Culiacán Valley horizon throughout 1958[8] as progress seemed stalled: in the year following the first UGOCM invasions fewer than 2,000 hectares had actually been distributed. In addition, the investigatory commission, which had contributed to the UGOCM's strategic decision to retreat in February, still had not made its report.

When President López Mateos declared in January 1959, a month after taking office, that security of land tenure would be guaranteed, he aggravated an already volatile situation. Jacinto López was reported to have threatened to invade all of Sinaloa and Sonora. Immediately thereafter the Mexican army began to patrol the International Highway with machine guns to protect lands under cultivation.[9]

In early February UGOCM leaders met with President López Mateos in Cananea, where he was distributing the Sonora lands occupied by the UGOCM one year earlier.[10] He sent a personal envoy to Sinaloa to give the UGOCM and CNC campesinos material possession of the lands they had been promised a year earlier.

Attention now focused on the Humaya lands, which were actually the most valuable lands available for distribution at this time. The Agrarian Department chief noted that property titles would be respected except in the Humaya region, where private property would be reduced to 30 hectares. The creation of ejidos in "Las Bocas" and "El Venadillo"

---

*When the UGOCM referred to "foreigners," they meant principally the Mexicans of Greek extraction who maintained a tight community with an emphasis on cultural heritage and who controlled a good deal of the winter vegetable production; see Rubio Félix, *Cuando tomamos la tierra*, passim. Sinaloa growers are also of German, French, Chinese and Spanish ancestry.

was cited as a precedent for bringing agrarian reform to the 130,000 hectares of the Humaya region.[11] The UGOCM was confident that they would be the chief beneficiaries of this distribution. The CNC had been accused, even by the quasi-official press, of having abandoned the agrarian struggle, and it was evident to all that the UGOCM had been the catalyst for the progress achieved since 1957.[12]

Nevertheless, the federal government decided to marginalize the UG-OCM in the distribution of the Humaya lands. Of the 130,000 hectares in this region of the irrigation district, 60 percent were distributed to ejidatarios, an outcome directly attributable to the pressure tactics of the UGOCM. The UGOCM itself, however, received few lands, and campesinos quickly abandoned the independent union in favor of the official union and a chance to partake of the bonanza. As a result, the UGOCM faded from Sinaloa land politics for a decade.

Growers Take The Offensive (1975–1976). Following a lull in the sixties, tension over land began to grow again in the 1970s, this time on a national scale.[13] Between January and October 1975 Sinaloan farmers experienced more than 70 invasions, and at times over 50,000 hectares were under the control of the invading campesinos. In September the Ministry of Agrarian Reform (SRA, formerly the Agrarian Department) announced that it would continue its investigations of illegal landholdings. Spurred by the actions of the federal agrarian bureaucracy, land invasions proliferated in October in southern Sonora and northern Sinaloa; campesinos from the UGOCM and members of local unions took part in the occupations. In all cases the campesinos refused to negotiate with local authorities and private farmers, demanding instead to meet directly with national authorities.[14] In Sonora, Hidalgo, and Veracruz, blood was shed in encounters between invading campesinos and the army, police, and property owners.

In a hurried attempt to distribute lands and moderate campesino unrest, an expropriation was carried out in Sonora which affected forty-one small farmers with parcels of between 5 and 20 hectares, clearly an illegal step under the agrarian legislation. The Sonoran farmers' association was quick to pick up on this case to demonstrate their defense of small farmers faced with arbitrary government action.[15] On November 21, 1975, Echeverría expropriated 2,500 hectares in the disputed Montelargo region of the Culiacán Valley,[16] promised to campesinos back in the days of the 1958 land invasions. The leader of the campesinos benefiting from the Montelargo expropriations claimed this success was only the beginning.[17]

On November 24, 1975, 4,000 hectares just north of Culiacán planted with vegetables for export were occupied. The next day 150 campesinos took over 500 hectares in the Culiacán Valley. The secretary of the SRA, Félix Barra García, arrived in Culiacán to confer with Governor Alfonso G. Calderón, but refused to confer with representatives of the Sinaloan rural elite, rejecting allegations that campesinos had occupied private lands in Sinaloa. Growers announced a work stoppage to put on pressure for an immediate end to the land invasions; to demonstrate strength on an issue they realized would be settled through politics and not merely litigation; to restructure the channels for class-state negotiations; and to unite all private farmers behind their organizations.[18]

The state responded to the pressure of the campesinos and the farmers by creating a national tripartite commission (Comisión Nacional Tripartita Agraria—CNTA) to bring each of the three parties in the conflict to the negotiating table; local branches (CTA) were also created. The CNC and the UGOCM agreed to expel any members who took part in land invasions. The private sector sought a negotiated solution by offering to invest 150 million pesos to create small and medium-sized industries in rural areas so as to decrease the unemployment which, in the farmers' view, was the cause of the land invasions. The federal government also contributed to creating a climate for resolving the crisis, as it announced that Echeverría would travel to Sinaloa to distribute 3,000 certificates of agrarian reform immunity to small farmers.[19]

On May 3 a special commission on land invasions was created with personnel from the Ministries of the Interior and Justice, the Mixed Agrarian Commission, and the army. More than 2,000 members of different police agencies were involved.[20] Action was also taken against the private sector. On July 14, 732 individuals from 31 families who allegedly owned 39,000 hectares were notified that they had thirty days to present SRA with their defense of legal ownership or their lands would be distributed.[21] But invasions continued as peasants, fearing their interests would be sold out once again, would not follow their leaders on this issue.

The SRA again refused offers by the Sinaloa farmers to sell and donate land as a solution to the problem of landless peasants. Barra García noted that the SRA would "definitely" not buy land in Sinaloa or Sonora, but would only apply the law. Barra García also informed campesinos that 100,000 hectares which presently belonged to 130 families[22] would be distributed before the end of Echeverría's term, some three months away. Governor Calderón joined the bandwagon by declaring that 40,000 hectares in Sinaloa would be distributed and the SRA would begin investigating another 25,000 hectares.[23]

Following several weeks of uncertainty, Echeverría made his move. On November 18 and 19 the president expropriated 100,000 hectares (including 37,000 irrigated) in Sonora. While Sonoran farmers were reacting to a fait accompli, Sinaloan farmers were still hopeful of avoiding such an outcome. On the 23d, 702 farmers received provisional injunctions against expropriations.[24] Three days later representatives of the Sinaloa rural elite met with President Echeverría in Mexico City. The farmers reiterated their offer to resolve the crisis in Sinaloa through donation, sale, and incorporation of new lands. Once again the state refused to buy land from the farmers, but this time Echeverría accepted the farmers' donation of 10,000 irrigated hectares and 3,500 rain-fed hectares. After the president and the farmers worked out this agreement, the campesino unions were called in to talk,[25] and the CNC walked away with the bulk of the land.[26]

Thus on November 26 the land invasion crisis in Sinaloa reached a temporary solution once again. The basis of the solution was the same which the rural elite had repeatedly offered—the donation rather than the expropriation of land from the rural elite—but the timing was all Echeverría's. The campesinos of Sinaloa were not pleased by the solution; in the final two weeks of November, 20,000 hectares were occupied.[27] But the context within which independent campesinos maneuvered changed dramatically with the end of Echeverría's term. President López Portillo, with the campesinos' leadership and the governor following his lead, took a definite stand against land invasions, thus undercutting any support independent campesinos could gain from a waffling presidential policy on the matter.

ACTORS' STRATEGIES AND REWARDS

Peasants. Peasant politics in the earlier period revolved around the UGOCM, but in the 1975–1976 invasions nonaffiliated groups as well as wildcatters in the UGOCM became the key actors. The UGOCM can be seen as an initiator at the local level, while the CNC reacted to actions taken by the UGOCM, independent campesinos, and the state.

In the earlier period, a rift within the Revolutionary Elite during an election year helps explain why the UGOCM was active and why the state responded with moderation to the land invasions. But it does not shed light on why the UGOCM was able to gain a foothold in the Culiacán Valley. Joaquin Salgado, a young CNC leader in the Navolato area of the Culiacán *municipio*, headed a group of *colonos* and ejidatarios attempting to force the local sugar mill owners to honor various aspects of their production contract. Since the state CNC leadership did not respond to their needs, Salgado sought support elsewhere. He contacted fellow Sinaloan Lázaro Rubio Félix, himself a CNC leader in Sinaloa during the bloody 1930s and 1940s* and now secretary of campesino affairs for the UGOCM.[28]

In early 1957 Salgado established a local UGOCM affiliate in Culiacán, the Federación de Obreros y Campesinos del Valle de Culiacán. Only "three or four" ejido groups presented official delegations at the founding congress, but "more than 1,000" campesinos attended, mostly out of curiosity. Salgado was elected secretary general and Roberto Arriaga secretary of organization.[29]

In an effort to publicize the continuation of agrarian reform as a key national issue and to map out a strategy for action, the UGOCM called an Interstate Congress for March 30–31, 1957, to be held in Los Mochis, Sinaloa. The chief result of the congress was the promulgation of "Agreement Number One," which called for occupation of lands held in violation of the agrarian laws if the government took no action on the matter.[30] Shortly after the Congress, ex-President Cárdenas arrived in Los Mochis on his tour of the northeast, during which he stirred emotions with his condemnation of the CNC as unrepresentative of campesino interests and called for a return to the policies of the 1930s.[31] The tenor of his remarks at the very least lent indirect support to the UGOCM mobilization.†

In late November 1957 the UGOCM met in Mecixo City and reiterated

---

*See his reminiscences in *Sinaloa, Campo de sangre: la quinta columna nazi en acción* (Mexico: Federación Editorial Mexicana, 1978).

†The *Excelsior* coverage of Cárdenas' Los Mochis visit made no mention of the UGOCM Congress, nor did the Mexico City daily refer to it in any time. Lázaro Rubio Félix, *Cuando tomanos la tierra*, does not mention the Cárdenas trip, nor do Gerritt Huizer's references to the Los Mochis Congress (see bibliography). Nevertheless, both

its call for the president to carry out the land reform in the northwest, or "Agreement Number One" would go into effect. The Ruíz Cortines administration turned a deaf ear, and in January 1958 the UGOCM called for a meeting to discuss implementation of the agreement.[32] Lelegates from seven states representing 30,000 landless campesinos attended the meeting in Culiacán.[33]

Discussion of the threatened invasions was heated and by no means unanimous. Ramon Danzós Palomino (a local Communist party leader who had just returned from Moscow)[34] and others advised that before taking a "dangerous path with uncertain results" the UGOCM should first gain "the solidarity of the masses on a national scale" to avoid repressive acts by the government. They found themselves in the minority, however, as the assembly decided that Jacinto López would lead the invasion of the Cananea *latifundio*; FOCVC would be in charge of the occupation of the *latifundios* of "foreigners" on the Sinaloa coast; and the other federations of the UGOCM would stand ready to carry out any further decision as events unfolded.[35]

The UGOCM now concentrated upon stepping up the pressure on agrarian authorities. The following day more than 7,000 UGOCMistas marched in front of the Sinaloa governor's office in Culiacán. The march demonstrated the union's ability to mobilize thousands of campesinos and clearly challenged official claims that no agrarian problems remained.[36] The march and meeting also prepared the participants psychologically for the coming land occupations. Finally, given later FOCVC actions, one can assume that there were hopes that this show of strength would convince the authorities of the need to negotiate.

Peasant reaction was not all favorable. The secretary of the Liga proclaimed that the Liga knew that "sooner or later" peasant desires would be met without resorting to violent acts.[37] Some UGOCM campesinos themselves were unwilling to take on the rural elite and the state in direct action: in San Pedro 249 ejidatarios dismissed the UGOCM leader and refused to support any illegal actions.[38]

The FOCVC leaders appear to have decided , despite the accords of the earlier UGOCM strategy meeting, to allow more time for a nego-

---

the timing of the two events and the personal links among Jacinto López (UGOCM secretary general), Lombardo Toledano (UGOCM founder and CTM leader under Cárdenas), and Cárdenas suggest that some coordination of the two events may have taken place.

tiated solution. When Jacinto López took the Cananea lands, the FOCVC failed to occupy simultaneously the Culiacán Valley lands, as had been decided at the earlier strategy meeting. Instead the FOCVC published a manifesto in the press justifying the Cananea invasions. According to Rubio Félix the FOCVC did not act because they still lacked sufficient popular support for the invasions. Nevertheless, he himself recognized that there was pressure from López to carry out the occupations, and he presents no evidence that when they did invade five days later public opinion had significantly shifted to the FOCVC's side.[39]

Occupying the land for four days and obtaining favorable agreement from the president's envoy emboldened the FOCVC. In a review of the events of the past half year (February–August), the FOCVC's executive council enumerated the following problems: a) a total examination of private property in the Culiacán Valley was required; b) the secretary of agriculture's February promise to create a commission presided over by the governor and endowed with executive power to investigate the existence of disguised *latifundios* had not yet been carried out; c) an "enormous" amount of land on the coast was in the hands of "foreigners"; and d) 50 percent of land distributed recently went to CNC members despite their nonparticipation in the struggle; in addition, the CNC distributed their share of the land to people who had no roots in farming and therefore abandoned it shortly after receiving the land. The group also heard calls for renewed efforts in the fight for land from Rigoberto Arriaga, secretary of organization, just back from Prague where he had attended the World Congress of Working Class Youth.[40]

Despite the rhetoric, the UGOCM undertook no new invasions in Sinaloa. Their strategy appears to have been to keep issues on the table during the transition of power (López Mateos had been elected in early July, but would not take office until December 1), but not to provoke the outgoing president. Although 15,000 UGOCMistas demonstrated in Culiacán on the day of Ruíz Cortines' final state of the union address, no civil disorder was undertaken.[41]

But the new president's early pronouncements on the issue of agrarian reform (ordering the military to impede land invasions) did not please the UGOCM. They therefore made direct protestations to the president and sought to enlist the support of the Sinaloa governor. The FOCVC, without informing the national UGOCM, threatened to concentrate

10,000 campesinos in front of the governor's offices in early March of 1959. The state branches of the electric workers', teachers', telegraph workers', and railroad workers' unions, already mobilized due to the general ferment in Mexican labor politics in this period, all announced their support for the campesinos' petitions.[42] Through the efforts of Governor Leyva Velázquez and the Agrarian Department chief, a special envoy from the president was sent to give campesinos from both the UGOCM and the CNC material possession of the land they had been promised as a result of the February 1958 invasions.[43]

The FOCVC's Arriaga led UGOCM leaders in a three-day demonstration in front of the governor's office. The action allowed the union to demonstrate strength, keep the issues in the public mind, and cultivate the governor's friendship. Other officials, state and federal, had attempted to negotiate a solution with the UGOCM, but it was not until the governor personally intervened that the UGOCM ended the demonstration, although he offered nothing new.[44] The governor, therefore, was encouraged to feel that he had a special relationship with the union. Governor Leyva Velázquez, ex-secretary general of the CNC and a general in the Mexican Army, was thought to be a good ally, though he ultimately played a minor role which did not favor the UGOCM to any important degree.

In 1959 the federal government was still not ready to distribute the 130,000 prime hectares of the Humaya region. UGOCM strategy emphasized distribution of the lands in the San Lorenzo region promised as a result of the 1958 occupations and the credit to make these productive, apparently in order to give the government time to organize its distribution plan.

By summer the UGOCM reactivated the struggle for land distribution. In late July 1959 the Agrarian Department chief arrived in Culiacán to give symbolic possession and credit to the ejidatarios of "Los Bocas" and "El Venadillo." FOCVC leaders, apparently to underscore their view that the present success was but a small step forward, did not appear on the podium despite the fact that their members were among the beneficiaries and that CNC leaders were present. Instead Salgado made further demands of the federal government: the modification of constitutional statutes which limited ejido plots to 10 hectares if the land were irrigated; measures to stop the de facto concentration of land in a few hands; and the suspension of certificates of agrarian reform immunity until all campesinos had land.[45] UGOCM leaders also protested that the union should have exclusive rights to these lands because it had begun efforts to obtain the land via expropriation even before the Humaya dam had come under construction.[46]

After the credit situation was resolved in August 1959, the UGOCM turned its attention to distribution of the Humaya lands. But precious time had been lost. López Mateos had already begun efforts to revitalize and legitimize the CNC in the eyes of the campesinos and the country as a whole (see chapter 3). Federal revitalization of the CNC, which included continued support for the CNC and a weakening of the support given the UGOCM, was perhaps the most important factor contributing to the decline of the UGOCM in Sinaloa.

As a result of this change in national policy, during the fall of 1959 Liga strategy in the Culiacán Valley shifted to a more combative stance. The Liga utilized three basic tactics in this period: it espoused a more active pro-agrarian reform policy;[47] it denounced "communist agitation" on the part of the UGOCM;[48] and it claimed to be the sole beneficiary of federal policies.[49]

The new policy at the national and local levels quickly bore fruit: on March 16, 1960, the most important independent ejido organization in the state, the Sociedad de Interés Colectivo Ejidal para la Emancipación Proletaria, affiliated with the CNC. Three weeks later the UGOCM members in "Las Bocas" switched campesino unions, and UGOCM desertions continued to mount through October.[50] López Mateos could now accelerate land distribution and regain much of the tarnished legitimacy his actions on the labor front provoked, without contributing further to the strength of the chief rival of the official campesino union. Thus the CNC monopolized the distribution of some 70,000 hectares in the Humaya region, and the UGOCM fell temporarily by the wayside.

Within a decade the CNC had sacrificed the legitimacy López Mateos gave it in the early 1960s. Because of its corporatist nature, the CNC had supported Díaz Ordaz's record-breaking distribution of useless land and his repressive policies toward political dissidents. It therefore once again found itself by the early 1970s in a weak position to lead the campesino movement.

In the northwest the UGOCM was the chief beneficiary among the campesino unions of the decline of the CNC influence. But this was not the same UGOCM as that which had led the struggle in the late 1950s.

Jacinto López had broken with Lombardo Toledano and the Partido Popular Socialista (PPS), and upon López's death the UGOCM had split in three.[51] One of the splinters, the UGOCM-Jorge Orta, retained its independent stance vis-à-vis the state as indicated by its refusal to join the Pacto de Ocampo, an attempt by the Echeverría administration to coordinate campesino unions.[52] It was this UGOCM which operated in the Culiacán Valley during the invasions of 1975–1976. But the reformist nature of the UGOCM leadership (so useful in 1958), its blatantly demagogic rhetoric, the advanced degree of the general agricultural crisis, and the acute conflict between the state and the national bourgeoisie, all contributed to the decline of the UGOCM's legitimacy before large members of very active and often nonaffiliated independent groups of campesinos.

Thus both the UGOCM and the CNC increasingly found themselves unable to lead large numbers of campesinos effectively. Nevertheless, the reaction of each of the two unions differed dramatically. The UGOCM consistently reevaluated its strategy in an attempt to regain its leadership of the independent campesino movement. The CNC, on the other hand, sought to marginalize the independents by ignoring their obvious strength or condemning their tactics.

The CTA provides a good example of this pattern. All four campesino unions (the CCI and the CAM included) supported the CTA's call for an end to the occupations in mid-December 1975. Invasions nonetheless continued, carried out by rank and file members of the CNC and UGOCM as well as those without any affiliation. By mid-February the UGOCM, however, reevaluated its strategy in light of its rejection by membership. UGOCM leader Gambino Heredia announced its separation from the CTA,* accusing the SRA of hindering the process of agrarian reform; in a return to the rhetoric of the late 1950s he threatened to invade 10,000 hectares in the hands of "foreigners." In addition, he reported that no occupied lands would be evacuated for the present,[53] neglecting to mention that such was the case because the union had lost the ability to control these particular groups.

This pattern was repeated throughout the crisis.[54] Once the agreement between state and growers was negotiated, however, UGOCM

---

*Neither the UGOCM nor the private sector representatives ever formally presented resignations; they simply avoided meetings

leaders went along quietly, although independent-minded campesinos continued to protest by occupying lands.[55]

Two lessons in particular stand out from the analysis of campesino politics in these two periods of land tenure conflict. First, once the transfer of presidential power had been completed and the new president made clear that he did not support the independents and would move against illegal actions, land occupations were not sufficient to keep the land tenure issue at the crisis level necessary to pressure the state into moving forward with the agrarian reform. Thus it is clear that at particular historical moments, not controlled by the campesinos themselves, they can make the state take action in their favor; once the historical moment has passed, however, the same efforts by campesinos will not produce similar results. Second, although the state may be pushed to distribute land through the efforts of campesinos acting on the margin of the law, the state will favor its own unions in the actual distribution.

Growers. In 1957 when the UGOCM began to make threats to support their demands for the acceleration of land reform, the growers behaved as did most other groups in Mexico, including the president: they wrote off the UGOCM as a marginal group with little following in the countryside. The January 1958 meeting to discuss the implementation of "Agreement Number One," however, aroused concern among local farmers. The FEPPS issued a veiled warning to government officials by announcing that to avoid giving the matter undue importance, no petitions had been made. Any comments were deemed superfluous, given that the authorities were required to uphold the law and the threatened invasions were clearly illegal.[56]

The UGOCM's march immediately following their strategy meeting forced the rural elite to take them more seriously.[57] A week later the FEPPS censured the threatened invasions, claiming that private farms were within legal tenure limits. Attempting once again to defuse the issue and to warn the government, FEPPS leaders stressed the "harmonious" relations between private farmers and the membership and leaders of the CNC and noted that occupying private property was illegal.[58]

Once the invasions were actually carried out, the growers reacted quickly, demanding government intervention.[59] More than 150 Culiacán farmers established a Permanent Committee to negotiate with the authorities; the committee included representatives from local and national agricultural producer, industrial, and financial organizations. The president of the bankers' group noted that credit would have to be restricted in view of the instability and that this would affect production. The president of the National Chamber of Commerce underlined the fundamental link between agriculture and commerce.[60] Thus the entire private sector closed ranks in the face of this challenge to private property. CAADES also took the situation to the national level by requesting the state delegate of the national farmers' confederation (Confederación Nacional de la Pequeña Propiedad Agrícola—CNPP) make the situation in Culiacán known to its members nationwide and request that members protest to the president.[61]

When the president sent the minister of agriculture to negotiate a settlement to the February 1958 invasions, the farmers presented him with a memo outlining the damages caused by the occupations. Culiacán Valley farmers also sent the president himself a memorandum on the land problems in which they stressed that "only the federal government—through decisions which are fully in accord with the Constitution of the Mexican Republic—will solve the problem."[62]

The following day a full page advertisement appeared in the regional press. Among the phrases which stand out are the following:

. . . [the authorities] *have not acted with sufficient energy to repress these acts* so they will fail and thus protect not only the particular interest of the state's economy, but also avoid setting the precedent of ignoring the violent form of the proceedings which may generalize themselves throughout the country, *because nothing stimulates proselytizing as much as the offering of the distribution of someone else's goods* . . . [emphasis in the original].[63]

The growers were sufficiently politically astute, however, to realize that they had to negotiate a solution and attempted to do it from a position of strength. In response to the governor's suggestion, "in light of the agricultural bonanza they enjoy"[64] (1957–1958 was the "golden year" for tomato exports), AARC undertook a campaign to raise the admittedly "insufficient" wages.[65] Nevertheless, the growers considered the continuing threat sufficient for CAADES to make the Committee for the Defense of Private Agricultural Property permanent,[66] with a budget of 1.5 million pesos for 1958.[67]

In their defense growers played by the rules of the agrarian reform.

Both the CNPP and the FEPPS acknowledged the right of the state to destroy *latifundios* to help landless campesinos; their contention was that their properties complied with the letter of the laws governing land tenure. The fact that the traditional *latifundistas* had not played a role in the grower organizations, and that the new rural elites were modern commercial farmers who had little in commom with the traditional nonproductive *latifundistas* who were keeping land off the market for purely social prestige purposes, probably explains some of this new rural elite's willingness to recognize this particular right of the state. In addition, the ability of the growers to utilize various mechanisms to avoid the concentration of land in one name (see chapter 4) meant that the letter of the law was complied with and the state could choose not to force a confrontation over the spirit of the law. Growers would certainly press for the formal interpretation.

After the initial pressure upon the state immediately following the February invasions, the growers maintained silence on the issue, despite UGOCM rhetoric, for over a year. Two factors shed light on this be-havior. First, the actions of the state in resolving the crisis at this point did not appear to threaten grower interests. The land distributed came from an area where the vegetable producers who formed the elite and ran the organizations did not have holdings. In its present state the land was almost worthless, and the dam designed to irrigate the San Lorenzo area was still in the planning stages. In addition, the governmental committee designed to investigate landholdings in the irrigation district and which had the power to affect the vegetable lands never filed a report.

Second, the agrarian bureaucracy was moving slowly on the matter of the lands to be distributed in the Humaya region. The UGOCM was occupied in solving the short-run problems, which included actually obtaining possession of the lands of the ejidatarios of "Las Bocas" and "El Venadillo." Thus there was little chance that the UGOCM would extend itself to take on new problems before the ones which legitimated the union in the eyes of the campesinos were resolved.

But by August 1959 the UGOCM could turn its full attention to the Humaya, and the growers took action. CAADES noted to its members the importance of stopping such actions (by demonstrating that the properties in question were legal possessions according to the Mexican Constitution) *before* the bureaucratic procedures began, and converted the problem into a social rather than a juridical one. In addition, CAADES called on the government to defend private property.[68] Another tactic was to strengthen local growers' associations' defense of private property by freeing state organizations from the control of a national confederation whose interests lay in Mexico City. To this end, CAADES joined with six other state delegations in the national meeting of the CNPP to demand the reorganization of the confederation to strengthen state associations so they might be better equipped for defending farmers' interests.[69]

Despite this preparation no conflict occurred when the distribution of the Humaya lands was actually carried out, even though 60 percent of the land was distributed to ejidatarios. The comparable figure for the Culiacán system of the district, already in operation, was 40 percent. Various factors probably contributed to this unexpected reaction. A technological change in the production of tomatoes that tripled yields at a time of glut in the international market (beginning in the 1958–59 season and lasting to the 1960–61 season) diminished the importance of land for the vegetable farmers, who no longer sought to expand their acreage. In addition, the soils of the Humaya area are not particularly suitable for vegetable production. The new crops of sorghum, soybean, and safflower, which would become so attractive in a few years, still had not established themselves in the Culiacán irrigation district. Rather than spend political and economic capital on a serious conflict with the state over the Humaya lands, they chose not to respond to the distribution of lands which were not critically important.

The response was also surprisingly mild because of two other factors. A variety of means existed to disguise the size of holdings, avoid the agrarian laws, and retain the best land in the area. Such was the case with the Montelargo area of the Humaya region (which would be the spark that ignited the 1975–1976 round of invasions). In addition, by renting ejido lands (illegal under the agrarian laws at that time) the growers could actually control much of the land in the Humaya region; one estimate is that before 1976, 80 percent of the ejido land in the Humaya was rented.[70]

All of these factors help explain the surprisingly peaceful distribution which took place in the Humaya. The situation was dramatically different in 1975–1976 although the amount of land in question was a fraction of that disputed in the conflict of fifteen years earlier.

With the advent of the Echeverría administration and renewed agitation in the countryside, growers responded with a proliferation of organizations and activity in defense of private property. AARC created its own department to watch over property rights,[71] while CAADES pressured the CNPP national assembly to provide greater defense of private property at the national level.[72] The CNPP responded by joining the groundswell in favor of a nationwide investigation to strip ejidatarios who were not working their lands of usufruct rights.[73] In addition, growers announced their intention of playing an active role in the PRI through membership in the popular sector of the party (CNOP).[74] Institutional infrastructure was also set up to deal with the problems perceived on the horizon: a coordinating committee was created among the Liga, CAADES, the Regional Cattlemen's Union, and the state government.[75]

In attacking the invasions throughout the Echeverría period, growers repeatedly stressed the economic importance of the region for the nation, particularly in exports, and urged change in emphasis from the distribution to the production phase of agrarian reform. They also noted that even extensive land distribution would not enable all landless campesinos to benefit. Therefore, the growers proposed employment generation as a substitute for land distribution.

After the Montelargo expropriations and the land occupations which followed, FEPPS and CAADES decided to go directly to the president. Although the farmers were fighting a situation which they were convinced Echeverría had provoked for his own political reasons, they realized that any solution had to go through him. Their strategy consequently emphasized pressuring the president.

After voting for a work stoppage, CAADES declared that processing plants would join the stoppage and farmers would refuse to sell their harvest to the national food subsidy agency, CONASUPO, and would shift their bank accounts out of the country if the first stage of their response did not produce the desired results.[76] This action appears to have been a means of measuring the resolve of Echeverría and of the campesinos. Once it became obvious that neither would be frightened into retreating, the growers decided to negotiate in order to cut their losses.

Before serious bargaining could take place, the growers had to be sure that their organizations would defend their interests and not those of the state. Thus when the CNPP leadership accused transnational corporations of fomenting the work stoppage, the Sinaloa farmers took a bold step. The FEPPS president condemned the CNPP as "an organization created and maintained by the federal government" whose leader, Guerra Castaños, "has turned his back on us." One week later, farmers from eighteen states formed the Unión Agrícola Nacional (UNAN), an organization parallel to the corporatist CNPP. In obvious deference to the leadership role played by the Sinaloan rural elite, CAADES president Lauro Díaz Castro was elected president of the UNAN.[77]

Conflict between the Sinaloa farmers and the CNPP dates to at least the 1958 land invasions, but it was not until this point that a formal break, lasting for the duration of the crisis, actually occurred. In mid-1976 a further break came. CNPP's Guerra Castaños announced the confederation's complete support for Echeverría and Calderón's agrarian policies. The CNPP also accused FEPPS leaders of utilizing legitimate small farmers to defend *latifundistas* and therefore withdrew recognition of the FEPPS leadership.[78]

Although the state, through the corporatist CNPP, withdrew official recognition of the Sinaloa leaders, the expelled FEPPS leadership continued as de facto representatives of the private agricultural sector in Sinaloa. The Sinaloa farmers responded to the CNPP action by withdrawing its recognition of Guerra Castaños as CNPP president and offering FEPPS president Angulo as a candidate to replace him.[79]

The Sinaloa farmers-CNPP conflict was the only time the rural elite clearly violated the structure of the authoritarian-corporatist regime. Nevertheless, even at this point they did not directly attack the president himself, thereby respecting what is perhaps the main tenet of Mexican politics. An indication of how far the rural fraction of the national bourgeoisie had actually come in gaining autonomy from the state is Echeverría's continued negotiation with the rebel FEPPS leaders in the search for a solution to the agrarian crisis in Sinaloa.

Pressure tactics and the components of the farmers' offer in the negotiations changed in accord with the development of the crisis and the state's own position vis-à-vis the issue. The CTA, because it brought all sides together, was perceived by the Sinaloan farmers as a mechanism which would facilitate negotiation for immediate return of occupied lands to the private sector. On December 8, 1975, the Permanent Assembly, established by the growers a week earlier to oversee the conflict, was officially closed.

The farmers went to great lengths to contribute to a settlement: when some of the invaders agreed to leave the parcels if they were paid for their work in preparing and sowing the lands while they were occupied, AARC quickly recommended such payments be undertaken.[80] But the CTA's efforts to bring calm to the Sinaloan countryside failed as thirty-two new occupations occurred in the first half of January. The farmer representatives then denounced the failure of the CTA, withdrew from it, and made their first offer to invest in rural industrialization.[81] This offer was rejected.

President Echeverría's announced visit to Sinaloa in early March set off a new wave of invasions in February. On February 20 the Sinaloan farmers called themselves into permanent session once again, denouncing forty-one invasions still in progress. Two days later the private farmers took the offensive by declaring for the first time since November that the land invasions were a part of a premeditated plan to create chaos in the countryside;[82] later, Díaz Castro warned that credit sources, even official ones, were reluctant to invest in Sinaloa due to the political climate. CAADES' president denounced SRA efforts to create tensions within the private farm sector and the demagoguery of erroneously accusing certain families with Spanish surnames of being foreigners.[83] He also announced that the private sector would request guarantees for "authentic" small private farmers, but would support the distribution of *latifundios*, if any existed.[84]

Echeverría made some peace overtures during his trip to Sinaloa and left the agricultural minister to find a solution to the conflict. The SRA chief failed at his mission and the growers, frightened by the mobilized invasions but terrified by the autonomous ones, took the offensive once again after a two-month lull. FEPPS, in order to close ranks, denounced the practice of paying the invaders for work done on the parcels while occupied, claiming that this only stimulated further invasions by making them a profitable business.* In addition, farmer spokesmen once again accused the authorities of having "lost respect" because of their passivity in the matter, thereby encouraging arbitrary actions.[85] In a nine-day

---

*When AARC recommended this procedure, there had been some hope of a negotiated settlement.

period (June 15–23) the farmers undertook a massive advertising campaign to garner public support and pressure the state. Throughout their attack on the state, the farmers remained respectful of the script of Mexican politics: they accused PRI president Augusto Gómez Villanueva and Barra García of not understanding the president's policies and of breaking the laws of the land.[86]

On July 7 the Sinaloa growers met for several days with President Echeverría and his agrarian team. Growers again accepted the principle that concentration of land in violation of the agrarian laws should be broken up, if any existed, while the president noted that such action would be carried out within thirty days. But the state assented to two points of the growers' program: lists of possible beneficiaries of any distribution would be culled to eliminate those who no longer qualified, and ejidatarios and farmers would be encouraged to work together so as to maintain efficient units of production rather than creating more infrasubsistence farms (*minifundios*).* The farmers also agreed once again to invest 150 million pesos in the Altos region and to prepare 10,000 hectares for use as irrigated farmland at their own expense.[87]

Despite the fact that the agreement reached incorporated the solutions proposed by farmers, it was obvious that interpretations (and therefore relative political weight) would determine actual events. The SRA notices given out in mid-July informing farmers that their landholdings were the subject of agrarian investigations pushed the growers to counterattack. A press campaign with full-page advertisements was undertaken with a series title of "The Agrarian Distribution Corrupted." On August 6 the UNAN held its first national assembly in Mexico City. More than 2,000 farmers discussed possible solutions to the rural problems facing the country.[88]

After the president's threatening state of the union address, the Sinaloa growers increased their offer to sell 20,000 hectares, donate 10,000, and clear another 20,000 to make them suitable for cultivation. The Sonoran delegation offered, in turn, to sell 20,000 hectares and donate another 5,000. Both groups made it clear, however, that their offer did not imply renunciation of legal defense of private property.[89]

---

*This is a delicate issue, because as a measure to protect ejidatarios from becoming peons of private capital, the Constitution prohibits renting of ejido land. In 1980 President López Portillo's new agricultural development law allowed association of ejidatarios and farmers under strict guidelines.

When the offer was not accepted, growers continued legal efforts to protect their properties. In November, just after the president renewed his attack on large landholders, a suit was filed against the SRA secretary alleging the illegal expropriation of three farmers in the Montelargo region.[90] Sinaloa farmers responded to the Sonora expropriations not only by undertaking a short-lived work stoppage in support of their neighbors but also by filing for 702 provisional injunctions against expropriations.

The perseverance and flexibility of the Sinaloan growers paid off as the crisis reached what can only be seen as a temporary solution (given the constantly increasing demand for land). The Echeverría administration did not move against the farms singled out in July, one-third of which were vegetable lands, but rather settled for even less than the rural elite was willing to give. To understand this response we move to an analysis of state strategy.

State. State action in the two periods of land crises varied considerably. Two factors were key to the responses of the federal government to local pressures on this issue. One element was the implication of the expropriations for the production of foreign exchange and employment-generating export production: in 1958 the lands in question did not cover vegetable area, while in 1975 they did. Another factor was the depth of the political crises faced by the political system in both periods: in 1958 peasants were just beginning to pressure the authoritarian-corporatist regime (see chapter 3), so the state had plenty of room to maneuver; in 1975, by contrast, reformist solutions which had not been tried were few, and thus there was more need for at least the appearance of more "radical" solutions.

In addition to these two elements, others specific to these historical moments placed significant constraints upon presidential reaction to the land tenure crisis. Each of the three presidents involved had a goal in mind when he confronted the issue. Ruíz Cortines sought to distribute as little land as possible and, if pushed, to parcel out the least desirable lands. López Mateos and Echeverría, on the other hand, recognized the political and economic need to distribute vast amounts of cultivable land, but attempted to do so in such a way as to strengthen corporatist structures at the same time, thereby increasing the state's ability to dominate events in the countryside and avoiding total alienation of the private farm sector. López Mateos, dealing with a reformist union with national aspirations, was able to occupy it at the margin while he prepared the official corporatist union to control the largest distribution in Sinaloa's history. Echeverría, however, faced a rank and file peasantry which operated on purely local, short-term criteria, a national bourgeoisie he had already alienated by the middle of his term, and little land left to distribute in Sinaloa without affecting the rural elite.

The response of the Ruíz Cortines administration, in accord with its desire to distribute little land, contributed to UGOCM combativeness. When the president did not even acknowledge the problems raised by the union (and because the presidential election year provides dissidents political space to air some complaints), the UGOCM took direct action. Again, the lapse of time in granting first material possession, then credit, provided the impetus for UGOCM mobilization for a year and a half after the only invasions were actually carried out. Ruíz Cortines thus took the easy way out and left the resolution of the land crisis to his successor.

López Mateos responded by granting material possession of the lands and credit. At the same time he recognized the need for a revitalized CNC in the countryside and undertook the necessary efforts to revitalize the organization. Until the CNC could lay claim to spokesmanship for the campesinos, however, López Mateos channeled resources to the reformist UGOCM, in this manner offsetting some of his own legitimacy problems for actions taken in the railroad strikes.

López Mateos' support for the UGOCM, however, was not unconditional. The president took a strong stand for the sanctity of law; the state would only expropriate where it had the right to take land for distribution. Thus peasants would receive land, but legitimate farmers would also receive certificates of agrarian immunity to protect their farms. In his first month of office he ordered the attorney general to guarantee the security of private property and declared that land invasions were to end, as well as "unjustified" petitions for land distribution. In addition, it was made clear that certificates of agrarian reform immunity were not required for protection to be accorded the private sector.

In 1975–1976, in contrast, Echeverría's populist rhetoric since before taking office provided a catalyst to peasant mobilization. Peasants now felt they had someone in office who sympathized with their plight, while the national bourgeoisie perceived themselves as the scapegoat for a president confronting political legitimacy problems and economic crises. But, as noted in chapter 3, Echeverría's efforts to construct a new populist ruling coalition suffered from at least one serious flaw: the supposed members of the coalition believed they should play major roles in the decision-making process, thereby posing a threat to the elite-dominated structure.

In the following analysis, therefore, Echeverría's actions are interpreted as efforts to bring both the rural bourgeoise and the independent campesinos to accept his right and ability to determine the path agrarian reform would follow in Sinaloa at this time. Given that Echeverría recognized the political need for land distribution, his strategy appears to have been to push the rural elite to accept expropriation of their land while controlling the mobilization of campesinos in order that distribution could strengthen the state's influence over them.

Echeverría began the 1975–1976 phase of the larger state-bourgeoisie conflict by seeming to discard past protocol with regard to the agrarian question (one which favored the farmers). The Montelargo lands which were expropriated were actually given to the campesinos the day of the expropriation, a rare occurrence.[91] When the president sent the SRA minister to Culiacán to investigate the movements going on among the peasants, he refused to confer with representatives of the Sinaloan growers, rejecting allegations that campesinos had occupied private lands in Sinaloa.[92]

When the Sinaloa and Sonora farmers undertook a work stoppage to protest what they considered arbitrary action by the state, the SRA and the corporatist organizations representing campesinos and private farmers denounced the strike. CNC secretary Celestino Salcedo Monteon called the work stoppage "sabotage," and the CNPP's Guerra Castaño went so far as to accuse transnational corporations of responsibility for the action.[93] The fact that the corporatist organization representing the growers at the national level condemned the action suggests that though rhetoric and political maneuvering were acceptable tools of opposition, the state perceived the work stoppage as more threatening and exceeding the bounds of acceptability.

In an effort to increase the state's control over the situation in Sinaloa and elsewhere, which appeared to be getting out of hand, the state set up the CTA to institutionalize state, farmer, and campesino negotiations. In this type of arena the state's ability to mediate between social forces was expected to increase. Nevertheless, the reticence of the peasants to relinquish possession of land they had little hope the state would ever give them prevented the CTA from playing this role.

In an effort to have more influence over events in Sinaloa, President Echeverría paid two visits to the state during 1976. His visits, however, provoked more tension: peasants stepped up the land invasions and growers the tenor of their accusations as both jockeyed for exposure prior to the arrival of the president.

Barra García and the minister of hydraulic resources served as Echeverría's vanguard for the March trip. Before traveling to Sinaloa both made statements which justified the need for agrarian reform to continue in Sinaloa, indicating that the concentration of benefits (land and income) of Sinaloa's development was responsible for the understandable response of the peasants. To offset any stimulation for independent action these remarks might have upon the peasants, the SRA chief asked them to beware the "reactionary elements which sought to push the country into chaos," and also warned that peasants who occupied lands could not hope for favorable SRA resolutions because they would have broken the dialogue.[94]

During his stay in Sinaloa Echeverría sought to convince both peasants and small farmers that his agrarian plans would benefit them. Speaking before some 20,000 campesinos in the highlands region, far from the turmoil in the valleys, the president announced that SRA's Barra García would remain to resolve the disputes. He also promised to return "in a few more weeks" to sign relevant presidential resolutions. In an appearance before the private sector the president handed out certificates of agrarian immunity covering 16,500 hectares throughout the state, a minimal amount which could not convince the growers that their farms of thousands of acres each were safe, but which illustrated to small farmers his intention that the private sector remain a part of the Mexican countryside. For the growers' consumption, Echeverría claimed that "new solutions" would be found shortly to end the land invasions,[95] apparently an indication that their offer to create jobs would be part of any solution.

Though Barra García's efforts failed totally, the president continued to pressure the peasantry to allow him to resolve the issue in his own way. In mid-April, one of the most dramatic agrarian reform meetings took place in southern Sonora. Echeverría, accompanied by all thirty-two governors, informed the 40,000 to 50,000 campesinos in attendance that "the way of the law is still good."[96] This was followed by Governor Calderón's announcement that the SRA had already detected lands subject to the agrarian reform and that the president's express orders were to coordinate the police power of the state to end all the invasions in Sinaloa.[97]

The president met with the leaders of the Sinaloa growers in early July, just before the SRA made public the progress of its investigations. Echeverría accepted part of the farmers' bargaining package, but had the SRA push ahead. When the SRA announced publicly that thirty-one families holding almost 40,000 hectares had been served with thirty-day notices to justify the legality of their holdings, it appeared that the state had decided to act unilaterally to end the land tenure crisis in Sinaloa. Expropriation at the end of the thirty days was plausible, given the precedent of the November 1975 expropriations in Sonora and Sinaloa.

Growers vehemently protested the notifications, so it appears that this is not what they expected to emerge from the negotiations with the president. But Echeverría did not act upon the SRA resolutions at this time. Why not? The answer probably lies in developments taking place in the national political economy. The impending devaluation of the peso would most certainly have great political costs. It is therefore likely that the president chose not to face at the same time the response to the devaluation and the political crisis which would surely follow any massive expropriations in the northwest (as indeed did happen in Sonora).

This argument about the repercussions of the devaluation upon the agrarian process in the northwest would seem to be supported by the fact that in August the president made the only conciliatory remarks he would make until the resolution of the conflict in November. On this occasion he declared that the country needed the food and foreign exchange which Sonoran and Sinaloan farmers produced, precisely the farmers' argument against the proposed expropriations.[98]

These conciliatory gestures, however, proved to be only a temporary lull in the land tenure disputes of the northwest. A solution had to be reached, one which would preferably contribute to state power. Thus in new meetings with representatives of the growers, the president once again refused to accept the farmers' offer to sell and donate land to resolve the crisis. He followed up the meetings with a state of the union address which carried a threatening tone for the farmers. The SRA followed this lead by publicly declaring that it would not buy land from the private sector, thus rejecting the basis of the bargain the farmers hoped to strike.[99]

But once again Echeverría backed off. He arrived in Sinaloa in mid-November to attend the governor's annual address and blamed the agrarian problem on the population explosion. The solution, he said, was twofold: everyone had to obey the law, no land invasions but also no *latifundios;* and industrialization had to create jobs for those who could not make a living in agriculture.[100] The president thus suddenly appeared to leave the door wide open for a negotiated solution which accepted the basic premise of the rural elite's package.

Shortly thereafter Echeverría met the leaders of the private farm sector for the third time in the last five months and appeared anything but conciliatory. He announced that all outstanding presidential resolutions on land reform would be signed in fifteen days. Following the governor's state of the state address, the president accused *latifundistas* of fomenting "false" invasions in order to create a picture of rural unrest.[101]

With Echeverría's term set to expire in a few weeks, the moment had finally come for a solution. The move against Sonora surprised everyone; nevertheless the Sinaloan rural elite kept its head and continued to press for a negotiated solution. A week after the Sonora action Echeverría met with the Sinaloa farmers. The president rejected their offer to sell land, but accepted the donation of 13,500 hectares as a means to resolve the conflict. In a telling move which clearly illustrates the role of campesino organizations, Echeverría informed the unions of the agreement and channeled the bulk of the land to the CNC.

CONCLUSION

Comparison between the land tenure crisis of the late 1950s and mid-1970s provides another illustration of the state-grower alliance's defense of vegetable production. But once again we find that the existence of the alliance does not preclude other social forces from benefiting. In this case distribution of land has occurred. Why does the state-grower alliance, particularly the growers, oversee the redistribution of private property? And how does it affect vegetable production? The answers to these two questions are intertwined and related to the interests of the two partners.

In both periods the peasants' ties to the state had weakened by inattention in the preceding years. As important groups began to manifest their dissent from the shift in public policy (labor against "stabilizing development" and capital against "shared development")[102] the state sought to revitalize the state-peasant relationship. Independent unions and groups of campesinos were allowed to put the land tenure issue on the agenda where it commanded presidential attention. Although such an occurrence is not what one would expect in an authoritarian-corporatist regime, these cases suggest that it is crucial to the continued operation of the system. Official control over the CNC renders it incapable of confronting a legitimacy crisis in the countryside. Consequently, reformist unions provide the state with the opportunity to address the land tenure issue without subjecting the system to the intense polarization between campesinos, farmers, and the state which would inevitably occur if the CNC took the lead. In fact, these are precisely the times when the state can revitalize the CNC itself.

While it is fundamental to note that independent movements play such a crucial role, one must also be aware of the limits to this reformism: in the actual resolution of the crisis they have little influence. As is argued throughout this book, in Sinaloa the needs of winter vegetable production have been determinate in any major issue involving agriculture. Problems of oversupply in the 1950s market made the vegetable producers keenly aware that new lands could not be brought into vegetable production; in addition a technological revolution was beginning in tomato production which would triple yields in these years. Thus the land invaders' demand that land in the new section of the Culiacán irrigation district be distributed to them did not directly threaten the rural elite's continued production for export. In the 1975–1976 case the campesinos demanded distribution of the vegetable lands and therefore the response of the rural elite was bound to be stronger.

The winter vegetable trade also gave local actors resources to use in their bargaining with the state. The ability to threaten the production of vegetables which provided both foreign exchange and employment helped give the landless campesinos in Sinaloa the means with which to attract the state's attention. At the same time, however, the trade also gave the rural elite two elements with which to bargain with the state. First, the continued production of the vegetable farmers had to be guaranteed. And second, the financial and organizational resources provided by their participation in the trade gave them the ability to circumvent the corporatist channels set up by the state to minimize input from social forces on the resolution of policy issues.

Comparison between the November 1976 resolutions in Sonora and Sinaloa provide additional support for this interpretation. The ability of the Sinaloa rural elite to avoid the fate of their Sonoran counterparts stems from the difference in production patterns and the leverage accruing to Sinaloan producers because of their greater contribution to the needs of the state. The wheat produced in southern Sonora provides few jobs and can be produced by ejidatarios; the vegetables of Culiacán, in contrast, employ thousands, bring in foreign exchange, and are beyond the productive capacities of ejidatarios because of the large investment requirements and the high risk. Thus Echeverría was able to expropriate in Sonora and regain political legitimacy in the eyes of the campesinos, but the economic needs of the state dictated a more conciliatory position in Sinaloa.

6

MANAGING LABOR COSTS

In this chapter we examine the response of the state-grower alliance to the demands of farmworkers for greater participation in the benefits of vegetable exports. The alliance confronts two potentially divergent interests: to produce vegetables at internationally competitive costs and to keep farmworkers loyal to the state's labor organization. The challenge to the state-grower alliance arises in periods of overt conflict between these interests. In such cases resolution of the challenge demands short-run sacrifices by one or both of the partners.

This chapter has three sections. First, the labor market for Sinaloa's vegetable production is analyzed. In this section we are given an appreciation of the objective conditions in which growers and farm-workers confront each other. The second section examines the strikes of the late 1950s and mid-1970s. Section three analyzes the response of growers, farmworkers, and the state to the evolution and resolution of the conflicts.

THE WINTER VEGETABLE LABOR MARKET

Sinaloa, because of its northwestern desert location far from the central plateau of Mexico, has throughout its history suffered from a shortage of labor.[1] In 1897 one of the haciendas around Culiacán attempted to attract labor from throughout Mexico by offering good wages in addition to subsidizing the cost of housing and food (see figure 3).

A decade later the same producers undertook to bring 1,000 Japanese peons to work in both the sugar cane and vegetable fields.[2] Winter vegetable production in particular has been characterized by an inadequate local labor supply since its beginnings in the early 1900s.[3]

Labor shortage threatened to become acute as Sinaloa's agriculture evolved into its diversified double crop per year that became characteristic with the advent of large-scale irrigation facilities in the 1950s. In response, a variety of labor flows developed, and the rural social structure evolved to include a large class of farmworkers. Farmworkers may be distinguished by whether they are stationary or migratory, permanent or temporary. Farmworkers are also identified by whether they have their home base in the valleys or migrate from the Sierra foothills of Sinaloa or come from other states. In addition, farmworkers can be distinguished by their dependence upon wages: some supplement their income from wage labor while others are entirely dependent upon selling their labor power.

The labor cycles for tomatoes have been studied, but there is scarce information for that of the other vegetables. On the tomato-tomato circuit, campesinos work the Morelos tomato fields in central Mexico for the domestic market, then come those in Culiacán, move north to Guasave, across the Gulf of Cortez to La Paz, and end the cycle in Ensenada on the Pacific coast. The tomato-cotton cycle begins in Culiacán with tomatoes, moves to Guasave for tomatoes and cotton, and then follows the cotton harvest to Ciudad Obergon in Sonora state and on to Mexicali on the U.S. border. Veracruz state provides two flows for Culiacán vegetable producers at the end of the sugarcane and coffee harvests.[4] An indeterminate number of farmworkers continue on to the U.S. labor market after the Mexican northwest labor cycle is complete.

Data on the specifics of employment of farmworkers in Sinaloa are not readily available, generally unreliable, and not systematic. In 1960 the population census recorded 65,746 *jornaleros*. This figure is not disaggregated and appears to count only permanent workers, or at most migrants from within Sinaloa. The Ministry of Hydraulic Resources and the Fuerte River Commission reported that over 2 million people per month were employed in the five Sinaloa irrigation districts during the 1974–75 season.[5] In perhaps the only study based on some field research, investigators estimated that 180,000 farmworkers labored in the Culiacán Valley's winter vegetable fields. Of these workers, 45 percent (81,000) are residents of the valley, with the other 100,000 migrating for the season. In 1974, 20,000 of the total farmworker labor force labored

"Important Notice"

We have the pleasure of announcing that our sugarcane harvest will begin from November 15 to December 1. All farmworkers, or children of any age who present themselves will have work, with those families of two or three persons able to make

SEVEN TO TEN PESOS DAILY

Since the company continues its other activities, in addition to the sugar harvest, we have weeding, different work on irrigation canals, which means that we can employ as many workers as come. The lowest daily wage one can make is five *reales*: but in the other chores on contract one can make up to

ONE PESO DAILY

This is paid daily. To all our peons, we give them free, a house in which to live, a plot of irrigated land of 60 *aras*, equivalent to 2 *almudes*, plows and mules so they may plant, without charging any rent for all this. Those families which come from outside the area and which stay to live and work in the company, in addition to facilitating the above, we shall give them free of charge: One lot so they may construct their house, wood for construction, half a day off during the time of construction, with the house to be used in benefit of the family. We shall sell them a cow and calf, to be paid at a rate of 50 *centavos* weekly. There is a well-stocked store which sells everything cheaper than in Culiacán. We have made arrangements so that our workers can buy corn, beans, meat and lard, at cost, cheaper than in all the coast and even more so than in Culiacán itself. There are inns which can accomodate workers without families for twenty-five *centavos* daily, in which case a worker can save three, four, and six *reales* daily. No other business in the State has as many favorable conditions for the farm-worker, in which they offer continuous work, good wages, the good things of life, and the principal ones at very low prices, allowing the worker to save daily half of his wages, to buy clothes or whatever he needs.

Navolato, Hda. "La Primavera", October, 1897
"JESUS ALMADA Y HERMANOS"

SOURCE: Gilberto López Alanís, *Ciencia y Universidad* 1.

for nine to eleven months, with 160,000 temporary farmworkers averaging 7.2 months. Of the 100,000 migrants, some 75,000 depended solely upon their wages and therefore continued on to harvest elsewhere: approximately 10,000 returned to their place of origin to work their infrasubsistence plot. Some 15,000 migrants seemed to have stayed on in the valley in 1974.[6]

If this rough picture is correct, then these farmworkers are much better off in Sinaloa than the national average.* Nationwide, the average number of days worked by farmworkers has been declining since 1950: 190 days in 1950, 100 in 1960,[7] and 65 in the 1970s.[8] But in Sinaloa those farmworkers who have the relatively good fortune of working on these export farms receive minimum wages and work an average of seven months in Culiacán and then either return home to plant or move on to work elsewhere.

Nevertheless, these farmworkers live in miserable conditions. For example, the legal minimum wage has been paid regularly only since the 1960s. Part of the wage paid is in housing, the majority of which consists of a long building of cardboard structure with dirt floors, on the edge of an irrigation canal. The canal provides water for drinking, cooking, and washing even though the detached latrines stand on the edge of the canals. Buildings are 60 meters long and 10 meters wide, with each room measuring 5 meters by 5 meters[9] and often inhabited by a number of families.

To understand the poor living conditions in which farmworkers find themselves, despite the shortage of labor in the fields, we must examine the structure of the winter vegetable labor market both in terms of demand and supply. Table 6.1 illustrates that demand for labor is dramatically higher in the export-oriented crops than in other crops. But the demand for labor is not uniform over the season. There is an inherent extreme seasonal fluctuation with most of the demand coming at harvest time. One other factor affecting demand for labor is the fluctuation in the international market, which often leaves the grower with little choice but to let part of his crop rot on the vines. Consequently, there exists excess supply of labor for most of the season, but farmers face serious labor shortages at certain crucial times.

This characteristic of the demand for labor theoretically presents

---

* For a general discussion of farmworkers' conditions in Mexico, see the works cited in this section and Rodolfo Stavenhagen, "Los jornaleros agrícolas" and Iván Restrepo Fernánedez, "El caso de los jornaleros agrícolas en México."

TABLE 6.1

Employment Requirements of Staple and Export
Crops in Irrigated Districts

Crop	Number of Workdays per Hectare
Staples	
Corn	14
Beans	12
Rice	9
Wheat	6
Exports	
Cotton	47
Chick-peas	15
Stalked tomatoes	143
Ground tomatoes	66
Cucumbers	66
Other vegetables	56

SOURCE: AARC files.
NOTE: Table covers the Culiacán, Guasave, Los Mochis, Guamuchil, and El Rosario zones.

farmworkers with a bargaining tool in their struggle with capital. But here the political structure of the supply side becomes determinant. In the context of the general ferment in the Mexican labor movement just before and during the Cárdenas presidency, farmworkers in Sinaloa had undergone a mobilization effort which yielded at least thirty-two farmworker unions in 1934 with over 6,400 members (table 6.2). These unions, however, had weak roots among the work force and when Cárdenas prohibited the CTM from organizing or supporting rural unions (which in 1937 accounted for 43 percent of CTM membership),[10] these unions faded into the labor court's archives.* The CTM contented itself with informal recognition (they had no farmworker union registered in Sinaloa) of their official role as spokesmen for labor.

*I would like to thank Kevin Middlebrook for suggesting a possible link between Cárdenas' decision and the disappearance of the rural unions in Sinaloa. The history of these unions is oblique, even their affiliation, but it is clear that all of the rural unions disappeared after Cárdenas left power. The winter vegetable industry was in its infancy in the 1930s (cotton, chick-peas, and sesame seeds were other major export crops at that time), and analysis suggests that the experience of the 1930s had a minor impact on the successes of the 1950s. It is clear, however, that the whole issue of unionization in Mexican agriculture in the 1930s calls for serious scholarly treatment.

TABLE 6.2

Farmworker Unions in Sinaloa, 1934

Registration Number	Name	Membership
6	Sindicato General de Obreros y Campesinos del Estado de Sinaloa, San Lorenzo	48
8	Sindicato de Obreros y Obreras, Campesinos de Villa Unión, Villa Unión	61
16	Sindicato de Obreros y Campesinos de Cualia-cancito, Culiacancito	57
17	Sindicato de Obreros y Campesinos Progresis-tas, Los Mochis	1104
22	Sindicato de Campesinos de El Dorado	?
30	Sindicato de Obreros y Campesinos Leales de Navolato	415
31	Sindicato de Obreros y Campesinos del In-genio de El Dorado	236
32	Sindicato de Campesinos "Fuerza y Accion" de la Hacienda El Sufragio, Espza-Los Mochis	?
33	Sindicato Revolucionario de Obreros y Cam-pesinos de El Dorado	?
36	Sindicato de Obreros y Campesinos, Ingenio El Roble	83
41	Sindicato de Campesinos "Fuerza y Accion" El Sufragio	208
42	Sindicato de Obreros y Campesinos de Esta-ción Verdura	104
43	Unión Femenista de Obreras y Empleadas del Ramo Tomatero y Similares, Los Mochis	379
44	Sindicato de Obreros, Campesinos y Agraris-tas de Charay	441
45	Sindicato de Obreros, Campesinos y Agraris-tas de San Miguel	277
46	Sindicato de Obreros y Campesinos del In-genio de San Lorenzo	356
48[a]	Sindicato Agrario "Guadalupe Rangel" Hig-ueras de Zaragoza	200
49	Unión de Trabajadores de Empaque y Campos Tomateros, Los Mochis	252
50	Sindicato de Obreros, Campesinos y Agraris-tas de Mochicahui	296
57	Sindicato Fraternal de Obreros Campesinos, Los Mochis	40

TABLE 6.2 (*Continued*)

Registration Number	Name	Membership
67	Sindicato de Obreros y Campesinos Unidos de Sinaloa, Sonora, Los Mochis	102
70	Sindicato Unión de Obreros y Campesinos de Los Mochis	1104
2164	Sindicato de Campesinos de Orba Bamoa-Bamoa	38
2167	Sindicato de Obreros y Campesinos de Bamoa	19
2170	Sindicato General de Obreros y Campesinos del Distrito de San Ignacio	28
2171	Sindicato de Campesinos de Espinal, San Ignacio	54
2174	Sindicato de Campesinos de San Juan, San Ignacio	96
2175	Sindicato de Campesinos de Charay	80
2176	Sindicato de Campesinos de Ixtagua, San Ignacio	42
2181	Sindicato de Obreros y Campesinos de Al-huey, Culiacán	58
37	Unión de Estibadores y Jornaleros,[b] Suc. 1, Topolobampo, Sinaloa	76

SOURCE: Estados Unidos Mexicanos, Departamento del Trabajo. *Directorio de Asociaciónes Sindicales de la República Mexicana.* Oficina de Informaciónes Sociales, 1934.

[a] This union is also listed under registration no. 19 with 66 members.

[b] This union falls under federal rather than state jurisdiction.

THE STRIKES

Spreading the Wealth in Time of Plenty. In the 1954–55 and 1955–56 seasons exports of tomatoes from Sinaloa fell 70 percent (see chapter 8), leading to widespread unemployment among the rural work force.[*] In addition, in January 1957 social security was extended to farmworkers in southern Sonora, but the Sinaloa growers had not yet agreed on the

[*] Cotton production was also off as world market prices fell due to U.S. cotton policy (see David R. Mares, "The Evolution of U.S.-Mexican Agricultural Relations," pp. 14–19). Cotton is produced in northern Sinaloa, but I could uncover no written or oral information on the influence of unemployed cotton pickers on the vegetable workers' strikes, which extended into the northern part of the state.

mechanics of participation.[11] In this context, the CNC, UGOCM, and CTM sought to organize the farmworkers. When exports recovered in 1957, the incipient farmworker unions began to make demands for minimum wage, overtime pay, and legal benefits accorded urban workers.

The UGOCM farm labor unions were never recognized by the labor courts, ostensibly because they included ejidatarios who had no legal standing as workers.[12] The CNC apparently failed to attract any farmworkers[13] and thus the field was left to the CTM and its state federation, the Federación de Trabajadores de Sinaloa (FTS).

Despite scattered informal agreements, growers refused to sign labor contracts, arguing that the volatile nature of the international market did not allow for stability in labor relations.[14] Several attempts to form unions, notably by Antonio Vizcarra, triggered mass firings beginning in mid-1958;[15] Vizcarra's support among workers nonetheless strengthened his negotiating position[16] and helped mark him for future co-optation by the FTS and rural elite leadership. The labor court (Junta Central de Conciliación y Arbitraje, JCCyA) worked against the unions, however, refusing to give them legal standing through 1958.[17]

But Vizcarra was not to be denied. He researched the labor court's archives and discovered a union, the Sindicato de Obreos y Campesinos de San Pedro (SOCSP), which had been registered in the ferment of 1935, but had subsequently faded away. In mid-November 1958 the SOCSP was revived and presented the labor courts with its first threat to strike.[18] Vizcarra's success stimulated other independent groups in search of the labor court's recognition to review history.[19] But Vizcarra stayed in the forefront of the movement by affiliating his union with the FTS,[20] thereby bringing on his side an ally which the state would seek to appease. Despite Vizcarra's early denunciations of FTS' collaboration with growers, the SOCSP's first demands included that employers collect union dues and pay a union employee to watch over fulfillment of the contract.[21] In an attempt to guarantee his usefulness to the FTS, Vizcarra demanded that growers sign agreements directly with the SOCSP and not the FTS.[22]

In January 1959 AARC made its first complaint to Governor Leyva Velázquez about the union. The growers' association also protested to the Culiacán labor court that the SOCSP had ceased to exist because it had violated its statutes by not holding elections every two years.[23] AARC then persuaded a CAADES emergency meeting to declare that if the labor courts recognized the legal existence of the SOCSP, the rural elite throughout the state would declare a work stoppage.[24] Through January and February Vizcarra threatened twenty-one growers with strikes. Demands included overtime pay; a paid day off on Sunday; and back pay and severance pay for fired workers in addition to the two aforementioned demands to benefit the union. Tensions were fueled in early February as some tomato harvesting was suspended when prices in the U.S. market fell, leaving 1,500 workers temporarily unemployed.[25]

The immediate crisis came to an end on February 5 when the Culiacán labor court refused to grant the SOCSP legal standing, ostensibly for irregularities in its internal elections.[26] The SOCSP and FTS protested and continued to threaten action, although none was carried out. At the end of the 1958–59 season the labor court accepted the revised registration petitions from four unions, among them the SOCSP. The labor court's decision meant that the confrontation between growers and unions would take place in a more legitimate setting in the next season.

In the 1959–60 season the basis for the temporary resolution of the labor conflict was set. Growers continued to reject the desirability and even need for collective contracts. On the labor side, Vizcarra was pressured out of the scenario by a rebellion among his union members, joined by the state government, against his alleged deals with the growers.

Market conditions and technological change in vegetable production at this time altered the context within which capital and labor interacted. Confronted by an international market unable to handle an ever increasing volume from Mexico, Culiacán producers were beginning to take measures to regulate supply and make production for export a profitable enterprise once again. In addition, producers in Culiacán were turning toward producing a vine-ripened tomato grown on stakes; yields increased threefold over the traditional ground-grown tomato, but labor requirements also increased significantly. In these circumstances, the more progressive growers were becoming aware of the need to settle the labor disputes on a basis which would provide at least medium-term stability, and measures were undertaken to relieve some of the tensions arising over living quarters and educational opportunities for farmworkers' children.

The understanding growers sought could well be achieved with the official trade union, the CTM, which had demonstrated its willingness to support capital with a minimum of conflict ever since Fidel Velázquez assumed control of the CTM.[27] By at least the beginning of the 1962–63 season a verbal agreement existed between the AARC and the FTS union (now renamed Sindicato de Obreros Legumbreros y Conexos, SOCLyC) in which the growers' association agreed to intercede with the growers themselves if any violations of the labor code were denounced by the union.[28] In return the CTM received rights to a closed shop in the fields. The state-mediated resolution of the labor tensions was formalized in 1963 when AARC and the CTM signed a *convenio* (agreement), rather than collective contract.[29]*

The resolution given the labor disputes at this point greatly benefited both growers and the CTM. Farmworkers also received a benefit: minimum wages were increasingly paid. But other stipulations of the labor code which were standard for urban workers (such as overtime payments, sick pay, disability insurance, vacation pay, and Christmas bonus) were ignored by the CTM union.

Cutting Losses in Times of Crisis. In the last half of the 1970s labor tensions in Sinaloa broke open once again. Two of the conditions of the previous period of intense labor conflict were present: a very good year for the vegetable growers following some bad seasons, and a new union in the fields. With the minimum-wage situation more or less resolved during the years following the 1957–1960 struggles, farmworkers and their unions turned their attention to benefits guaranteed by the Labor Code.

In October 1977, 4,000 farmworkers from two labor camps presented a petition before the state labor bureaucracy, the Dirección del Trabajo

---

*A *convenio* can be signed between any two parties, while a *contrato* must be signed by an employer and a union before a labor court; in signing a convenio, growers did not recognize the existence of the union and could not be brought before the labor courts for violation of a contract when the convenio was repeatedly violated. I would like to thank Kevin Middlebrook for making the distinction clear to me.

y Previsión Social (herein DT),* for vacation pay and Christmas bonus. Six months later, with no action taken on their demands, the Federación Independiente de Obreros Agrícolas y Campesinos de Sinaloa (FIOACS) struck two labor camps. Four new demands were added: installation of electricity, latrines, and washing facilities in the camps and reduction of Sunday's work schedule to four hours. The growers accepted the demands but did nothing. In December FIOACS called a work stoppage, which proved successful in forcing the growers to implement the agreement.[30]

Thus began the movement for better living and working conditions among migrant workers in the Culiacán Valley. From May 1978 to January 1980 there were strikes in twenty-five camps in which some 35,000 farmworkers participated.[31] AARC, the CTM, the DT, and the labor courts all opposed FIOACS' efforts to gain recognition as a bargaining agent. The CTM, DT, and the labor courts recognized the importance of the CTM corporatist system. Growers had successfully dealt with FTS leaders in the past and preferred that known route to labor peace at minimal cost. Nevertheless, FIOACS' de facto power in the fields required a more flexible response from the growers than that given by the government and corporatist institutions: despite the fact that FIOACS had no union registration, individual growers temporarily negotiated informal agreements with the union in order to maintain production.[32]

The formula of the early 1960s repeated itself in 1978–1979: growers and the CTM union revitalized their relationship, this time via a collective contract, on the understanding that each would contribute to the goals of the other. The previous two seasons had been excellent for Mexican producers, and so this new arrangement between growers and union leaders could have augered benefits on all sides, with the farmworkers themselves once again receiving benefits, although relatively fewer than those received by the other two.

But these were years in which Mexico's position in the winter vegetable market deteriorated. Rising real wages which outstripped those of Mexico's competitors for the U.S. winter market (see table 6.3)

---

*During the period of the first srikes the name of this state agency was Dirección del Trabajo y Acción Social. For simplicity I will merely refer to it as DT in both periods.

TABLE 6.3

Farm Labor Wages, Florida and Sinaloa

	Percent Increases 1977–78 to 1980–81			
	Florida		Sinaloa	
	Wages	PPI[a]	Wages	PPI
1977/78	7	8	16	41.2
1978/79	10	8	18	16
1979/80	8	13	22	18
1980/81	8	14	26	24

SOURCE: G. A. Zepp, "Trend and Outlook for Florida-Mexico Tomato Competition" presented at the Florida Tomato Institute, Naples, Florida, September 10, 1981. 1977/78 PPI for Sinaloa is calculated from the wholesale price index. *International Financial Statistics Yearbook 1985* (Washington, D.C.: International Monetary Fund), p. 273.

[a] Producer Price Index; PPI is for the year at the beginning of the winter vegetable cycle.

combined with poor weather and an overvalued Mexican currency to render the solution given the labor conflicts in 1977–1979 obsolete by the 1979–80 season. For the next three seasons, to 1981–82, Mexican winter vegetable exports to the United States declined dramatically (see chapter 8). Growers turned to labor costs as the key variable in their cost of production which could be influenced by them (the exchange rate and weather being beyond their reach).

ACTORS' STRATEGIES

Growers. The vegetable growers initially responded in both periods by relying on the state to diffuse farmworker mobilization without extracting any additional contribution from growers. Growers reacted to the increase in organizational efforts by prospective unions as a problem of public order, and provided the state attorney general's office (Procuraduria de Justicia) with two pickup trucks to facilitate a police presence in the fields.[33] Direct action was also taken. In May 1958 almost 200 farmworkers at just four labor camps were fired for union activities.[34]

Some growers understood that their workers had real grievances and that peace in the fields would be tenuous if these needs continued unanswered. By a majority vote, AARC voted to increase that season's wages in light of the bonanza (and labor agitation) experienced in vegetable exports.[35] But once the new season began in November, the same threats of unionization reappeared. Growers attempted to force more active state mediation. AARC president Atilano Bon Bustamante, while admitting that growers had to increase the standard of living of their labor force, argued that the uncertain nature of the winter vegetable industry meant collective contracts were ill-suited there. He argued that the economy of Sinaloa was threatened, and therefore he expected the state government to resolve the conflict.[36] Two days later Governor Leyva Velázquez met with AARC leaders, who requested his direct intervention in resolving the question of SOCSP's legal standing. Farmer representatives vowed to fight the union in the labor courts, claiming that SOCSP had ceased to exist because they had not held the requisite biannual elections.[37]

As SOCSP activity increased, growers put further pressure on the state government: farmers threatened to strike themselves if the union were granted legal standing. Other segments of the private sector were mobilized. The financial and commercial organizations of Culiacán met to discuss and denounce the possibility of a worker, but not employer, strike in the fields. Farmers sought to impugn the reputation of the labor leader Vizcarra by revealing that he had extorted some of them the previous year.[38] Access to the labor camps and the public roads beside them was restricted.[39] When Governor Leyva Velázquez supported the right to unionize,[40] Culiacán growers reiterated their refusal to sign contracts and unanimously approved a tax on exports of vegetables to finance a common defense fund.[41]

Although the labor court initially found that SOCSP and another union (Sindicato de los Suarez) had no legal standing, some growers recognized this as only a lull in the evolution of farmer-labor relations. Antonio Amézquita, grower, banker and ex-president of CAADES, led this group. Amézquita proposed that AARC should construct schools and housing for the farmworkers and that the government should pressure the farmers to meet the needs of their labor force.[42] Education became the rallying cry for the farmers as they approved expenditure of 20 percent of AARC's gross income for the construction of schools in the labor camps. The association also requested that growers prohibit children from working unless they also attended school.[43]

Despite the efforts by the FTS to organize farmworker unions and Vizcarra's continued strike threats, for the remainder of the 1958–59 season the labor front was quiet. Two factors may explain the sudden lull. Most of the growers' attention was necessarily focused upon their external market: the U.S. demand was very weak, supply was up, and the U.S. government raised the import tax.[44] Perhaps most importantly, and in light of past admitted behavior as well as alleged future behavior, AARC's labor defense fund may have been successfully utilized to keep labor leaders at bay via personal payoffs. Certainly the fact that the labor bureaucracy and official union were spearheading the drive gave the impression that discreet monetary deals could keep the peace. But at the end of the season the JCCyA recognized four unions, one of them Vizcarra's SOCSP, thus setting the stage for an expected confrontation the following season.

At the start of the new season growers reiterated their ultimate threat. They were willing to pay "good" wages, but if union leaders attempted to force then to sign contracts, they would halt production. Noting that such an action would harm the economy, growers called upon the government to take action against labor leaders who, according to the growers, exploited the farmworkers' situation for personal gain.[45]

In the face of the state's decision to mediate capital-labor relations via FTS control over the unionization movement, however, growers capitulated. Payoffs to union leaders from the AARC defense fund seem to have continued. Unions whose leaders accepted this "understanding," chief among them Vizcarra's, were granted legal recognition by the labor courts and agreements by the producers. The fund also served to buy pickup trucks which were given to the military in an effort to increase patrols[46] and decrease agitation by union leaders who refused to play by the rules. But on the question of whether such distribution would continue on the basis of grower goodwill or legal obligation, growers and unions were still far apart.

Although they successfully rejected collective bargaining agreements, Culiacán producers were politically astute enough to realize this skirmish represented only a stopgap victory. Further efforts were undertaken to defuse the labor conflict by reforming some of their labor practices. A few growers began to respect minimum-wage laws and one even paid above that level.[*] Vegetable exports, already contributing to

[*] On November 25, 1963, the SOCLyC protested to AARC that only 9 growers paid minimum wages, and one, Manuel J. Clouthier, paid above minimium. ("Sindicato de

the construction of schools, were now taxed to fund construction of houses for permanent workers in the labor camps.[47]

Recovery of the profitability of Mexican participation in the international market allowed the growers to formalize their arrangement with the CTM union in 1963. As part of growers' recognition of a new situation in labor relations, AARC assumed many of the costs paid by individual growers for labor peace. The association distributed release forms so that workers who were laid off testified that they had been hired on a temporary basis (and were therefore ineligible for many of the benefits established by the Labor Code). In addition, AARC paid half of the severance pay for those workers with such rights.[48] The success of this strategy is indicated by the peace in the fields which reigned over the next fifteen years, despite the continued misery of the labor force.

With the renewal of labor conflict in the 1970s, growers perceived the need to introduce changes in their relationship with their workers, but to do so at minimum cost to themselves. In response to the FIOACS strikes of 1978, growers reacted as they had in 1958: they called on the state to maintain order in the fields and fired a number of workers. The two growers who were struck signed agreements with FIOACS pledging to pay a Christmas bonus (*aguinaldo*), vacation pay, and wages for overtime on Sunday. These agreements were on the margin of the law, since FIOACS had no legal standing as a bargaining agent.

The state proved incapable of halting the movement in the fields, and the growers found the need to take more serious action, still short of turning to overt violence. Growers used their association to sign a collective contract with the CTM union, and the first contract was signed on November 17, 1978.[49] By accepting a contract with the same union

---

Obreros Legumbreros y Conexos to Asociación de Agricultores del Río Culiacán," November 25, 1963. AARC Archives). To determine what percentage of the growers this represented is a complicated process. In 1961 there were 174 tomato growers (*SS*, June 18, 1981); by this count only a tiny fraction abided by the labor code on this matter. But 174 growers is a fictitious number designed to avoid agrarian legislation (see chapter 4). A more reasonable number would come from the number of packing houses. This would err on the low side, because some packing houses represent more than one grower, but the error here is less than with the other method. With this estimate of 59 ("Sindicato de Obreros Legumbreros y Conexos to Dirrección General del Impuesto Sobre la Renta," December 4, 1963. AARC Archives), it appears that about 20 to 25 percent of the growers paid at least the minimum wage. Particularly after five years of labor strife, this is still an appallingly low compliance rate.

that had ignored farmworkers' needs for years and whose leaders were widely rumored to accept payoffs, the growers believed the way was open for only marginal changes to be implemented. In addition, growers utilized their associations to create a buffer to direct interaction between themselves and the labor movement, even if it was the CTM.

Growers also sought to offset the political and economic costs of meeting the needs of farmworkers by bringing the state's social welfare apparatus into the fields. Although part of the stimulus of the 1950s conflicts was the extension of health services under the IMSS to the Sonora and Sinaloa countryside, such service was mediocre at best. Growers' costs for this service were subsidized by the federal government because farmer contributions were based upon a number of workers per hectare for each crop which was below that actually utilized.[50] In September 1978 this subsidy was probably further increased as AARC pressured IMSS to provide greater and better service in the fields and vetoed the agency's proposal to nearly double the cost of employer contributions for the service.[51]

On the housing front, AARC followed a similar track. In the 1960s, this effort had been financed entirely from grower contributions. Now a state program of worker housing and low-cost construction loans, financed by contributions from the state, employer, and employee, began to bring portable housing to the fields with a lower cost to growers.[52]

As part of the same concern over mitigating the worst features of farmworkers' lives, AARC also attempted to persuade individual growers to construct public washing facilities and replace outhouses on irrigation canals with better facilities.[53] As an incentive, the funds earmarked for the 1960s housing project were made available to offset individual grower's costs on these projects.[54] AARC also began a mobile dental service program free of charge to laborers and their families, staffed by two dentists.[55] The social conscience and self-defense reaction of the growers also extended to measures to lower the cost of living of farmworkers so that their salaries would go farther. Various farmers donated land to the association so that it could operate grocery stores which would be supplied by the National Food Subsidy Program (CONASUPO).[56]

The success and rate of implementation of these reforms is guided by the profit and labor militancy perceptions of the growers rather than the needs of the farmworkers. With the CTM the only legal bargaining agent for the farmworkers and a weakening international market for Mexican winter vegetables, progress in this area has been excruciatingly slow since 1980. The portable housing project proved a failure, sanitary conditions remain dramatically poor, and implementation of benefit programs proved sporadic. The service provided farmworkers under the IMSS-grower auspices remained far below that given to urban workers. Farmworkers were entitled to utilize passes which gave them medical service at an IMSS clinic, but these passes were distributed by the institution to the growers in accord with a system which underestimated the size of the labor force. In these circumstances passes were in short supply and gave the grower control over one more resource of interest to the farmworker. In addition, farmworkers were entitled to only 50 percent pay when suffering a work-related temporary injury, while the general labor force received 100 percent pay when ill even if the causes were nonwork-related. None of the other benefits provided to urban workers under the IMSS legislation are given to farmworkers.[57]

Growers have not limited their response to rising labor costs and militancy to reforming some practices, shifting some of the cost of reforms to the public treasury, and letting time and the CTM demobilize workers. Wages constitute the single most important factor in input prices in both Florida and Mexico; therefore, their costs must be controlled in the extremely competitive environment of the international market. During this period of labor tensions, Mexican growers began to lose this battle. Although wage rates are significantly lower in Sinaloa than Florida (about one-fifth in 1978), the rate of increase of Mexican wages doubled that of Florida from 1967–68 to 1973–74. The devaluation of the peso in 1976 broke the pattern of ever increasing Mexican real wages, but by 1978–79 the predevaluation rate had been equaled.[58]

In response to their dramatic loss of market share from 1978–79 to 1981–82, Mexican growers have turned to labor-saving measures. Tomato growers are increasingly planting tomatoes that can be harvested green, by fewer workers, or even by machine, and gassing them to give them color. Two growers have patented machines which speed up a variety of tasks in both the preharvest and harvest stages. The most successful of these machines saves up to one-third of the labor previously utilized in these tasks and is even being marketed in the United States.[59] The 1982 devaluations in Mexico may halt this trend toward mechanization temporarily, but it is clear that growers have discovered the ultimate weapon to discipline labor militancy and bring wages into line with grower profit expectations.

Farmworkers. The success of the Culiacán growers in the 1957–1958 season stimulated a hope in the labor force that they would enjoy some of its fruits. But the local branch of the CTM, the FTS, was disposed to channel any such distribution into their own personal and organizational hands. CTM corruption and disregard of farmworker needs created a space for someone to step in and organize an effort to mobilize farmworkers in defense of their own self-interests.

The UGOCM, already mobilized around the issue of land reform, attempted to step in to fill this vacuum. But the very success of the UGCOM in organizing landless campesinos with agrarian rights worked against the UGOCM on this issue. For the state to allow the reformist and action-oriented UGOCM to compete for the allegiance of farmworkers would have given the organization too important a role to allow it to be discarded once its role in the political crisis of the late 1950s was complete (see chapters 3 and 5).

Elimination of the UGCOM did not mean that others were not tempted to take advantage of the opportunity. One man who spoke out against the labor bureaucracy and its collusion with the growers was Antonio Vizcarra, a laborer at the Evangelatus camp.[60] Little is known about the origins of Vizcarra, alias "the Black Devil." It was reported that he was an ex-UGOCMista,[61] but in the agrarian climate of the late 1950s such an "accusation" may have meant only that he opposed the established order of things. One grower erroneously claimed he was a member of the CCI,[62] while the CTM union denied any link between Vizcarra and the CTM, claiming he was a member of a rival labor union, the Confederación Revolucionaria de Obreros y Campesinos, CROC.[63] The following he attracted over the next two years, despite his alleged personal corruption, suggests that he was a dynamic and charismatic person (he wore two guns, which he was known to brandish) who knew how to take advantage of a situation. In any case Vizcarra soon became premier labor leader in the Culiacán Valley.

Vizcarra's behavior after he filed his surprise SOCSP strike petition in 1958 was suspicious. After filing strike petitions in November, he backed off from those demands without securing any concessions from growers, for the farmworkers at least. December saw a repeat of this performance.[64] Later events would indicate that Vizcarra was more concerned with extorting growers for personal gain rather than negotiating with them to secure benefits for the farmworkers. These November and December tactics would come back to haunt him.

Vizcarra understood that political pressure would be necessary if his union were to be recognized by both labor court and growers. Respectful of the organizational and political support which the CTM controlled, and overestimating his own ability to maneuver within it, Vizcarra affiliated his SOCSP with the same FTS he had previously accused of being corrupt. He was politically astute enough to realize that his value to the FTS depended upon his brokerage role and sought to guarantee a direct relationship between the SOCSP and growers. To his demands for wages and benefits Vizcarra added that growers collect union dues and pay the salary of one FTS representative.[65]

Under pressure from the farmers, the JCCyA initially rejected the SOCSP's legal standing. The basis for the labor court's decision was technical (election procedures) rather than absolute (the legality of unions in the fields) and consequently allowed the possibility of success in the future. Vizcarra bet that the state would not utilize its police power to implement the JCCyA decision at this time of national labor strife. In early March 1959, the SOCSP challenged the labor court's ability to set the terms of interaction in the Sinaloa countryside and called for a strike. Fear that Vizcarra would continue to organize and temporarily halt production enabled the union leader to meet with AARC representatives and state his case. Once again, the meeting did not result in any recognition of labor's rights, yet the strike threats were terminated.[66]

Recognition by the JCCyA of the SOCSP's legal standing gave Vizcarra legitimacy outside of his own membership. At the beginning of the 1959–60 season the FTS commissioned him to undertake a major organizational drive, which included denouncing growers who violated the labor laws. To some degree Vizcarra was restrained by a labor inspector from the DT who accompanied him on his rounds. The inspector filed petitions against growers found in violation of the labor code, and DT settled some disputes before Vizcarra could exploit them.[67] Vizcarra continued to present a public image as a progressive labor leader. He was reported to have presented growers with a proposal so advanced for the Mexican countryside that even in 1982 most of its provisions had not been granted. Among its components were the following:(a) a base salary slightly above the minimum wage, (b)equal pay for female workers, and (c) payment of the base salary when work is temporarily halted for reasons beyond the control of the worker.[68]

Growers rejected the program, but Vizcarra demonstrated that his outward limits were far beyond anything the growers could contemplate. It was clear that Vizcarra was a resource which neither growers nor CTM nor the state could confidently rely upon to play by the rules of the game.

Vizcarra alienated everyone with his unbridled corruption which benefited neither farmworkers nor union nor grower nor state. When the pressure for his expulsion came, he had no one to intervene on his behalf. After almost two years of activity with nothing to show for it, SOCSP members began to question his allegiance to the interests of farmworkers. Vizcarra denounced growers who he said were spreading rumors to counteract his efforts on behalf of farmworkers.[69] But it was too late for such tactics to save Vizcarra.

In early 1960 seventy laborers from "Trancas Nuevas" and the union's own secretary for labor conflicts petitioned the DT that they had not received any of the wages or benefits Vizcarra claimed to have extracted from growers in return for labor peace. The petition was supported by the state labor inspector. The SOCSP called a meeting of its members to judge their leader's record and the DT asked Vizcarra to explain the alleged discrepancies in his handling of union affairs. Vizcarra responded by getting an injunction against any actions taken by the DT in the matter. But the DT proceeded with the investigation and after the third citation for Vizcarra's appearance announced that it would turn the affair over to the proper authorities.[70]

The SOCSP held a secret meeting in April 1960, at which Vizcarra was stripped of his leadership. Vizcarra made a brief attempt to rebound as a force in the farmer-labor struggle the following week, putting fifty people in front of the Governor's Palace to protest the labor practices of the growers.[71] Although Leyva Velázquez summoned growers to discuss the accusations, Vizcarra mysteriously disappeared shortly thereafter. His wife reported he was arrested by the police. The police denied any knowledge as to his whereabouts and initiated a search for him so that he might answer accusations about fraud brought by some growers who had paid for his services in legalizing their property.[72]

The disappearance of Vizcarra remains a mystery. He reappeared briefly in 1961, announcing that he would mobilize farmworkers once again in defense of their labor rights and would avoid the errors he made before,[73] but his time had passed. Vizcarra had taken advantage of farmworkers' discontent for personal gain. In the process, the issues of minimum wage, housing, and education were forced upon the table where growers, the state, and the CTM made the necessary arrangements to guarantee labor peace and grower profitability. Once the agenda had undergone the required modifications, Vizcarra's expulsion from the Culiacán fields facilitated the understanding between the CTM union and the growers which evolved into the *convenio* of 1963.

Renewed tension in the Sinaloa vegetable fields in 1977–78 owed a great deal to a new generation which attempted to mobilize farmworkers. In late 1975 the CCI of Ramon Danzós Palomino changed strategies in its search for relevance to the class struggle in the Mexican countryside. Of Communist orientation, the CCI also wished to incorporate the rising number of rural proletariat which Mexican development was producing. In recognition of their new clientele, the CCI became the Confederación Independiente de Obreros Agrícolas y Campesinos (CIOAC). While the CTM's national farmworkers' union, Sindicato Nacional de Trabajadores Asalariados del Campo (SNTAC succeeded SCOLyC), concerned itself with permanent workers, the CIOAC focused on migrants.[74]

Culiacán was an ideal place for CIOAC to initiate operations. It had a large number of unorganized migrant workers who did not receive the obligatory legal benefits and lived in totally unsanitary conditions. In addition, the governor of the state, Alfonso G. Calderón, had had a serious conflict with the rural elite during the land invasions of 1976 (see chapter 5). Finally, the local university (Universidad Autónoma de Sinaloa, UAS) was dominated by the Mexican Communist party and had a history of participating actively in worker and campesino struggles. The Sinaloa federation of CIOAC, FIOACS, set up shop in a university building and received legal and political support (also most likely financial) from various UAS organizations and individuals.[75]

At the beginning of the 1977–78 season the FIOACS made its move.

The 1976–77 season had been one of the best seasons on record, and growers were anticipating that this season would be similar. In October the first warnings were given that FIOACS would mobilize farmworkers if growers were not forthcoming with significant benefits for their laborers. Growers ignored the FIOACS. As the excellent season wound down, they attempted to squeeze as much as possible as late as possible out of the market. The moment was ripe. On April 25 and again on May 16 under FIOACS direction, 3,000 farmworkers walked out of the fields at five labor camps. The success of the maneuvers was quite spectacular, as growers signed agreements with FIOACS (which had no legal standing as a bargaining agent) that promised farmworkers in the affected camps significant new benefits. Among these were Christmas bonuses, vacation pay, Sundays off with pay, construction of worker housing, and construction of toilet facilities and of a potable water tank.[76]

The FIOAC victory had not come cheaply. There were arrests by the police and some workers lost their jobs. Implementation of some of the terms of the agreement required another strike movement at the beginning of the next season. But the hard-won victories were irrefutable indicators that FIOACS was a force to be considered in the Culiacán fields.

Among those concerned with the presence of FIOACS was the CTM. Success of FIOACS would mean an end to the monopoly which the CTM's SNTAC had in the Culiacán fields. In addition, the tactics of the new farmworker organization illustrated that these leaders were willing to disrupt the productive process in order for workers to gain; such an understanding of the nature of employer-worker relations was anathema to the CTM and to the CTM's patron, the state.

In this context of labor strife the first collective bargaining agreement in the Culiacán vegetable lands was signed at the beginning of the 1978–79 season. Terms of the contract demonstrate that its purpose was to serve primarily the interests of the growers and the CTM, and only secondarily these of the workers. For example, growers were free to decide how many workers were needed at any particular time and discharge them permanently or temporarily without any responsibility.*

---

*Mexican labor legislation stipulates that employers must pay fired workers compensation. In addition, as early as 1959 Vizcarra had suggested that workers be paid for time off due to suspension of work caused by factors beyond the control of the worker.

Among the express conditions for discharge are conditions in the international or national market and behavior by the worker which impedes the normal pace of work. The CTM union is favored by a closed shop and automatic discounts of workers' salaries for union dues. Farmworkers themselves received limited benefits, mainly the minimum due them under law. Thus 80 percent of workers receive the minimum pay established in the contract, the inequality of IMSS for rural workers remains unquestioned, and housing provisions are ignored.[77]

The contracts between AARC and the CTM put a tremendous stumbling block in the way of the FIOACS. Growers argued that they could not sign agreements with FIOACS because they were legally bound by the AARC–CTM contract and that agreements with FIOACS were nonbinding because that labor organization has no union registration. The CTM provided growers with the names of workers suspected of FIOACS sympathies, and under the closed shop provisions, they were fired. Even the federal government intervened against FIOACS: one FIOACS leader, a bilingual Indian from Oaxaca who was advised by the UAS and had 4,000 followers, was allegedly beaten by the army upon his return to his home state. He is now reported to be a very quiet worker in the Culiacán fields.[78]

FIOACS continues to operate, but changes in both market and political conditions appear to have stunted its ability to develop beyond sporadic mobilizations which bring benefits only so long as the immediate pressure is on. As for the CTM, they have struck occasionally, but their efforts are less concerning to growers. Firs, a CTM strike does not mobilize the labor force; rather a few pickets make a presence, and the camp closes down.[79] Thus the consciousness-raising spinoff of a CTM strike is far less than that of a FIOACS one for the farmworker. Second, the demands of the CTM cost the growers less. The CTM strikes for the minimum the labor law provides for rural workers. Under the present situation farmworkers are once again in the position of waiting for the trickle down to reach them.

The State Intervenes. The local government becomes the focus of attention when the issue revolves around implementation of minimum-wage laws. Minimum-wage levels are set at the national level, but the struggle in Sinaloa was not over the level of minimum wage which farmworkers should receive, but rather over the implementation of wages and benefits already granted farmworkers by the federal government. In these circumstances, the governor, the labor court (JCCyA), and the local labor department (DT) played fundamental roles in state intervention in farmworker conflicts.

Once the farmworkers' struggle addressed the need to extend the social-welfare provisions designed for urban labor to the rural sector, federal bureaucracies became involved in a complementary manner. The housing and social security institutions involved in administering social-welfare programs, became directly involved in negotiating with the growers over which programs would be extended to the rural sector, how, and who would pay what. These bureaucracies stayed out of the struggle over which unions would speak for the farmworkers, preferring to let the governor and his people decide that issue.

In the late 1950s, Governor Leyva Velázquez's initial response to the threat of strikes by farmworkers gave priority to the economic health of the Sinaloa economy. Seeking to derail the unionization efforts which began in the 1957–58 season, the governor pressured the labor court, just before the start of the next season, not to register any farmworker unions.[80] The official national labor confederation, however, realized the potential of the farmworker movement and sought to dominate it at the outset. Labor boss Fidel Velázquez came to Culiacán to inform Governor Leyva Velázquez of the CTM's interests.[81] The governor now found himself in a complicated situation: while recognizing the rights of labor to organize, he had to convince the growers to work with the unions. Mediation, rather than total acceptance of growers' demands, became the strategy.

The SOCSP's aggressiveness in filing strike petitions forced the governor to move quickly. In a move most likely designed to win time for the state's mediation efforts, the JCCyA refused to register the SOCSP on a technicality, thereby nullifying the strike petitions of the union. After disposing of the immediate threat, the governor maneuvered to make progress on the labor front without having things get out of hand. The labor court recognized four unions, among them the SOCSP, at the end of the season. The recognition served to remind the growers that they had to come to grips with the new dynamics in the countryside, but was also too late to have any effect on the current (1958–59) season. There would be some six months to reach an agreement before the next season.

The growers' continued refusal to enter into legal contracts forced the governor to adopt further measures. At the beginning of the new season the DT labor inspector accompanied Vizcarra on an inspection tour of the labor camps, citing those growers found in violation of the labor code. Through the intervention of the DT some conflicts were resolved outside of the labor courts, thereby circumventing the issue of the union demands.[82]

But Vizcarra's violation of the discreetness of corruption in the labor movement, as well as his need to keep tensions high in order that the FTS and AARC continue to need his services, threatened to overwhelm the governor's efforts at mediation. When farmworkers in the SOCSP began to confront Vizcarra about his performance on their behalf, Leyva Velázquez seized the moment. The DT undertook an investigation of the labor leader, and a series of events culminated in Vizcarra's exit from Sinaloa.

With the absence of Vizcarra and the movement toward understanding between growers and the CTM, the state found its efforts at peaceful mediation successful. Until the renewal of tensions in the Sinaloa countryside in the mid-1970s, most disputes were discreetly resolved by the AARC and CTM with marginal assistance by the DT.

In the late 1970s the state again played a fundamental role in the development of the situation on the labor front. As noted, the antagonism between Governor Calderón and the rural elite provided CIOAC with some room to maneuver. In addition, there is some speculation that Calderón was able to exert some influence over the timing of the mobilization of FIOACS via his control over the purse strings of the state university.[83]

Calderón had another reason to stimulate FIOACS in the early stages. Apart from his poor relations with the growers, Calderón's relation to the CTM also influenced his behavior in this period. Before becoming governor, Calderón had been head of Sinaloa's branch of the CTM, the FTS. It was natural, therefore, for the governor to use the DT both to maintain the CTM's legal monopoly in the fields and to pressure the growers to revise their agreement with the CTM union to channel it more resources. In fact, not only did his court refuse to register the FIOACS union, but in an earlier case, when the growers attempted to create their own farm labor union in 1976, Calderón was reported to have had the police beat and run the "labor" leader out of Sinaloa.[84]

The change of governor in 1980, in which a financial magnate with ties to agriculture replaced a governor from the labor sector, did not significantly affect CTM-grower relations. Toledo Corro's own conflicts with growers (see chapter 3) hampered his ability to use the power of the office against the CTM. Consequently, the idea of a grower's union supplanting the CTM, although supported by some growers, has not prospered. The major concern of the growers appears to be that despite the popular perception of a ruthless *neo-latifundista*,[85] Toledo Corro could not keep the CTM from responding to the challenge by shutting down the fields.[86]

But there is a much more fundamental aspect at work. In the context of the present political and economic crisis of the country, the CTM is a pillar of support for the state. In order to maintain legitimacy the CTM makes demands, but these are relatively minor in the overall context. Thus in the face of an 80 percent devaluation in February 1982, the CTM struck the growers for a 20 percent wage increase.[90] The pragmatism of the political elite, including Toledo Corro, suggests that there will be no attempt from the top to push the CTM out of the Culiacán fields.

CONCLUSION

Examination of the labor conflicts of 1957–63 and 1977–82 provides a striking illustration of the interaction among the three levels of political economy. Within this dynamic interaction among levels of analysis, the case also sheds light upon the relationship among three political forces in the Sinaloa countryside as they maneuver to affect the distribution of benefits generated by the vegetable exports.

In the case of the growers, we see the bias in the Mexican political economy in their favor: since the state is not willing to put its scarce resources into this highly risky venture, the private sector must be supported in production of these export crops. But the bias in favor of capital does not determine the form in which the decision as to the distribution of wealth between capital and labor will be carried out. Here growers' organizations play a fundamental role in facilitating acceptance of the formula advocated by capital that limits the redistributive aspects of the integration of Sinaloa into the international market via winter vegetables.

In the context of an expanding market and increased demand for labor, the distributional question could be resolved with a minimum of tension. The existence of a non-zero sum alternative from 1957 to 1963 meant that growers were able to begin to establish their independence from the state (chapter 3) and foreign capital (chapter 7) and still distribute benefits to a small part of the farm labor work force via capital investments (housing and education), and less so through a wage increase (i.e., paying legal minimum wages). The ability of the growers to speak with one voice and threaten to halt production became crucial in ensuring that the state would mediate the grower-farmworker face-off of 1957–1960 so as to allow the implementation of a solution along the parameters of the 1962–63 agreements between AARC and the CTM.

The labor conflicts of 1977–82 took place in a different context. In this recent period Mexican growers began to lose their competitive edge in the international market, and thus the non-zero sum solution of the earlier period was no longer possible. Once again the organized farmers were able to mobilize their resources to bring about a situation in which the cost of the redistribution made necessary by FIOACS' mobilization of farmworkers would be minimal to growers themselves. The economic costs were shared with state social welfare agencies, most likely disproportionately in favor of the growers, while the political costs of marginalizing FIOACS were borne by the CTM-state alliance.

The redistributive impact in this latter period was limited not only by sharing economic costs with the state and shifting political costs to other political actors. Through their control over the productive process itself, growers began to meet the pressures from the international market and a sporadically mobilized labor force by mechanizing production and thereby decreasing demand for labor. As chapter 7 will demonstrate, growers could have met the demands of international cost competitiveness via a variety of mechanisms, but took advantage of the situation to push the cost of adjustment onto the labor force and in the process strike a blow at labor militancy.

The state intervened in the labor conflicts through the governor and social welfare agencies. Each of these played an important role in mediating tensions in the Sinaloa fields. Perhaps most importantly, the presence of the state was most critical in setting the parameters for farmworker organization. The CTM had originally unionized the Sinaloa fields but the most radical of Mexican presidents had expelled it from the countryside. In the late 1950s a deal was apparently struck between the CTM and a new president to allow the official labor movement to organize farmworkers in Sinaloa's vegetable farms.

Given the lack of nonpoliticized analysis of the relationship among the state, CTM, and farmworkers, here I can only present a hypothesis about this decision taken at the center but which had enormous implications for the local level. During the late 1950s, independent movements, in which the Mexican Communist party played a significant role, were posing a serious challenge to the corporatist control over the labor sector which the state had constructed. In the Sinaloa vegetable fields good economic times, following some very bad seasons and corruption of CTM leaders with no link to the farmworkers, made the region ripe for union organizers. Not only was the region a potential site for further inroads by reformist groups (as chapter 4 demonstrated, the UGOCM was already active in the area), but individual leaders like Vizcarra were already proselytizing among the farmworkers. The importance of the vegetable trade for Mexico made it logical for the state to extend its corporatist network to Sinaloa; Fidel Velázquez's trip to Culiacán signaled such an effort.

Grower control over the production process and state determination of the basis for organization and mobilization of the farmworkers have doomed efforts to wrest significant benefits from the industry for the benefit of labor. In the 1957–63 period the incipient farmworker labor movement was captured by the CTM, whose interests have very little in common with those of farmworkers. When national and local circumstances were conducive to a resurgence of a reformist movement in the Sinaloa vegetable fields, state and grower willingness to ally in defense of that corporatist structure condemned FIOACS to a sporadic movement. By taking advantage of the political (Governor Calderón's fight with the growers) and economic (the harvest cycle) moment, FIOACS has been responsible for some improvement in farmworkers' lives, but their housing, hygienic, and nutritional condition stand in stark contrast to the fortunes which vegetable exports created, or supplemented, in the private sector.

III

FOREIGN CHALLENGES TO OWNERSHIP AND TRADE

7

SUBORDINATION OF FOREIGN INVESTMENT

The examination of the U.S. fresh winter vegetable agribusiness commodity system presented in chapter 2 suggested that the system has been undergoing a process of change in the last decade. That very process presents some participants with opportunities to increase their weight in the system. In a dynamic sense, those opportunities are also limited by both the system and sociopolitical relations which are a part of the productive and commercialization process.

Of course, the existence of opportunities does not guarantee that any one particular group will either be interested or able to avail itself of them. One might just as well expect the "commercial element of the U.S. bourgeoisie"[1] to integrate backward and squeeze the Mexican grower even more in the competitive struggle with U.S. retailers and producers. In order to understand the ability of the Mexican growers to take advantage of these opportunities, it becomes necessary to analyze their organization and mobilization of resources in support of those efforts.

This chapter is arranged into four sections. The first section examines the organization of the Mexican producers, led by the Sinaloa growers, into a national union. The performance of the UNPH in serving the needs of the vegetable growers has been fundamental in their progressive domination of the agribusiness commodity system. Section two analyzes the efforts by Culiacán growers, first in Sinaloa and then nationwide, to regulate supply to the export market. The third section turns to an investigation of efforts to increase demand for winter vegetables. We shall see that controlling supply actually depends upon having a consistent, though moderate, expansion of market demand. In the final section, we address the actual integration forward by the elite of Mexican growers. Particular attention is paid to those domestic and international factors which at one point can be favorable to the evolution of Sinaloa growers' dominance of the agribusiness commodity system and at another moment threaten it.

ORGANIZING EXPORTS: A NATIONAL UNION OF PRODUCERS

The fresh fruit and vegetable export business has historically gone through periods of expansion and contraction as supply overwhelmed demand, toppling prices. In the late 1920s the first rush to corner the export market broke the two U.S. companies which dominated the northern Sinaloa operations.[2] The early 1940s were a boom period due to the war effort in the United States and Mexico's provision of primary products at higher than normal prices. Demand for Mexican vegetables, tomatoes in particular, continued high for the rest of the decade.[3]

As investors rushed in to benefit from the profitable export market, supply outdistanced demand and the bottom dropped out of the market. The almost 50 percent drop in exports from 1953–54 to 1954–55 (see table 7.1) not only pushed many producers out of tomato production but also suggested to the remaining growers that some regulation of supply was necessary. In late 1955 Sinaloa growers' statewide organization, CAADES, formulated the first serious effort to limit production of all export crops in Sinaloa. The proposal apparently included controls on area and quality (these latter would be in excess of USDA minimum standards) as well as the provision for temporary suspensions on picking. Only the Culiacán association voted to accept these guidelines, but even here the decision was not taken until the following season and did not include acreage limitations.[4]

Contraction in supply as a result of falling prices in previous seasons pressured prices upward. In 1956–57 exports picked up and export controls were loosened. The following year Floridian production was hit by a disastrous freeze, and the door was opened to imports of large quantities of Mexican tomatoes at high prices. The 1957–58 season went down in Sinaloan history as the "golden year," and any concern to limit supply disappeared. Success once again stimulated increased investment in vegetable production. Cooler heads tried to prevail, warning that area planted was beyond requirements of the market, but it

TABLE 7.1
Tomato Exports from Sinaloa

Seasons	Total A	Culiacán B	Percent B/A	Others[a] C	Percent C/A
1950–51	75,496	45,457	60.2	30,039	39.8
1951–52	79,529	45,581	57.3	33,948	42.7
1952–53	89,727	65,448	72.9	24,279	27.1
1953–54	67,394	50,700	75.2	16,694	24.8
1954–55	37,649	28,701	76.2	8,948	23.8
Average 1950–55	69,959	47,177	67.4	22,782	32.6
1955–56	19,938	17,172	86.1	2,766	13.9
1956–57	62,331	46,784	75.1	15,547	24.9
1957–58	102,375	63,985	62.5	38,390	37.5
1958–59	112,995	63,736	56.4	49,259	43.6
1959–60	124,759	96,459	77.3	28,300	22.7
Average 1955–60	84,480	57,627	68.2	26,852	31.8

SOURCE: *Boletín Agrícola*, AARC, May and June 1961, p. 24.
[a] Guasave, Los Mochis, and Guamuchil.

proved impossible to secure the votes to restrict area within AARC's jurisdiction.[5]

But the 1958–59, 1959–60, and 1960–61 seasons were poor as Mexican production fell into a cycle from low-supply to high-price to over-supply to decline-in-price to decline-in-supply. In 1958 Mexican export volume increased 86 percent, but the value of total production fell 8.5 percent; for the next two years volume increased slightly and value continued its decline, although at a slower rate.[*] In Culiacán 90 percent of growers lost "considerable" amounts of money, 5 percent broke even, and only 5 percent made what were reported to be small profits.[6]

Control over supply going to the export market at any particular moment was in the hands of the growers. Sometimes the U.S. distrib-

---

[*] These figures are not entirely satisfactory for our purposes. The volume figures are for total Mexican exports, while the value is for total Mexican production, i.e., it includes domestic consumption. Leonidas P. Bill Emerson, Jr., *Preview of Mexico's Winter Vegetable Production for Export*, p 33. We can reasonably assume, however, that the price in the export market declined if volume of exports increased and the value of the crop fell. Given that the value is quoted in current prices, the real decline was even greater.

utors who financed and marketed the vegetables would request that growers impose certain restrictions upon supply. Internal documents of AARC indicate that despite financial dependence, grower committees made the final decisions.[7] This evidence of substantial grower autonomy suggests that U.S. distributors as a whole (some individual distributors may have had the desire to control their growers carefully) had only a marginal interest in the growing side of the operations.

The attempt to control supply via harvesting and quality regulations proved ineffectual at best and usually caused further downward pressure on prices. Growers merely picked more tomatoes on those days harvesting was allowed, thereby increasing supply in the packing sheds. The temptation presented by having the product on hand proved too much for some producers, who then attempted to hide poor-quality tomatoes under good tomatoes.[8] If the load passed inspection by the U.S. Department of Agriculture at the border, supply in the terminal markets would be increased, but with poor-quality tomatoes. In addition, buyers were aware of the potential supply in the Sinaloa fields and lowered prices accordingly.[9] Thus supply and quality forced prices down.

In this context there was renewed pressure for effective supply controls. Producers were aware that Culiacán, or even Sinaloa, could not regulate their own production without growers in other areas increasing production to replace Sinaloa volume. Such an outcome would mean that Sinaloa sacrifices would be in vain. Culiacán growers, therefore, renewed efforts to get at least regional participation in regulation of supply.

In July 1957 AARC and CAADES had organized the First Convention of Horticultural Producers of the Northwest. Initially only the Sinaloa associations, their Arizona distributors (WMVDA), and the railroad which transported the vegetables (Ferrocarril de Pacifico)* were scheduled to participate.[10] When the states of Nayarit and Sonora and the Ministries of Agriculture and Livestock and of Treasury and Public Credit decided to participate, the convention took on a regional significance.[11]

At the 1957 convention AARC presented a proposal to combat the

---

*These three groups had been meeting annually since 1951 to discuss transportation problems in the winter vegetable industry.

tendency toward oversupply. Regulation, complete with sanctions, to decrease supply through quality and packaging controls in both the export and domestic markets was suggested. But there was no consensus to support AARC's efforts in 1957 because at that moment U.S. demand was very high.

In June 1959, with a weak international market, AARC complained that quality controls initiated under the 1956 AARC regulations were being ignored, with the result of increased supply at "giveaway" prices. Distributors for the domestic market were also accused of exporting tomatoes (not meeting export quality standards) through Texas ports, rather than through Nogales, Sonora, where CAADES had its inspectors. Finally, the association pointed out that producing large quantities of tomatoes in hopes that Florida would suffer a freeze was bad business. Planning was necessary, and even though Culiacán producers had restricted acreage in recent years, other areas had increased theirs. The bad seasons and the logic of AARC's arguments facilitated transforming the regional meetings into national ones to discuss coordination of the industry in all its phases.[12]

The first National Convention of Horticultural Producers was held in 1959, although the only new participants were growers from the northeastern state of Tamaulipas. But at the second national meeting, held the following year, Michoacán and Puebla were represented, thereby ushering in a new phase in the Mexican industry. In the 1959 convention the AARC representatives again proposed that production regulations be implemented, and in the 1960 convention a committee was created to formulate a proposal for a national union which would have regulation as a priority. But CAADES did not move on the mandate given it until growers in AARC prodded the commission into action.[13]

In 1961 the conjunction of three factors gave life to the dream of Culiacán producers: a national union of horticultural producers (Unión Nacional de Productores de Hortalizas, UNPH). First, a poor market for three years running convinced producers from various parts of the country, with different market positions and therefore different interests,* to agree on goals and functions for the organization. Second, the

---

*The problem of organizing supply agreements with production distributed asymmetrically among many producers has been treated extensively in the literature on international commodity agreements. One of the chief obstacles is that supply agree-

state had become concerned over the health of the industry because of its importance to the generation of foreign exchange and employment creation. As representative of state interests in the agricultural sector, the Ministry of Agriculture put its Department of Small Property Owners* to the task of working with the Culiacán growers in this endeavor. Finally, there was the all-important personal link to policymakers. Luis Gaxiola Clouthier, member of the aforementioned Gastelum-Gaxiola-Clouthier clan (see chapter 3), was president of both AARC and CAADES in 1961 and was able to enlist the support of his friends in the Sinaloa and federal governments to back the project.[14]

With the basic outline of the UNPH agreed upon at the Third National Convention of Horticultural Producers, delegates from nine producer organizations (five from Sinaloa and two each from Sonora and Tamaulipas) met on October 14 in Mazatlán, Sinaloa; in addition three representatives from the secretary of agriculture were present.[15] The UNPH was established to perform five basic functions for its member associations (membership was confined to local and state producer organizations): a) regulate horticultural production; b) promote the vertical integration of the producers into marketing and industrialization of their product; c) coordinate and stimulate cooperative efforts among its member associations; d) represent members before relevant public and private organizations; and e) provide production services for its members.[16]

The UNPH is formally regulated by the same corporatist legislation to which state and local associations must conform: the 1932 and 1934 federal laws. It, too, has proved a successful vehicle for the articulation and defense of the interests of horticultural producers for both the export and domestic markets, although less so than CAADES or AARC (more

---

ments tend to freeze market share, thereby presenting a high cost to smaller producers who believe that in times of crisis they could better their position in the market. For an excellent treatment of the subject, see L. N. Rangarajan, *Commodity Conflict*. This situation is replicated at the national level, indicating the usefulness of this literature for producer-controlled supply agreements. In all successful commodity agreements, one group (in this case Culiacán growers) disproportionately pays the costs of regulation. Sinaloa producers agreed to absorb the costs of regulation in a disproportionate manner such as Brazil in coffee and Saudi Arabia in oil.

* In light of the UNPH's contribution to the strength of the Sinaloa vegetable growers, and the analysis of this book, it is ironic that it was President Cárdenas who created this department in 1938.

on this below). The UNPH has taken an active role in obtaining import permits for all types of horticultural inputs, including transportation. International trade disputes also provide a forum for the UNPH to come to the defense of its producers (see chapter 8). The union has also become active in promoting the export of a variety of horticultural products and in realizing another goal of early Culiacán producers: the organization of the domestic market to provide a quality product at prices profitable to the producers. With this expansion of activities and the accumulated successes, the UNPH has grown rapidly: in 1961 nine associations from three states constituted the UNPH;[17] by 1979 there were 54 member associations from 19 states[18] representing 19,000 producers.[19]

Culiacán's Domination of the UNPH. Although the UNPH represents horticultural producers for both the export and domestic markets, the strength of the union lies with the export sector. This is logical, since the creation of the organization was a response to the needs of export producers. From the very beginning Culiacán growers were concerned about dilution of their influence in an organization which would agglomerate all horticultural producers in the country.[20] (In the 1955–59 period Sinaloa was responsible for only 19 percent of Mexico's total horticultural area.[21]) Chapter 3 of the UNHP regulations was specifically designed to safeguard those interests; it notes that on matters that are the concern solely of export producers a special assembly of export producer organizations will legislate.

Export producers have controlled the union through their monopoly of its administration and its heavy dependence upon taxes on exports for funding.[22] In 1961 Luis Gaxiola Clouthier was elected president in recognition of his role in the creation of the UNPH (he thus held the presidencies of three of the most important rural elite associations in the country—AARC, CAADES, and UNPH—simultaneously). Ever since, there has been an implicit agreement that the president shall hail from Sinaloa and the vice president from Sonora. With the expansion of membership the posts of secretary and treasurer have been given to the Michoacán and Guanajuato associations, respectively.

But the expansion of membership to states which produce vegetables primarily for domestic consumption has led to increased tension between export and domestic producers within the Unión Nacional. This

TABLE 7.2

Presidents of the Unión Nacional
de Productores de Hortalizas

Period	
1961	Luis Gaxiola Clouthier, Culiacán
1964	Adolfo A. Clouthier, Culiacán
1967	Alfredo Careaga Cebreros, Culiacán
1970	Manuel J. Clouthier, Culiacán
1973	Roberto Tamayo Muller, Culiacán
1976	José Carlos de Saracho C., Guasave
1979	Jorge R. Ibarra Castañeda, Culiacán
1982	Emilio Gastelum Angulo, Culiacán

SOURCE: UNPH, *Convención anual*, annual reports for 1961–1982.

tension has coincided with the state's attempt to defuse recent efforts by the rural elite to become involved in official party politics and has led to a polarization of forces within the UNPH.

In 1976 José Carlos de Saracho, the first UNPH president to hail from a local association other than AARC (he is from Guasave, just north of Culiacán; see table 7.2), outmaneuvered his fellow Sinaloa producers and obtained the nomination for federal deputy through his personal ties. He enraged Sinaloa producers, especially those in AARC, whose candidate was CAADES President Diaz Castro, who had defended the growers so well against Mexican President Echeverría (see chapter 5). In preparing for the 1979 UNPH elections, Jorge R. Ibarra Castañeda, an intimate friend of de Saracho, failed to be nominated by his local association (AARC)* or by the state confederation. Nevertheless, at the national convention Ibarra joined forces with domestic producers† in an alliance against the Sinaloa exporters and their allies. In an extremely close vote, Ibarra defeated the Culiacán candidate, Emilio Gastelum Angulo, who was at that time also the president of CAADES.

Upon defeat, the Culiacán association threatened to expel Ibarra from AARC for having ignored association decisions, namely that Gas-

---

*He also lost the 1979 elections for AARC president.

† Ibarra had an opportunity to culitvate this relationship in his capacity as president of the committee which regulates Sinaloa's vegetable supply to the domestic market (Comité Regulador de Hortalizas Frescas del Estado de Sinaloa, para el Mercado Nacional).

telum Angulo was to be the Sinaloa candidate, not Ibarra. CAADES also threatened to withdraw from the UNPH because, although the financial burden of the UNPH was shouldered by CAADES' export producers, voting procedures based on acreage were biased against the more land-intensive export producers. Thus shortly after his election, Ibarra, recognizing that withdrawal of Sinaloa would mean the end of the UNPH, began working to revise the electoral system of the organization.[23]

In the meantime, AARC and CAADES were successful in pulling a special fund financed by export vegetables out of the UNPH and into the jurisdiction of local associations. Because the Sinaloa vegetable export contribution to UNPH funds represented 50 percent of total UNPH funds from all domestic and international sales during the 1979–80 season, this action can be of major consequence for the UNPH.[24] It is still too early to tell whether the UNPH controversy will herald a significant decline in the Sinaloan export producers' influence in that organization. Again, as in the case of the AARC presidency, it may just signify the low point in their influence; the election of Emilio Gastelum Angulo as president for the 1983–86 period suggests this may be the case.

Past experience indicates that internal divisions among private farmers cannot alone check the power of export producers. So long as the national and state economies depend heavily upon export of agricultural products, those producers will continue to wield influence in those policies of direct concern to them. And if the control of those local and state organizations is wrested from them, they most likely would resort to the creation of parallel organizations as they did in 1976 (see chapter 5).

REGULATING SUPPLY TO THE INTERNATIONAL MARKET

One of the first tasks the Culiacán growers set for the UNPH was to extend production controls to the country as a whole. In this effort the Culiacán growers had to meet challenges on three fronts: within the Culiacán association itself, from the producers in the other regions of Sinaloa, and from growers in other states. The strategy utilized combined the carrot and the stick: quotas were manipulated to allow smaller producers to continue to undergo slow growth in production, and the federal and state governments were persuaded to lend their police power to enforce export quotas.

Despite the fact that the calls for regulation were coming out of the Culiacán association, experience had demonstrated that even within AARC it proved difficult to convince growers to institute controls and abide by them. Once it was clear that the UNPH would be created, those growers in AARC who were advocates of production controls renewed their efforts to get the most powerful local association in the country to institute such controls in its region. Toward the end of the 1960–61 season informal meetings of vegetable growers were held, and it became clear that within the Culiacán group an internal revolt was brewing.[25]

Lacking the votes to pass restrictive legislation, pro-restriction growers turned to the state to tip the balance. The irrigation district's directive committee (CDA)* announced that water would not be available for those who planted in excess of the area necessary to supply the international market. AARC was then asked to conduct a study of precisely what those needs would be. The fact that AARC was given the task of undertaking the study and that it was completed in a few days indicates that the pro-restriction growers in AARC had circumvented the opposition within AARC. The study concluded that production could be reduced by 45 percent.[26] Now that Culiacán growers were faced with the need to reduce dramatically the area they planted, they had to face the question of how the cuts would be distributed.

On June 17, 1961, a meeting of vegetable growers in AARC was held. Of the 174 vegetable growers 89 were present, and the feelings were running high against the large growers. For some growers the question of supply control had to begin by running a newcomer out of the fields: staked tomatoes. In the late 1950s a few Culiacán producers began to experiment with tomato plants grown vertically on a stake instead of horizontally on the ground. The results were incredible, as yields increased dramatically (see table 7.3). But capital requirements were also significantly higher, particularly because labor requirements increased manyfold. The smaller producers began to fear that not only was the staked tomato ruining the market at this time, but also that any recovery

---

*For a discussion of the CDA and irrigation politics, see chapter 4.

TABLE 7.3
*Culiacán Valley: Tomato Hectarage
Harvested and Yields*

Season	Hectarage	Yields
1956–1957	7,760	6.0
1957–1958	7,563	8.5
1958–1959	12,255	5.2
1959–1960	14,718	6.6
1960–1961	19,043	3.1
Average	12,268	5.4
Production Controls		
1961–1962	8,462	9.8
1962–1963	6,004	16.2
1963–1964	6,387	16.1
1964–1965	7,218	15.8
Average	7,018	14.5

SOURCE: "Las necesidades de crédito para la horticultura," presented by AARC to the UNPH General Assembly, Guadalajara, Jalisco (c. 1965), p. 3. AARC Archives.

would be limited to the few rich producers who could afford the higher costs of staked production. These growers mobilized and sought to ban production of these tomatoes in 1961.[27]

But the rural elite understood the potential of the new tomato in their battle with U.S. competitors: to increase yields by increasing labor costs played to the Mexican producers' relative strength. These growers defeated the initiatives by growers of ground tomatoes, and the costs of production all but finished off those producers who would not switch. Whereas in 1956–57 ground tomatoes accounted for 97 percent of the tomato area cultivated in Sinaloa and represented 91.6 percent of the value of its exports, by 1964–65 the shares had fallen to 24.5 percent and 7.7 percent, respectively (see table 7.4).

The decision was made, therefore, to confront the market with a heavy reliance on the advantage of cheap and abundant labor. A different strategy could have been adopted, one that Florida growers themselves would implement in the face of increased competition from Sinaloa: increase yields in ground tomatoes through technological

TABLE 7.4
*Culiacán Valley: Hectarage and Export Volume of
Mature and Green Tomatoes*

	Preproduction Controls			
	Hectarage		Export Volume[a]	
Season	Staked	Ground	Mature	Green
1956–1957	230	7,530	3,929	42,855
1957–1958	490	7,073	11,006	52,979
1958–1959	1,060	11,195	14,085	49,651
1959–1960	1,710	13,008	27,298	69,161
1960–1961	4,820	14,223	32,373	26,600
Average	1,662	10,606	17,738	48,249
	Production Controls			
1961–1962	2,330	6,132	52,676	30,051
1962–1963	3,294	2,710	69,339	28,707
1963–1964	3,876	2,511	85,868	18,395
1964–1965	5,211	1,695	103,686[b]	8,619[b]
Average	2,942	3,262	77,892	21,443

Source: "Las necesidades de crédito para la horticultura."
[a] Brute tonnage.
[b] Approximate figure.

change. The strategy adopted by Sinaloa growers meant gaining a market advantage at that time and coming to some understanding with an incipient farmworker movement in their fields (see chapter 6), but it also sowed the seeds of disaster fifteen years later.

This reliance upon a high-yielding product made supply controls all the more pressing and kept tension over distribution of area high. Although in June 1961 large growers were able to defeat the attempt to ban the production of staked tomatoes, they were not successful in keeping the group from voting to limit tomato area for individual farmers to 50 hectares. Those voting for this limit claimed outright it was an attack on the large producers. They also understood that a variety of means would be found to circumvent the limits, but felt that the increased costs of doing so might bring them benefits.[28] If the larger growers were forced to seek more associates, small growers would increase their chances of surviving in the volatile market, albeit in association with a large grower.

The larger growers regrouped and forced another meeting to discuss production quotas. At this two-day meeting it was decided to decrease area so as to provide a supply of 60,000 tons of tomatoes, which implied a reduction of 45 percent in area harvested. The distribution of costs was to be spread across the spectrum of producers, with a concession to the smallest. The basic principle was that all producers who harvested tomatoes in the 1960–61 season would cut area by 45 percent, except those producers who, as a result of such a cutback, would find themselves limited to less than 45 hectares could plant up to 45 hectares. The remaining area which was allocated after this process would be distributed with preference given to those growers who had sat out the 1960–61 season but had planted tomatoes in the four previous seasons; whatever was left would then be allocated to new growers but limiting them to no more than 45 hectares and/or only up to half of their land holdings. In addition, the productivity advantage of staked tomatoes was compensated in these acreage controls by making 1 hectare of staked equivalent to 3 hectares of ground tomatoes. The assembly also authorized AARC to regulate supply for peppers, cucumber, green beans, and eggplant. In hopes of guaranteeing compliance, the assembly also voted to hire two inspectors to patrol the fields and packinghouses.[29]

With the resolution of internal disagreement over the manner in which to control supply, AARC turned to the matter of convincing growers in Sinaloa's other vegetable zones to accept the AARC proposal as a guideline for their own policy. Here the Culiacán growers ran into more problems because the area allocated by AARC for their own producers was sufficient to supply the entire demand for Mexican tomatoes. Growers to the north of Culiacán believed that AARC was attempting to shift a disproportionate share of the adjustment onto them. At the CAADES meeting to discuss the AARC recommendations, northern Sinaloa growers refused to limit their area. Since these areas accounted for 30 percent of Sinaloa's tomato exports in this period (see table 7.1), the failure of AARC to convince them to participate in this effort was a major setback for AARC's regulatory program. AARC producers retaliated by setting only minimal quality restrictions on their supply as the season progressed, despite northern Sinaloa growers' efforts to impose severe quality control.[30] AARC's strategy was apparently to allow supply to remain high in the belief that they could withstand the weakness of the market better than the northern growers.

The possibility of continued disorder in the international market attracted state intervention, with the Sinaloa representative of the Ministry of Agriculture intervening in the 1963–64 program to control production.[31] Although the Ministry's agent was apparently able to smooth over the tensions by limiting Culiacán's area, these growers were able to petition the governor to intervene to increase Culiacán's quota.[32] The following season, AARC went one step further in pressuring their neighbors: implementation of any controls (area or quality) on supply from the Culiacán Valley was made contingent on statewide acceptance of the same measures.[33]

But northern growers saw their participation in the market at stake and refused to yield. The Culiacán group was in a difficult position, for to carry through on their threat to disrupt the market once again implied costs few of the growers wanted to pay. As a result they capitulated: until 1967 only the Culiacán growers were subjecting themselves to acreage controls,[34] and oftentimes quality controls were handled in the same manner (push the costs to AARC).[35] Confronted by this threat to the market and to the UNPH, concerned growers apparently decided to save the organization and hope that Florida's volume would be weak enough to save the market. Although the CAADES committee to study the needs of the U.S. market recommended that only 8,700 hectares of tomatoes be planted in Sinaloa during the 1967–68 season,[36] CAADES' assembly of tomato growers allocated 25 percent more. In this manner programming of acreage could be claimed to be a success in terms of grower acceptance.[37] Now, if only the market would hold . . .

With unity in Sinaloa achieved in this manner, attention turned to the UNPH's ability to implement it on a national scale. Here the Culiacán growers saw little need to expend political capital required by their leadership position to control area planted; Sinaloa's 90 percent to 95 percent share of tomato exports allowed them to accept adherence to quality controls as sufficient for growers outside of Sinaloa. For 1963–64 AARC's tomato regulations thus noted that Culiacán growers' acceptance of these regulations was dependent upon area controls being implemented statewide but only quality controls nationwide.[38]

The state's interest in developing a stable environment for this important industry led it to intervene once again. It contributed to the UNPH's monopolization of resources to enforce these decisions by delegating to the UNPH important governmental functions. First, the UNPH was given sole authority to control distribution of permits and certificates of origin for marketing tomatoes either in the domestic or external market.[39] Shortly thereafter, the Finance Ministry amended the Customs Code to require presentation of this UNPH documentation for export.[40*]

For 1962–63 acreage restrictions were again in effect, with total area planted in Culiacán rising by about 3 percent. But the composition of that area changed dramatically, with implications for the concentration of production in the area. Between 1961–62 and 1962–63 area in ground tomatoes fell by 56 percent, while that of the staked variety increased by 41 percent.[41] The shift toward a more expensive investment at a time when the market was only beginning to be profitable once again led to a decreased number of producers and concentration of production in a few hands within that number. Whereas in 1960–61 there had been 174 tomato growers, in 1962–63 there were only 117. In addition, while in 1961–62 growers had been limited to a maximum of 45 hectares of tomatoes, the following season lack of such restrictions led to the distribution noted in table 7.5.

Fear of monopolization of production of such a lucrative crop brought forth protest from other growers (as we have seen) and other sectors of Mexican society. For example, the magazine *Novedades* ran an article denouncing area restrictions and the destruction of supply deemed by the growers to be in excess, and calling for a reevaluation of state policies supportive of these growers.[42] In response, the major tomato growers made some concessions. Beginning in 1967, the area which any one individual grower could plant was limited to 100 hectares. Another concession was to restrict packinghouses to processing the crop from a maximum of 400 hectares.[43]

If the concern was monopolization of control, these requirements were ineffectual, for, as chapter 4 illustrated, ownership/production was

---

*When grower control over these licensing measures threatened to disrupt Mexican participation in the U.S. market, the state would reassume these functions (see chapter 8).

TABLE 7.5
Distribution of Tomato Area in Culiacán Valley, 1962–63

Growers	Area (has.)	Group Total	Average
25	1–45	710	28.4
19	46–60	993	52.3
8	61–75	540	67.5
9	76–90	762	84.7
56	>90	9,205	164.4
117		12,210	104

	Relative Shares	
Growers	Total Producers	Total Area
25	21.4	5.8
19	16.2	8.1
8	6.8	4.4
9	7.7	6.2
56	47.9	75.4
	100.0	99.9

SOURCE: Notes from AARC *Archives*, Tomato File, dated September 13, 1963.

often listed under various family and friends' names, when in fact a single individual can control the group. This practice provided a means to evade the processing restrictions on packinghouses, since the composition of groups was amorphous enough that several group members were allowed to process the crop from 400 hectares. The popularity of this mechanism is illustrated by the fact that in 1965 there were twenty-nine "groups"* of growers but forty-two packing sheds.[44] For the 1967–68 season, fewer than ten growers produced 60 percent of the tomatoes exported, and with the poor seasons of the early and late 1970s that concentration most likely increased.[45]

In one very important respect, the concessions were important in distributing some of the benefits of this booming industry. By renting land and through bringing in more partners, the major producers were forced to share the wealth, although to a significantly lesser degree than if the restrictions were adhered to in spirit rather than merely the letter.

Over the years the UNPH has developed an elaborate computer

---

*A group is generally comprised of a number of growers who associate on the basis of financial and/or packing ties.

simulation model to predict an optimal level for Mexican exports. Some analysts have argued that this means that the organization exercises extremely tight control over production.[46] But this analysis of the market serves at best to guide the UNPH grower assembly. It is here that the decisions of how much area will be sown are made, and growers do not feel bound by the decisions of the UNPH technicians on this matter. Acreage and export permits are allocated by the organization to its regional affiliates, who in turn distribute them to the individual growers.* (In 1974–75 acreage controls were extended to cucumbers and bell peppers.)[47]

Even with acreage controls, Mexican producers have found it necessary to regulate the volume of produce sent to market. In order to implement these measures, committees for each of the major crops meet weekly with government representatives and establish quality requirements for export. Initially this committee was constituted by three representatives from the Arizona distributors, CAADES, and the UNPH. In 1970 its membership was expanded to thirteen: one each from the UNPH, CAADES, the Sonora growers, and the Los Mochis and Guasave local associations; two from the Arizona distributors' association; and six from AARC.[48] The quality controls voted by this committee are usually significantly more stringent than those which the USDA has established as minimum requirements for imports. Grower controls can have a large impact on supply: AARC estimated that the volume controls implemented in the 1966–67 season were responsible for keeping approximately 10 percent of total supply off the market.[49]

Of course, creation of a mechanism to control supply via production regulation and quality control does not necessarily mean that it will be implemented successfully. An examination of its functioning since 1961–62 is necessary.

Cuba's expulsion from the market and the reduction in Sinaloa area brought about a slow recovery in the profitability of tomato production for export. In 1963–64 acreage controls were eliminated and regulation of supply depended upon quality controls which were triggered by a combination of price and volume criteria which varied as the season evolved and were different for staked and ground tomatoes.[50] For this

---

*One of the benefits of this procedure is to strengthen the organization of local producers.

season acreage planted in tomatoes increased 13 percent over 1961–63.[51]

From 1963–64 to 1973–74 there was a constant expansion of Mexican tomato area due to the shifts in the international supply side of the U.S. market (Cuba and California's exit from the market and Florida's economic and climatic problems) which demanded more supply from Mexico. The increased Mexican supply became an issue of great concern for the Florida producers, leading to trade conflicts between Mexico and the U.S. in 1969 and again in 1978. As it became clear that Mexican producers were insensitive to the political ramifications of attempting to push U.S. growers out of the U.S. market, the Mexican state reappeared as a direct actor in the industry. In 1970 legislation to return export controls to the Agriculture Ministry were enacted which made UNPH grower assembly decisions on area cultivated subject to approval of the state. These powers were used to overturn grower decisions in 1970–71, 1973–74, 1978–79, 1979–80, and 1980–81 (for an elaboration, see chapter 8). But the market continued to call for increased Mexican supply, and the restrictions proved irrelevant in each of the seasons except 1973–74 (in 1980–81, for a variety of reasons discussed in the next section, supply was less than that programmed).

In light of steadily increasing Mexican production, recovery of Florida's production in the early seventies meant the supply situation became problematic once again. The best indication of this loss of control by Culiacán growers is the return to picking holidays in the 1972–73 season as the quality regulations proved insufficient to bring supply into line with expected prices in the market (table 7.6 provides an example of seasonal regulations). In response, Mexican growers cut acreage by one-fourth for the following season and instituted planting schedules to avoid concentration of production for the most lucrative months, January through March.[52] A major freeze in Florida during January 1976 opened the doors to significantly increased Mexican supplies, and once again Mexican area climbed upward. The new trade controversy and Mexico's loss of cost competitiveness reined in supply beginning in 1980–81.

Efforts to control supply to the U.S. and Canadian markets could not be limited to area and quality of those tomatoes selected for export, but had to include vigilance over the supply to the domestic market. The Mexican market is a residual market for most producers: tomatoes

TABLE 7.6
Mexican Tomato Shipping Holidays, February–June 1973

Date of Decree	Provisions
February 13	Total suspension of picking, packing, and shipping for February 13, 18, 21, and 25; partial suspension (picking to throw away), February 14 and 22
February 27	Total suspension, February 28 and March 3
March 7	Total suspension, March 9, 10, and 11
March 8	Suspension rescinded for March 9 and 10
March 21	Total suspension for all Sinaloa tomatoes on March 21 and for all of Mexico on March 25; after March 22 no 7×7 tomatoes may leave Mexico
March 29	7×7 exports allowed after March 30
April 16	No 7×7 tomatoes may be exported; total suspension on April 15 (*sic*); after April 16 a minimum of 5 percent green allowed
April 18	Partial suspension (picking to throw away) for April 19, 20, 22, 24, 25, and 29
June 7	7×7 tomatoes released for export; 7×8 and smaller restricted
June 19	7×8 tomatoes released for export

SOURCE: Florida Tomato Committee, *Annual Report 1972–1973* pp. IX–XI.
NOTE: Refers to the number of tomatoes in the rows and columns of a tomato crate. They are packed in crates of 7×8, 7×7, 6×7, 6×6, and 5×6. Size restrictions regulate the minimum and maximum diameter of a tomato that can be packed in a particular crate size.

which do not meet USDA minimum standards or AARC standards when in effect (which are always higher than USDA ones) are dumped on the domestic market for pennies on the dollar or fed to cattle in the area. In the early 1960s buyers for the domestic market often shifted destinations and exported these low-quality tomatoes through the Texas border. In this manner increased supply and poor quality had a negative impact on prices in the U.S. market.

Initial efforts to halt the diversion of this residual supply to the U.S. market attempted to use a registration and deposit mechanism. In August 1960 buyers for the domestic market were required to solicit licenses from CAADES and deposit a portion of the buying price which would be returned to the buyer once the sale in the Mexican terminal market had been made.[53] A year later it was clear that this system had not worked and a new strategy was embarked upon. At the beginning of 1961–62 one buyer for the domestic market, the "Compañía de Distribuidores de Legumbres del Noroeste", agreed to post a bond of 1 million pesos to supply the domestic market.[54] In return, the company was to have sole rights to market Sinaloa tomatoes in the domestic market. CAADES appears to have enlisted the support of the Sinaloa government for this effort to regulate supply to the domestic market.[55]

This decision split the growers in AARC on a new front. Some growers had marketing and financial ties to other distributors which were jeopardized by this latest step. The monopsonistic position this gave the company also worried growers. As a result, many growers simply refused to abide by this policy.[56]

Dissident growers forced an assembly of vegetable producers in CAADES in which, less than three months after the decision to provide a mandatory outlet to the domestic market, the membership watered this down considerably. The new decision was to open up the marketing channels to all buyers who would post a bond of one-half million pesos as a guarantee that the supply would not be diverted to the export market.[57]

But even this attempt proved impossible to implement as distributors refused to post the required bonds, some because they were buying specifically to export, while others objected to the increased cost of doing business. Resolution of this problem, at least temporarily, required a conjunction of three factors. First, there had to be actual control over the points of export on the border; this necessitated state action. In addition, supply had to be more in line with demand. Thus the second and third factors were regulation over Culiacán's supply and expanded demand from the market. As these factors came together in the second half of the 1960s, and the state limited export to certain ports,[58] diversion of supply from the domestic to the export market, although still engaged in,[59] ceased to be a major source of downward pressure on prices in the U.S. market.

Given the perception in 1961 that control of Mexican supply was fundamental to the survival of the Mexican fresh winter vegetable export industry, how important does history show supply control to be and how effective were the attempted controls? If one examines UNPH records it appears that control over production and export is very successful, with compliance rates of over 90 percent.[60] The experience of 1963–64 to 1980–81 suggests that one reason the UNPH has been successful in limiting area to that authorized is because its steady expansion of area gives most growers the opportunity to expand in a market whose relative stability depends on their actions. To the credit of the UNPH (actually of AARC) one can probably say that in the absence of the UNPH, Mexican supply would have continued in over-supply of market demands until bankruptcy forced out speculators and weaker producers. In addition, control over Mexico's supply has been facilitated by state actions in support of those growers who realize the value of stringent controls but are unable to convince other growers who want to increase their participation in the industry.

Under the pressure of the economic crisis in Mexico which began in 1982, this elaborate system of production and export control is under severe strain. The attraction of earning dollars via exporting winter vegetables has led to an increase in contraband exports. To offset the attraction of contraband, the UNPH has further loosened its area con-trols to make room for other exporters, even at the expense of weakening the market.[61] (Increase in production from other UNPH regions is illus-trated by the fact that Sinaloa was responsible for 99.6 percent of vine-ripe tomato exports from 1975–76 to 1979–80, but in 1981–82 its share fell to 89.7 percent).[62] The Culiacán growers appear to be responding to this challenge from other Mexican areas head on, confident that their experience and economic power will make them the survivors. In this context, limiting production becomes a secondary concern to reasserting dominance over Mexican supply. The process is under way: Sinaloa area harvested with bell peppers in 1982–83 increased 37 percent over the previous season, but total exports declined 30 percent. For other vegetables, the increase in applications for permits in 1983–84 varied from 58 percent (for tomatoes) to 124 percent (for eggplant and cucumbers).[63]

This examination of efforts to control supply points to the need to bring the demand side of the market into the analysis. Of fundamental importance in the evolution of Mexican participation in the U.S. market in particular has been the increased demand for Mexican produce in light of expanding consumer demand and production problems in com-petitive areas (first Cuba, then California, then Florida; see chapter 2). The importance of the dynamics of the market brings us to the analysis of grower efforts to expand demand for their product in a variety of international markets, as well as the domestic one.

EXPANDING DEMAND FOR WINTER VEGETABLES

As sophisticated businessmen, some Culiacán growers have been aware that efforts can be undertaken to expand the demand for Sinaloa's vegetable production. These efforts are oriented toward three different markets: the established export markets (the United States and Canada); the potential export markets (Europe and Japan); and the domestic market. Each of these markets is in many ways independent of one another, and the needs and strategies of Mexican growers vary in accordance with each.

The United States is the dominant foreign market, receiving about 90 percent of Mexico's fresh winter vegetable exports. Geographical proximity and the income levels of its consumers make it the ideal market for these highly perishable commodities. Population growth and rising per capita consumption of out-of-season produce keep the potential for expansion of demand in this market high, and it is still believed to merit the most attention.

When Mexican growers first focused promotional efforts on the U.S. market, their concern was to overcome a perception in the U.S. market that Mexican tomatoes were of poor quality.[64] Luis Gaxiola Clouthier, wearing his CAADES presidency hat in the early 1960s, sought to convince growers to earmark funds from a government tax rebate program for a publicity campaign in favor of Mexican vegetables.[65] But it was not until 1967 that growers agreed to undertake such a campaign. It was carried out in conjunction with the United Fresh Fruit and Vegetable Association, the United States-based international arm of the industry. The effort was principally underwritten by the growers, with the UNPH picking up 80 percent of the cost and the Arizona distributors the rest.[66]

The decision to carry out the promotional effort and the structure of financing for the campaign illustrates substantial independence of the Mexican growers with respect to their U.S. financiers, the distributors. An indication of the seriousness with which this program was viewed by the Mexicans was their decision to limit the program to tomatoes because the other export vegetables still had not reached the category of "excellence."[67]*

---

*In an effort to upgrade quality, the 1965–66 UNPH regulations for tomatoes extended packaging criteria to eight other fruits and vegetables. "Reglamento para el

Success on the quality front and in consumer acceptance, helped enormously by the free publicity given Mexican tomatoes in the first "tomato war" (see chapter 8), enabled growers to turn their attention to promoting consumption of fresh vegetables in general. In 1974 Mexican growers struck out on their own. The UNPH contracted with a U.S. company, Food Business Associates (which lists among their clients large U.S. agribusiness transnationals such as Chiquita and Dole, as well as a number of U.S. industry groups)* to carry out an advertising campaign in the U.S. market.[68] One of the interesting characteristics of these campaigns is that they are primarily oriented to the retailer, suggesting ways in which to display the fresh vegetables to attract consumers. The success of these efforts is difficult to judge, but probably interacts in a dynamic fashion with health and economic trends to stimulate consumer demand.

These promotional efforts have been temporarily sidetracked because of political and economic changes affecting Mexican exports to the U.S. market. In 1979 the UNPH commissioned their U.S. advertising agency to undertake a special campaign to publicize the Mexican defense against the dumping suit filed by Florida growers which touched off the second "tomato war."[69] This extraordinary effort necessarily diverted funds from consumption-oriented efforts. The final blow came when growers finally realized that they had lost cost competitiveness to their Florida counterparts. Growers then decided to divert all funds from advertising to research.[70]

Canada is the second market for Mexican fresh winter vegetables. When the U.S. market presents problems, such as in the tomato wars, Mexican growers begin to express increased interest in this northern market. In more general terms, however, growers appear to consider Canada to have reached its limit and channel few funds in this direction. Some growers do ship 25 percent to 35 percent of their produce to this

---

empaque, embarque y cruce de tomate de exportacion," Articles 23–25, *Boletin Agricola* (September–October 1965), 9(5):23–28.

*Among these for 1979 were four California crop groups (avocado, tree fruits, strawberries, and table grapes); the Washington Apple Commission, the Idaho Potato Commission, Sunkist Growers, Inc., and the Potato Board; all of these are major actors in the U.S. food market. Food Business Associates, "Nature's Winter Sunshine from Sunny Mexico," 1979 Promotion Report, p. 176. The UNPH budget for 1977–1979 for the FBA contract was over U.S. $210,000.

market but they are in the minority. One of the major problems appears to be that U.S. brokers are used to reach the Canadian market, with their added cost leaving growers with unattractive profit levels.[71] Another major impediment may be Canadian retailers' preferences for mature green tomatoes, which continue to represent only a minor part of Mexican production.[72]

The European and Japanese markets have attracted Sinaloa growers' attention since at least the late 1960s. These are markets in industrialized countries, with consumers presumably willing and able to spend a little extra to taste fresh vegetables out of the domestic growing season. The potential of these markets is also attracting U.S. distributors, some of whom have made initial investments in expanding their operations overseas.[73]

In 1971 the governor of Sinaloa organized the first trade mission to feature Sinaloa vegetables in Japan.[74] Given the family nature of the fresh produce industry, a potentially more fruitful line of attack is being undertaken. One of the growers with his own Arizona operation has a Japanese son-in-law who has been attempting to structure marketing channels to link Mexican supply with Japanese demand.[75] Nevertheless, the Japanese market poses some problems for Mexican growers. Among these are protectionism by the Japanese government.[76]

In the European case, marketing contacts also appear to be a problem.[77] But the chief problem with both these markets continues to be shelf life. Perishable fresh produce does not make the boat trip from Mexico's production areas to retail shops across the oceans very well. Some Mexican growers have experimented with cold storage to extend shelf life, but with less than satisfactory results. Air transport has been used, but the costs to date have been prohibitive. In consequence, until plant geneticists create vegetables with significantly extended shelf lives, the European and Japanese markets remain just out of the reach of Mexican growers.

Quality control by Mexican growers and the USDA implies that not all of Mexican production is exported. In the case of some speciality crops not common to the Mexican diet, such as eggplant and bell peppers, what is not exported is destroyed. But for the two most important crops, tomatoes and cucumbers, Mexico has a very large domestic market: about one-third of Sinaloa's tomatoes and one-eighth of its cucumbers wind up there.[78] The chief domestic terminal markets for

Sinaloan winter vegetables are in Guadalajara, Monterrey, and Mexico City.

Since at least the late 1950s Culiacán producers have been aware that the domestic market offers a potentially important contribution to returns on investment.[79] Prices to the consumer generally are not the key problem: one buyer for the domestic market who is now a grower himself commented that grower ignorance of the marketing side of the business enabled him to make "millions" of pesos buying for the domestic market.[80] Rather the major problem has been in getting the domestic distributor and retailer to pay the grower remunerative prices. The obstacle seems to lie in the tight control which a few individuals have over these terminal markets and their unscrupulous exploitation of producer and consumer.*

In search of a profitable relationship with the domestic market, Culiacán producers have adopted a three-pronged strategy. One is to organize the smaller domestic retailers and to offer an alternative to their present lopsided commercial relationships. If successful, Sinaloa growers would be able to keep the distributors under surveillance and reap more of the profit in the domestic market. More recently, growers have sought to increase the quality of the product and regulate its supply and are oriented toward inducing the upper strata of Mexican society to pay a higher price.

The first attempt to map out a strategy for the domestic market came in the UNPH annual meetings of 1965. AARC's delegation warned of a growing dependence upon the export market and lamented the marginalization of a domestic market which had very good potential. According to the Culiacán growers, the chief problem with the domestic market was a lack of control over sales by the growers. This situation allowed intermediaries to operate as buyers under oligopsonistic conditions and sellers under oligopolistic conditions. Under this schema both growers and consumers preferred to stay out of the market: from 1951 to 1960 supply to the domestic market declined 11 percent although population increased 30 percent. AARC recommended eliminating the intermediary and conducting a promotional campaign to get retailers to set prices at

---

*Even the state has found it difficult to replace or break the power of these intermediaries; see Merilee S. Grindle, *Bureaucrats, Politicians and Peasants in Mexico*, *passim.*

an attractive level for the consumer and to convince the consumer of the nutritional qualities of fresh fruits and vegetables.[81]

But once again producers at the national or regional level were unwilling to undertake sacrifices unless the Culiacán growers made significant concessions to reduce the possibility that they would gain disproportionately if controls were introduced. It took another two years for AARC to decide to lead the way by example. At the end of the 1966–67 season AARC commissioned a tour of the U.S. points of entry and the Monterrey and Guadalajara domestic terminal markets. The committee's report condemned the quality of tomatoes marketed in these two Mexican cities, laying the blame on packing and transport procedures, and recommending that supply be regulated.[82]

At the beginning of the following season Culiacán growers agreed to regulate quality and supply to the domestic market. Requirements were implemented for quality selection, packaging, and labeling of tomatoes, with registration of labels in AARC and UNPH also required. Aware of the limited ability of the association to directly sanction intermediaries, AARC made each individual grower responsible for the behavior of the intermediary handling his produce.[83]

This effort by the Culiacán group was not seconded by any other group at either the national or regional level. No evidence could be found that at this point AARC saw any need to make the concessions which would draw in other producing areas. Events the following season, 1968–69, suggest that the supply situation in the domestic market was not yet perceived serious enough so that Culiacán acting alone could not have the desired impact. In that 1968–69 season, the eruption of the first tomato war diverted a large supply to the domestic market with a consequent large fall in price. Responding to that situation, AARC's vegetable growers' assembly unanimously decided to institute controls which dropped their volume to the domestic market by 30 percent.[84]

The disruption to the domestic market was significant enough that the assembly decided to ask CAADES and UNPH to extend the regulations to producers in northern Sinaloa and southern Sonora, respectively.[85] Within two weeks a meeting between growers in Guasave, Sinaloa (the second most important producing region), and Culiacán led to an agreement to constitute a state-wide committee which would regulate supply to the domestic market on a weekly basis.[86] The payoff to the Guasave growers for joining their Culiacán counterparts appears to have been substantial: they were allocated 50 percent more volume on an acreage basis* for the domestic market.[87]

Once again enactment of controls coincided with a significant expansion in demand to relieve growers of supply and price problems. The boom in U.S. demand for Mexican vegetables (more or less constant from 1970 to 1979) dissipated the diversion of supply to the domestic market. Under these conditions, interest in the domestic market waned anew. With it went efforts to push the domestic intermediary out of the market.

But by 1979–80 Mexican growers began to suffer the consequences of losing cost competitiveness in the U.S. market, and the interest in the national market rekindled. At this time, not only was demand in the U.S. market low, but the petroleum-fueled historically high growth rates of the Mexican economy, coupled with an increasingly overvalued currency, made the domestic market extremely attractive to Sinaloa growers. To give an example, in mid-December 1981 tomatoes were selling for U.S. $6.50 a carton in the United States, whereas the Mexican market was paying U.S. $16.00![88] The Mexican market was so attractive that even U.S. distributors were expressing an interest in it.[89] With the boom came renewed calls for eliminating the intermediary and organizing the growers to sell directly to retailers in the major cities.[90]

As Mexico succumbed to the international economic crisis in 1982 and 1983, experiencing negative growth rates, grower interest in the national market disappeared. The UNPH's annual bulletin reporting events at the national convention did not even mention the national market in 1982.[91] But the dream of making the residual market a profitable one, thereby decreasing vulnerability to the export markets, will not let Sinaloa growers forget the domestic market for long. As hopes of a beginning in Mexico's recovery surfaced for 1984, Culiacán growers began studying the domestic market once again.[92]

EXPLAINING MEXICAN FORWARD INTEGRATION

Production of fresh winter vegetables in northwest Mexico for export began in 1906. From its beginnings the industry was dominated by foreigners, both as growers and as financiers/distributors of Mexican

---

*Culiacán significantly outplants Guasave, so it is not that they offered a major inroad to their market share, but they did make it attractive for Guasave growers to cooperate.

growers. The nationalist revolution which shook Mexican society and politics intervened to guarantee Mexican participation in the export-oriented vegetable industry. Constitutional stipulations reserving ownership of coastal lands, which in this part of Mexico are best suited for vegetable production, to nationals forced foreign entrepreneurs to either violate the law or enter into partnership with Mexicans.

Some foreign growers, particularly the Greek-Americans who came to Sinaloa before the Revolution, violated these Constitutional provisions for years. But Mexicanization of their production was relatively simple as foreign growers followed a pattern often seen throughout history everywhere: they married into local notable families, and their offspring were born into their adopted nation.* Other foreign entrepreneurs were interested in participating in the business only as financiers and/or distributors. They sought business ties with the local sociopolitical elite.

This local elite accepted partnership with the foreign financier for a combination of three reasons. First, from its inception until the mid-1960s, production of vegetables for export was a very high-risk venture. The U.S. entrepreneur represented a low-risk way to participate in the trade because of the second factor: his offer of credit. In this context of high risk with large profits in good years, it appears that most Mexican growers were willing to earn less in return for a lower exposure. A third reason for this arrangement lay in the U.S. distributor/financier's provision of a marketing channel into the U.S. market.

But these ties were reluctantly made. The boom years of the mid-1950s brought the first efforts to limit foreign penetration. Strong demand from the U.S. market from 1955 through 1958 suggested to Mexican growers that a shift in bargaining power and market potential was occurring in their favor. The first effort by the major growers was to seek a change in the nature of the relationship with the U.S. entrepreneurs. Up to this point most growers merely provided use of their lands, apparently participating in the benefits of the trade only in this manner. This type of relationship limited the returns to the entrepreneurial Mex-

---

*The Greek-Mexican families who dominated this group continue to have strong cultural ties to their ancestral home. But this situation only allows us to note the multiethnic make-up of Mexican society in Sinaloa, not to speculate about the national loyalties of individual ethnic groups as many observers and inhabitants of northwest Mexico are wont.

ican grower who, in the new context, was not content to function merely as a rentier. Dependence of U.S. distributors upon Mexican production stimulated growers to seek an associational, rather than contractual, relationship between foreigner and Mexican. In 1958 a group headed by Luis Gaxiola Clouthier asked the Vegetable Convention to forbid cultivation of vegetables by foreigners unless they did so in association with nationals.[93]

The glut which hit the U.S. market in the next few years could have put a stop to these efforts, because growers could have retreated back into a subordinate and less exposed position behind U.S. entrepreneurs. But the Culiacán rural elite opted instead to increase their market power through organization. Their efforts to control production and export volume pointed up a new conflict of interest with the U.S. distributor. Contractual relations between distributor and grower, as well as the former's domination of market information flows southward, allowed distributors to make a profit even while growers failed to recuperate costs of production. Thus while AARC was trying to control growers, individual distributors, particularly new ones who were attracted by the profit potential and relatively low barriers to entry, posed a challenge by financing new growers.

AARC attempted to resolve this conflict through cooperative efforts with the Arizona distributors through their organization, the West Mexico Vegetable Distributors Association (WMVDA). The regulations for tomato exports in the 1963–64 season solicited distributor adherence to the following:

1. To avoid the possibility that a particular Distributor provoke an excess of supply, each Distributor will be limited to handling a maximum of 1,200 has. of ground tomatoes, or their equivalent in staked production.
2. When a restriction on exports is decreed by the Association, each Distributor will inform the Regulatory Commission of their inventory, in order to facilitate detection of violations by packinghouses.[94]

This effort failed as a control on distributors, and other mechanisms were tried. As a means of counteracting their oligopoly control over fundamental market information, AARC installed a telex system. The distributors were asked to share part of the cost, but refused on the grounds that the system would not benefit them, as they already had ready access to USDA's daily marketing bulletin.[95]

Competition from foreigners, then, was unwanted. In 1961 a vegetable grower went so far as to warn of the "invasion" of the Culiacán Valley by foreign capital.[96] But the distributors performed valuable services in channeling U.S. capital into the hands of Mexican producers and selling their produce. The key issue confronting Culiacán growers, therefore, was how to provide the services they offered and thereby render them secondary to the industry. Two approaches to this problem surfaced: mobilization of collective resources and individual mobility. Of the two, the latter proved more effective, although it was helped along by progress on the former.

A number of attempts have been made to create a financial institution which could meet the needs of growers in a volatile market. Although total costs of production were large, production could be financed with a significantly smaller sum. According to an AARC study, harvest, packing, transportation, and export costs could be self-financed with a working capital whose rotation was fast—every five or six days.[97] Chapter 3 noted that when CAADES came into being a bank (Banco de Sinaloa) was organized and funded by taxes on all private agricultural producers. But this bank appears to have had little impact and was disbanded in the early 1960s amidst controversy.[98]

Some growers believed cooperative financing efforts for vegetable production would be more successful if capital were raised from the direct beneficiaries themselves. In early 1962, with the success of Culiacán growers in creating a national union still fresh in everyone's minds, Atilano Bon Bustamante proposed creation of such a finance company to service all of Sinaloa's vegetable growers.[99] But the proposal did not even get the support of Bon Bustamante's local association, AARC.

To explain the failure of this attempt to create such a financial mechanism, it is useful to divide the Culiacán growers into different groups and examine their interests with respect to a grower-financed production fund. This plan confronted three types of growers, each with a different need. Those at the bottom of the scale, with 1 to 60 has. (see table 7.5), were too small to reap much benefit from placing yet another tax on their production, this time to finance their own and other growers' production. This is the group that tends to produce sporadically, depending upon the market and zealousness of U.S. entreprenuers. One can hypothesize that he wasn't too eager to risk his own money if he could avoid it;* in fact, as Mexican forward integration ensued, this type of grower has sought financing from the Mexican integrated grower-shipper.

At the other extreme were the richest men in Sinaloa, some of them also bankers. An undetermined but small number of these were already self-financing or able to access capital through their banks.[100] Of this group at least one had his own distributorship in Nogales, Arizona, in the mid-1950s. These growers would only be marginally interested in cooperative financing efforts; in fact, time demonstrated that they were only waiting for the market to stabilize at a profitable rate to invest their own capital in expanding their enterprises beyond the production stage. Thus Daniel Cárdenas Izábal set up his own distributorship in the boom period of the mid-1950s,[101] while most of the other grower-owned distributorships date from the height of the other boom period, the early 1970s.

The marginal interest of the most powerful and weakest growers in a grower-financed collective fund probably left only the middle-range grower, and table 7.5 indicates that there are few of them, as a constituent for such a financing scheme. This group had neither the political power nor the numbers to push it through.

Once it became clear that the effort to replace the U.S. financier had failed, attention was focused on regulating the financial relationship between grower and creditor. In 1965 the export regulations explicitly recognized the right of grower associations to regulate these relationships.[102] The following season Culiacán growers included these stipulations about finance: "Those producers who are financed by private investors should annex to their application for permission to plant a copy of their financial contract, and if relevant, of distribution. A maximum of 10% commission will be allowed in such a contract."[103] This attempt to decree greater returns to growers failed, and by the 1968–69 season growers abandoned commission limits but continued to require disclosure-of-contract terms for both finance and distribution, presumably to give individual growers information which could increase their bargaining power with their generally foreign contractor.[104]

---

*One cucumber producer I interviewed was financed by a small central California distributor. After sustaining losses for two consecutive years, he walked away from his debts, leaving the distributor with the losses.

Tension between Culiacán's rural elite and the U.S.-owned distributors remains and flares up during periods of market crises when growers accuse distributors of speculating with their production,[105] or not wanting to contribute an equal share in combatting Floridian attacks on imports.[106] In 1969 an Inter-Association Relations Committee was set up to improve coordination and communication between growers and distributors.[107] Problems remained and the UNPH has set up a mechanism by which to adjudicate disputes between growers and distributors. Sanctions include ultimate revocation of UNPH licenses to distributors, which implies that growers can only do business with them at the risk of losing their production permits.[108] In 1983 the UNPH incoming president made delinquent payments by distributors to growers his top priority.[109]

At the same time growers were attempting to replace, and failing that, regulate, financing tied to U.S. distributors with grower cooperative efforts, they also sought to replace it with state capital. In 1967 the UNPH began to tap the National Bank for Foreign Trade (Banco Nacional de Comercio Exterior) for credit, but the state would not finance the production process itself.[110] Growers availed themselves of official financing for what was possible,[111] but still found themselves dependent upon the U.S. distributor for working capital.

Up to this point, the late 1960s, Mexican growers had failed to replace the U.S. distributor as a source of working capital because they had forgotten the third function he provided: a channel into the U.S. market. There had to be an alternative marketing channel before the financial ties could be broken. The cooperative efforts of AARC never addressed this need.* Replacement of U.S. distributor dominance of Mexican production and trade of fresh winter vegetables had to wait until individual growers were ready to invest their own capital in distributorships on the U.S. side.

As chapter 2 noted, low barriers to entry at the distribution stage of the agribusiness commodity system of fresh winter vegetables made it possible for growers to integrate forward. But the decision to invest in such integration did not come automatically. First the wealthiest of the growers had to be convinced that risk in the industry had declined

---

*Neither interviews, searches of AARC or CAADES archives, UNPH's public record, nor the local press turned up any indication that the idea was ever broached.

sufficiently so that it was more attractive to him to invest his own capital and reap larger profits than minimize his exposure by utilizing other entrepreneurs' capital and earn correspondingly less.

The dynamic growth of Mexican exports to the United States from 1965–66 to 1976–77, with increases in value averaging over 23 percent annually,[112] stimulated some growers to expand their participation in a variety of phases of the business. One grower has invested in an enterprise which fabricates packing materials, a number of growers now own their own trucking fleets to transport both their own produce and that of others who contract the service to the U.S. border, and by 1979 half of the distributorships in Nogales, Arizona, were grower-owned.

As growers set up their own distributorships they also began to access U.S. bank capital directly. In 1977 about 40 percent of total yearly capital needs were met by U.S. sources.[113] (Approximately 10 percent of the growers in the early 1970s already had the potential to be self-financing.)[114] This progressive elimination of the U.S. distributor as an intermediary in the financial link between U.S. bank and Mexican grower not only reduces the cost of that credit but also leaves management more directly in the hands of the Mexican growers.

The success of the winter vegetable trade brought forth a new generation of Mexican agricultural entrepreneurs. In the process the import side of the U.S. fresh winter vegetable agribusiness commodity system became thoroughly Mexicanized as Mexican capital and entrepreneurship replaced U.S. enterprises. Industrial characteristics were susceptible to this forward integration by southern producers, and state-supported grower organization and control of supply were also fundamental. But we must not forget those few powerful Culiacán growers who became determined to make the industry theirs. The trade publication of the U.S. fresh produce industry provides a very revealing description of these new Mexican entrepreneurs:

. . . confident, cocky, young breed, now growing much of the West Mexican vegetables. Wealthy and financially independent, many of these growers have thumbed their noses at their former U.S. distributors and have opened their own distributing operations in Nogales, calling the shots from down South.[115]

8

TRANSNATIONAL ALLIANCES IN INTERNATIONAL TRADE

In this chapter we are concerned with the ability of the Sinaloa vegetable growers to protect their interest against threats of a political (rather than economic) nature arising from the international arena. Analysis of efforts by competitors of Mexican growers to construct nontariff barriers (NTB) to the U.S. market brings together international and domestic politics. On each level economic and political factors interact to determine, if not policy formulation (often the result of purely political considerations), certainly policy implementation (where economic factors cannot be ignored). Consequently both the United States and Mexican governments find themselves embroiled in disputes *within* their countries at a bureaucratic and societal level and *between* their countries at the level of foreign economic policymaking.

In analyzing the politics of NTBs in the winter vegetable trade we encounter a variety of actors. On both sides of the border we have producers and bureaucratic actors responsible for trade and/or consumption concerns. Within the United States itself we find the commercial agents for both sets of growers, retailers, and consumer organizations. The reality of diverse interests which these U.S. growers face creates a classical situation of "transnational relations" in which nongovernmental actors play important roles in addressing the issues of interdependence.[1]

In view of the analysis of the progressive domination by Mexican growers of this commodity system, the bi-national character of the industry should be stressed: United States *and* Mexican companies work together as part of an agribusiness commodity system. This binational characteristic leads to transnational relations among the various components of the system based upon their mutual interdependence. Under such circumstances it should not be surprising to discover that many U.S. businessmen, consumers, and politicians have integrated a transnational alliance with their Mexican counterparts in defense against their common enemy: the U.S. winter vegetable producers who wish to diminish Mexican participation in the U.S. market.

The chapter has three sections. The first section describes the two major vegetable trade conflicts between the United States and Mexico. The ability of the Culiacán rural elite to bargain with international capital, work the United States political system to its advantage, and enlist U.S. domestic groups as allies forms the basis for the analysis in the second section. In the final section the relationship between the rural elite and the Mexican state with respect to vegetable export policy is investigated.

THE TOMATO WARS OF 1968 AND 1978

Mexican participation in the U.S. market has brought stiff Florida opposition at least since the inclusion of horticulture products in the Smoot-Hawley Tariff of 1930. The first intervention by Mexican producers in the U.S. Congress occurred in 1934 as the industry argued against the application of such tariffs.[2] There was relative peace until 1968 when the Florida producers reorganized themselves for a major fight.

The reorganization of the Florida growers came about because of the factors analyzed in chapter 6. Faced with economic hardship at home and increased competition from foreign producers, the Florida growers decided to organize themselves once again in the Florida Tomato Committee (FTC).* The perception of well-organized Mexican producers crowding out Florida producers was so strong that the FTC was structured using the Mexican producer organization as a model.[3]

On August 28, 1954, Congress amended the 1937 Agricultural Marketing Agreement Act with the addition of Section 8(e). This new piece of legislation subjected imports of certain fresh fruits and vegetables to

---

*The original FTC, organized in 1955, disbanded in 1958 because of internal disputes.

the same grade, size, quality, and maturity requirements affecting its domestic counterpart under a marketing order within the United States. Section 8(e) had originally been proposed by a Florida growers' association to apply specifically to tomatoes and other perishable commodities grown in Florida. Other producer groups also sought protection from "unfair" foreign competition and were able to enlarge the list to include a number of products grown elsewhere in the country. Irish potatoes, green peppers, cucumbers, eggplant, onions, etc., were added to the final version of the provision adopted by Congress.[4]

On the face of it, Section 8(e) appears to be a fair regulation, as it provides that both foreign and domestic producers must play by the same marketing rules. As such the cost of regulating supply in a sluggish market would be borne equally; consequently members of Congress referred to this legislation as a "golden rule agreement."[5] Nevertheless, certain production characteristics could be manipulated to discriminate against imports; this was precisely the issue which touched off the first tomato war in 1968.

Florida producers grew some 90 percent of their tomatoes on the ground and harvested them green by machine: the chief rationale for this type of production lay in its labor-saving characteristic. In contrast, 90 percent of Mexican tomatoes were produced on stakes and hand-picked when ripe, a logical process given the country's comparative advantage in cheap labor. Early in the 1968–69 winter tomato season the FTC recommended that the U.S. Department of Agriculture (USDA) approve size restrictions on two basic types of tomatoes: vine-ripe and mature green.* The regulations, however, specified greater size tolerance (smaller size allowed) for the mature green tomatoes produced by Florida than for the vine-ripe tomatoes imported from Mexico.[6] Consequently, although the marketing order applied to both Mexico and Florida, its effect was clearly to place a greater burden on Mexican production to diminish supply so as to keep prices at a profitable level for Florida.

The international conflict over Section 8(e)'s application was not resolved until 1975, when a truce was reached in court by USDA and Arizona distributors representing the Mexican tomato industry.[7] Never-

---

*Once USDA approves the recommendations, they become binding on the U.S. tomato market.

theless, the dual restrictions were in effect only during three seasons, 1968–69, 1969–70, and 1970–71. After these seasons market conditions and the USDA ruling in 1973–74 effectively terminated the use of dual restrictions.[8]

After their failure in 1975, the Florida producers turned to other tactics in their endeavor to stem the flow of imports. In 1976 and 1977 hearings were held in Congress on a measure to alter packaging requirements for the import of fresh tomatoes; USDA recommended against the bill and it passed the Senate, but not the House. In 1977 the bill, proposed once again, passed both chambers, but was dropped in conference. In February 1978 the Florida Tomato Exchange requested that Secretary of Agriculture Robert Bergland use his authority under Section 204 of the Agriculture Act of 1956 to seek an agreement with Mexican officials limiting exports of fresh tomatoes to the United States. In March the Senate Subcommittee on Foreign Agricultural Policy of the Committee on Agriculture, Nutrition, and Forestry began hearings on inspection standards of vegetable imports; three hearings were held in 1978. The following month the Exchange proposed before the House Committee on Ways and Means' Subcommittee on Trade that imports of tomatoes from Mexico be limited at times when oversupply depressed U.S. prices below certain levels.

A delegation of Florida growers met with Secretary Bergland in early May 1978. The producers requested that the secretary take various measures designed to protect the U.S. industry. Among these were (a) to extend the earlier request of limiting tomato imports under Section 204 to cover all fresh fruits and vegetables; (b) to improve inspection at the Nogales, Arizona, port of entry; (c) for the secretary to reexamine his position on the packaging bill which had already failed various times; (d) for USDA to support legislation requiring identification at the retail level of country of origin of all imported perishable agricultural commodities; and (e) for the secretary to investigate the possibility of supporting legislation giving him authority to regulate perishable fruit and vegetable imports according to trigger price mechanisms which would be related to parity prices. Secretary Bergland responded by creating an informal working group to discuss the problems of the winter vegetable trade with Mexican officials.[9]

Their inability to erect nontariff barriers through the official channels of Congress and USDA did not discourage Florida growers. On September 12, 1978, the U.S. producers acted unilaterally and filed a petition with the Treasury Department alleging Mexican violations of the Anti-Dumping Act of 1921. Five products which represented over 60 percent of Mexican horticultural exports in the 1977–78 season (tomatoes, cucumbers, bell peppers, eggplant, and squash) were alleged to have been sold below cost during that season. The anti-dumping statutes thus provided the Florida growers with a mechanism they could utilize to place their particular interest on the bilateral agenda despite the lack of USDA or congressional support.

The tomato war of 1978–1985 was an extremely complicated issue. It was initiated by U.S. producers acting on their own initiative and without the support of the U.S. government, which was concerned with broader national interest questions on the Mexico-U.S. agenda. In addition, investigators utilized a level of mathematical sophistication that had never before been seen in a dumping case. Finally, conflicting interpretations of the anti-dumping statutes became key issues in the conflict.*

Resolution of the dumping conflict favored Mexico. The Treasury Department adopted wholesale for its Preliminary Decision in October 1979 a regression analysis conducted under the auspices of the transnational alliance of Mexican growers/distributors and Arizona distributors which demonstrated the lack of statistical support for an accusation of dumping.[10] The study utilized by the Commerce Department to reach a Final Determination of "No Sales at Less Than Fair Value" used the transnational alliance's regression analysis to verify results obtained through other methods, thus implicitly accepting the validity of the pro-Mexican imports study.[11] Florida growers filed suit in Customs Court against Treasury and later against Commerce, alleging the departments failed to follow the statutes. The first suit was thrown out as the court ruled it had no jurisdiction in the matter, while in the latter case the New York City U.S. Customs Court ruled in favor of the Commerce Department.

---

* See the memorandum from the Justice Department to Treasury on the legality of a season-long time frame rather than the sale-by-sale technique which had been used in all previous dumping cases, even those concerning perishable produce. John H. Shenefield, Assistant Attorney General, Antitrust Division, Department of Justice, to Robert H. Mundhein, Esquire, General Counsel, Department of the Treasury, July 16, 1979; and see the Florida growers' suit in Customs Court disputing such legality.

TRANSNATIONAL POLITICS IN THE UNITED STATES

The intimate contact which Sinaloa growers have had with their Arizona business partners has given the Mexicans an appreciation of the functioning of the U.S. market and political system. In the 1960s the UNPH, in conjunction with the West Mexico Vegetable Distributors Association (herein West Mexico), commissioned a prominent Arizona advertising firm to promote Mexican tomatoes in the U.S. market.[12] During the first tomato war the Arizona distributors carried the fight in the United States while the Mexican producers observed. By the second war the producers felt prepared to enter the foray directly.

In 1974, after the Marketing Agreement controversy, the Mexican growers contracted Food Business Associates (FBA) to carry out a promotional campaign in the United States. As part of their work on the market FBA reported on factors which could possibly affect the Mexican supply of winter vegetables.[13]

With the dumping controversy in 1978 the UNPH believed it important to get the support of U.S. groups. FBA undertook two new campaigns. One was directed toward the leading produce executives; entitled "Why *Not* Mexico," it was aimed primarily at convincing U.S. receivers and retailers that they faced no jeopardy in the dumping case if they continued to market Mexican vegetables. In addition, a special one year project was created "to foster more favorable publicity for the Mexican side of the Floridian/Mexican controversy." In this effort FBA contacted congressional and White House officials; at the end of May 1979 the White House contacted FBA to "assure us that the President's staff is continuing to monitor the controversy and will do all it can to foster normal trade relations." In addition, Hodding Carter, Assistant Secretary of State, "pledged support on behalf of Cyrus Vance."[14]

This section analyzes the functioning of the transnational alliance among Mexican growers/distributors, their U.S. business partners, and U.S. consumer groups.

The Congress. The U.S. Congress plays an important role in the U.S.-Mexican horticultural trade by establishing the general rules which govern imports. Congress has refused to modify legislation for the express purpose of discriminating against horticultural imports from Mexico. Congressional action with respect to these imports for the domestic market, except for the depression years, has been characterized more by a "fair and equitable" orientation than by protectionist sentiment. For example, the 1954 addition of Section 8(e) to the 1937 Agricultural Marketing Agreement Act (which formed the basis for the first major tomato conflict) was clearly written in a language designed to place equitable burdens for market regulation on both domestic and foreign producers. It was not so much the law itself as the production characteristics of ground and staked tomatoes which allowed for its use as a protectionist measure. The 1921 Anti-Dumping Act also falls under the category of a measure designed to promote fair and equitable trade rather than merely to protect U.S. producers against "legitimate" competition.[15]

In the controversy over the Marketing Agreement Act, both the restrictionists and the defenders of Mexican imports attempted to pass legislation favorable to their views through Congress. The distributors, overwhelmingly Arizona-based and organized into the West Mexico Vegetable Distributors Association, contacted their congressional delegation both directly and indirectly through their Washington lobbyists, Masaoka-Ishikawa and Associates, Inc. By means of this latter channel, Senators Barry Goldwater and Paul Fanin and Representative Morris R. Udall were informed of West Mexico's views on the vegetable conflicts.[16]

The Mexican growers also became involved in the congressional game, although more as reactors than as initiators. Growers utilized both newspaper advertisements and telegraph to reach the Arizona congressional delegation.[17] Masaoka-Ishikawa helped educate the Mexican growers about the policy process in Washington. They were informed about Floridian successes to gain the support of the Texas, California, and Ohio (winter greenhouse tomatoes) congressional delegations.[18] Growers were also notified that both the executive branch and the chairman of the House Ways and Means Committee, Wilbur Mills, opposed import quotas for tomatoes.[19]

Notwithstanding the national reputations of Senator Goldwater and Congressman Udall, the congressional arena proved futile for the defenders of tomato imports. Congressman Udall's bill to exclude tomatoes from Section 8(e) of the Marketing Agreement (H.R. 5865)[20] went down in defeat. Actually Congress proved to be a public forum for attacks on the Mexican industry.

Senator Allen Ellender of Louisiana pointed out in Congress that Mexico discriminated against U.S. tomatoes by not allowing them in during the summer months. Congressman Dante B. Fascell of Florida, chairman of the House Subcommittee on Interamerican Affairs, announced the initiation of efforts to persuade the United States to limit agricultural imports "drastically." He warned that if negotiations did not bring "desired results," the United States could adopt new laws which could provoke "a serious dispute with Mexico" which "should and ought to be avoided." "Tomatoes are the vanguard of a serious threat to all winter fruits and vegetables of the U.S. Our people . . . who depend upon this industry to make a living deserve a national policy to protect their legitimate interests."[21]

But Florida and its allies could get nowhere in Congress, either. Congressman Paul G. Rogers of Florida introduced H.R. 9656 in March 1969 and in March 1973, while Congressmen L. A. Bafalis and James A. Haley, both of Florida, introduced H.R. 5413 before the House Committee on Ways and Means. The proposed legislation, known as the "Fresh Fruits and Vegetables Market Sharing Act of . . ." sought to impose quantitative restrictions on imports.[22] Both bills, however, went down in defeat.

The U.S. Congress also became the scene of efforts to revise the anti-dumping legislation to exclude perishable produce and to convince the Treasury Department that the intentions of the statutes would be distorted by its strict application in this case. With respect to the first tactic, Congressman Udall testified before the Trade Subcommittee of the House Ways and Means Committee in April 1979 that since Treasury seemed bent on a literal interpretation, Congress had to rewrite the law.[23] Nevertheless, the Floridians on the House Ways and Means Committee, Sam M. Gibbons (Democrat) and L. A. Bafalis (Republican), blocked the attempted revision.[24]

Congress also became involved in applying pressure on the Treasury Department. Congressman Abner J. Mikva (D., Ill.) and Senator Edward M. Kennedy (D., Mass.) led "a strong group in Congress" calling on the Treasury to avoid interpreting the Anti-Dumping Act in a way that would lead to an "illogical result."[25]

Thus Congress stymied the proponents of both the Floridian and Mexican positions. Neither side was strong enough to pass legislation changing the status quo of fruits and vegetables and had to content themselves with blocking each other's efforts.

U.S. Consumers. Three elements trigger consumer defense of Mexican tomato imports: price, nutrition, and taste. Due to production cost and climatic factors Florida cannot supply, at acceptable prices, the entire winter-early spring demand for tomatoes. Thus without Mexican participation (which varies from 40 percent to 60 percent of total supply), U.S. consumers would face shortages of fresh vegetables and resultant high prices. In addition, some consumers prefer Mexican tomatoes because they are vine ripened, a process utilizing more labor, but producing more nutritional and flavorful tomatoes (Florida's crop is harvested green and given color through gassing). U.S. consumer groups, therefore, have come to the defense of the Mexican tomato at various times.

Both Arizona distributors and the Mexican producer/distributors organized campaigns to get the U.S. consumer and his organizations actively to defend imports of Mexican tomatoes. In 1969 the Arizona distributors undertook a public relations campaign to reach consumers and convince them of the dangers to nutrition and price stability that the Marketing Agreement restrictions posed.[26] With the dumping controversy a decade later, the UNPH decided to become directly involved in this propaganda campaign themselves and utilized their FBA contract to do so.[27]

The U.S. consumer advocates responded well, appearing before both Congress and the courts. In the first tomato war, Bess Myerson, commissioner of consumer affairs for the state of New York, testified in Congress that the restrictions "eliminated most Grade U.S. 1 vine-ripened red tomatoes from the market." In addition, the associate director of the Center for Consumer Affairs in Milwaukee claimed Mexican tomatoes to be "just plain better than the Florida tomato."[28] When the U.S. Secretary of Agriculture reaffirmed his authority to institute dual size restrictions in 1972, four consumer groups were the first to file suit in U.S. district court for a reconsideration of the decision.

In the dumping case the consumer organizations took a much lower profile. Whereas in the Marketing Agreement case consumer groups played a direct role in the judicial process as plaintiffs in various suits, in the dumping controversy they did not become direct participants as co-defendants. Consumer organizations made known their concern over the probable effects of a positive ruling in the dumping case through a report sent to the Treasury investigators by the Consumers Union. Nevertheless, the weight of the organized consumer movement in the United States apparently diminished greatly with respect to the second tomato conflict.

Consumers were indirectly represented in the second tomato war. Despite the freezing of the anti-dumping investigation in July when Florida growers withdrew their petition, in October the chairman of the Council on Wage and Price Stability, Alfred Kahn, presented Treasury with a document which noted that Treasury analyses supported a finding of dumping and argued that his staff and that of the President's Council of Economic Advisors had reviewed and supported an alternative analysis. The paper concluded recommending that Treasury make use of its "wide discretion" under the anti-dumping statutes and utilize the methodology which supported a finding of no dumping.[29]

Treasury and Commerce. In investigating the dumping charges Treasury analysts attacked the problem in the same fashion they had in other dumping cases. Thus individual growers' sales were to be examined on a day-by-day schedule to determine if any were made below production costs. The Mexican growers and their allies argued, however, that in the case of perishable produce, price fluctuated rapidly, and the goal of the producer was to make a profit over the season, not on every sale.

The methodology initially utilized by Treasury virtually guaranteed that dumping would be found to have occurred; Treasury had early on stressed the need for negotiation precisely because of this expected outcome.[30] When the tentative determination was to be announced in July, the *Wall Street Journal* reported the Department leaning toward a positive finding, as did the *New York Times* just before the preliminary decision was actually rendered in October.[31] Even the Mexican producers were pessimistic about their chances if Treasury did decide to apply the statutes. In a memo to President López Portillo, the UNPH president noted that the chances of a determination of no dumping were "very remote". And during a meeting with U.S. officials from the State and Treasury departments, as well as the Office of the Special Trade Representative, UNPH representatives recognized that a strict interpretation of the statutes would find dumping.[32]

This outcome was especially distressing given the concern with importing energy from Mexico at the time. One Treasury official said, with regard to the winter vegetable case and the need for good relations with Mexico, "There's no linkage with the oil issue in the formal sense. But let's face it, we all live in the real world."[33]

The Mexican growers and distributors attempted to convince Treasury to recognize that up to 50 percent of below cost sales were normal in the fresh produce business, to look at costs over the season,* and to compare U.S. market prices with Canadian prices† rather than constructing a price composed of cost plus 8 percent profit.[34] These three aspects were incorporated in statistical studies submitted to the Treasury in July and again in October by Professor Richard L. Simmons, a consultant to USDA on the fresh fruit and vegetable market who was contracted by the Mexican defense to analyze the dumping charges. Employing regression analysis, a methodology never before used in a dumping case, the Simmons work demonstrated a lack of statistical support for the allegation of dumping.[35] This was the alternative study which the country's chief inflation fighter had advocated Treasury adopt.[36]

There seems to have been no indication that Treasury would actually adopt the Simmons methodology: witness the aforementioned newspaper report just before the tentative decision dates. On October 30, 1979, however, the Treasury Department finally issued its tentative determination and, adopting the Simmons methodology wholesale, found no evidence of dumping.

The 1979 Trade Agreement Act transferred authority on dumping cases to the Commerce Department; thus it fell to this agency to issue the final ruling on the dumping case. Commerce analysts began by taking a position parallel to that of the Florida growers and questioned the legitimacy of the Simmons methodology in this case.[37]

Commerce analysts notified the parties involved that three new approaches to the data were being considered, all of which differed sig-

---

*West Mexico submitted a brief on this point to the Treasury Department in early June.
†Florida and Mexico supply this market also.

nificantly from Treasury's approach.[38] The Mexican defense thus sought to support the Simmons studies before the Commerce group. In this tactic, technical arguments were marshaled: Simmons submitted an updated study; Professors Hendrick S. Houthakker of Harvard, William D. Nordhaus of Yale, and Richard A. King of North Carolina State,[39] all submitted affadavits supporting the statistical methodology employed by Simmons;[40] another USDA consultant, Professor Robert S. Firch of Arizona, submitted a study of the California lettuce industry demonstrating that 50 percent of sales under cost was an economic fact of life in the industry.[41] In addition, Professor Houthakker's affadavit testified that the statistical methodology employed by the Florida study submitted to Commerce was "no longer considered valid in the current theory and practice in the fields of econometrics and statistics."[42]

On March 24, 1980, the Commerce Department issued a final determination in which it found no sales had been made at less than fair market value. The Commerce ruling was based on a study which, although not a regression analysis as was Simmons', utilized the Simmons study to verify its results, thus implicitly accepting the validity of this work.

The U.S. Judicial System. In January 1969, under guidance from two West Mexico lawyers, Walter Holm and Co. filed for a temporary restraining order against the secretary of agriculture's enforcement of the January restrictions. The injunction granted by the U.S. district court in Phoenix, however, lasted only two days; the judge lifted his order after consulting with attorneys from the USDA and the Florida Fruit and Vegetable Association. The complaint was formally denied on January 16, 1969, as the judge agreed with USDA testimony that its "actions were within the scope of its authority under the Agricultural Marketing Act and the Administrative Procedures Act." The plaintiff filed for a new trial requesting an injunction pending appeal, but was again denied; an appeal filed in the U.S. court of appeals in San Francisco also failed. In April the company again filed suit, with similar results.[43]

The distributors' organization also suggested that Harry H. Price and Son file a complaint in the federal court in Dallas; a temporary restraining order against the secretary of agriculture also resulted in the suspension of the import regulations in USDA Amendments No. 3 and No.

4 for the season. (The FTC then recommended Amendment No. 2 regulations be reactivated as Amendment No. 5, and Secretary Clifford Hardin immediately approved, rendering it effective the same day.) After hearings on April 25 and May 2, 1969, the judge dismissed the case finding that the plaintiff, as a tomato repacker, had "no standing to bring action."[44]

When USDA announced restrictions for April 27, 1970, West Mexico, Walter Holms and Company, and "other tomato importers" requested a temporary restraining order against the Secretary of Agriculture. When the court denied the request, the plaintiffs then requested a hearing before a three-judge panel in federal court, a motion which was also denied. U.S. District Court in the District of Columbia became the next arena, as it received a request for a permanent injunction against the secretary to prevent his enforcing import orders, based upon the constitutionality of Section 8(e).[45]

When the district court ruled in favor of USDA, the importers appealed the decision to the U.S. District Court of Appeals. This court modified the previous decision, finding in March of 1971 that importers have the right to a hearing before USDA on "novel and crucial" issues.[46] In response, the secretary of agriculture held five weeks of hearings in Orlando, Florida, during the fall of 1971. An importer of Mexican tomatoes and two representatives of consumer groups were among the sixteen witnesses heard on the question of the differential regulation of tomato shipments depending on maturity. In March 1972 the deputy administrator of regulatory programs upheld the authority of USDA to impose dual size requirements.[47]

Late in August 1972 Secretary Hardin announced a final decision reaffirming his ability to continue the dual-size restrictions. Shortly thereafter four consumer groups and various importers brought suits in U.S. District Court in the District of Columbia against the decision.[48]

The legal battles, while inconclusive, effectively kept the FTC from recommending restrictions during the 1971–72 and 1972–73 seasons.[49] During the 1973–74 season Floridian attempts to utilize Section 8(e) of the 1937 Marketing Agreement Act received a crucial blow: USDA ruled that "imported tomatoes are not required to be graded and sized the same as Florida tomatoes but are only required to comply with minimum grade and minimum size."[50] The final judgment on the Marketing Agreement controversy was more of a *tiro de gracia.* In 1975 the district court consolidated the suits brought by consumer groups and distributors against USDA in connection with the tomato case in 1972. The plaintiffs and USDA negotiated an agreement to dismiss the suit, insofar as no dual restrictions had actually been in effect since the 1971–72 season. The settlement stipulated that if any future restrictions were considered, USDA would have to give consideration to the effect on prices due to dual restrictions, alternatives to the dual restrictions, and tomato quality in any proposed regulations.[51]

The courts were also involved in the dumping case. When Treasury gave a Preliminary Determination favorable to Mexico, the Florida growers filed suit basically alleging they had been sold out for Mexican oil and gas. Nevertheless, the Court of International Trade refused to rule on the case, citing its lack of jurisdiction. The Florida growers persisted. After Commerce found "No Sales at Less Than Fair Value" it its Final Determination, the Florida industry filed suit in U.S. customs court in New York City, this time utilizing much more technical rather than political arguments.[52] In early 1985 the court ruled that Commerce's interpretation of the anti-dumping statutes was within the discretion which had been written into the bill by Congress.[53]

PRODUCER-GOVERNMENT RELATIONS AND FOREIGN TRADE POLICY IN MEXICO

The tomato wars were not instances of the "U.S. versus Mexico"; many U.S. forces, official and societal, did not want to see tomatoes become an issue in U.S.-Mexico relations.[54] In addition, the victory of tomato exports to the United States does not necessarily represent a victory of the Mexican government in its trade relations with the United States: in the first tomato war diplomatic negotiations played a minor role which was unimportant in the solution given the controversy. The settlement of the dumping case was also not a direct outcome of bilateral relations.[55] Nevertheless, the Mexican government has had a voice in influencing the trade. Therefore, producer-government relations must be analyzed, as they affect both exports from Mexico and production within the country.

The Marketing Agreement Conflict. With the outbreak of this first major conflict, Mexican producers looked for their government to protest the discriminatory restrictions. The growers were encouraged to follow this tack by their Arizona business associates. The U.S. distributors believed Mexican government protest to the U.S. government would make the distributors' case more credible. As they put it, "if the Mexican producers themselves could not convince their own government of the many obstacles that had been raised due to the market restrictions . . . by the Florida tomato growers, it is quite comprehensible that the United States Department of Agriculture cannot be convinced of our representation in favor of the American importers and distributors."[56] West Mexico's lobbyist in Washington pointed out that the Mexican Embassy's efforts to convince the U.S. government had so far lacked force.[57]

West Mexico's consultants in Washington also stressed the importance of the Mexican president and cabinet giving "highest priority" to tomatoes in their meetings with Governor Nelson D. Rockefeller during his Latin American tour for President Richard Nixon. The firm pointed out to West Mexico that any information they provided would probably be refuted by the briefings of the State Department and USDA, and that thus the most effective tactic would be if "the President of Mexico brought up this matter on the highest possible level and as a matter of international politics, rather than as a possible internal argument between Florida growers and Arizona distributors." It was also suggested that the Mexican president, upon his return from western Europe and before the governor's trip, personally phone President Nixon to convey these feelings.[58]

Mexican producers, however, were cool to the idea of involving their president in the issue.[59] This reluctance to involve the highest political authority in the country, however, did not hold for any official office outside the presidency. In a joint memo by UNPH, CAADES, and AARC to the secretary of agriculture (SAG), the Mexican producers castigated the various branches of the government involved in the tomato controversy for their weak efforts. The Mexican delegation to the IX Interparliamentary Meeting between the two countries was accused of underestimating the importance of the problem, while the president of the Mexican delegation was censured for removing the issue from the agenda. The growers also lamented the lack of official protest on the part of the Mexican government; distributors, wholesalers, transportation companies, supermarket chains, and even U.S. housewives were reported puzzled and worried, the Mexican growers said, by the weak and ineffectual defense of the Mexican producer. Growers concluded by suggesting that the Mexican position in bilateral negotiations should reject export quotas on Mexican production, seek to coordinate Mexican and U.S. production, establish a regulatory committee comprised of producers and government officials from both countries, and stress the necessity of good relations among the United States, Canada, and Mexico.[60]

The Mexican government relied heavily upon input from its producers to formulate technical proposals to present to the U.S. government. From the very beginning, Ambassador to the U.S. Hugo Margaín asked the Mexican producers for precise data, certified by the Mexican secretary of agriculture and livestock, and for proposals to end the controversy. Representatives from the UNPH, CAADES, and AARC met with the Sinaloa governor's representative and SAG's general agent in the state and formulated three conclusions which were to be the cornerstones of the producers' proposals over the next five years:

1. The growers recognize the need for equitable measures to regulate prices when the market "requires" it;
2. That regulations for vine-ripe and mature green tomatoes be the same, given that it is the volume of the total product that influences the market and that reaches the consumer;
3. The Mexican producers propose that the formulas to regulate the market be applied in the following order:
    a) by quality; restricting U.S. Grade 3, then 2, so that the consumer is offered the best product at prices reasonable to both consumers and producers;
    b) if a) is not sufficient, then restrictions should be placed on sizes, affecting both vine-ripe and green tomatoes equally.[61]

According to SAG, 89.8 percent of Mexico's production was vine-ripe, whereas 81.2 percent of Florida's crop was mature green; hence the restrictions which affected both varieties in the $7 \times 7^*$ and 7×8 sizes, but only vine-ripe in the larger 6×7 size were discriminatory. In fact, of the total volume of tomatoes exported in the previous three seasons, the affected sizes were alleged to have constituted 40.8 percent with a total market value of 230 million pesos.[62]

---

*Refers to the number of tomatoes in the rows and columns of a tomato crate. They are packed in crates of 7×8, 7×7, 6×7, 6×6, and 5×6. Size restrictions regulate the minimum and maximum diameter of a tomato which can be packed in a particular crate size.

Bilateral negotiations failed to resolve the trade conflict during the 1968–69 season.[63] But the international branch of SAG persisted with the idea of reaching a market sharing agreement. In 1970 SAG readied a tentative proposal. A minimum quota for imports from Mexico would be set (for the 1969–70 season it was to be the average of the last three years) with annual increases as demand expanded, and Mexico allowed to fill Florida's share in periods when the latter's production fell. A bilateral commission with government and producer representation from both countries would also be created to implement the proposed treaty. There would be a five-year trial period, with the possibility of revisions, and the parties would be free to renounce the treaty with six month's notice. The advantages of such an agreement for Mexico were believed twofold: a minimum export volume would be guaranteed (which therefore allowed for some degree of planning, which would, in turn, reduce cost and risk) and the Mexican initiative might hold off further U.S. unilateral and stricter measures. Thus now that the United States demonstrated a "good disposition toward an agreement," SAG believed it would be propitious to attempt one.[64]

Nevertheless, the Mexican ambassador to the U.S. disagreed with SAG's assessment of U.S. receptivity to quotas. He argued that both the executive and congress were against quantitative restrictions, partly because neither wished to become involved in the political problems of allowing quotas on only one particular product. Consequently, the idea of a quota would have only Mexican support and the ambassador felt it would not be in Mexico's interest to restrict itself.[65]

Other objections were also raised. Contrary to SAG's view, the Mexican diplomat felt that even if the United States were to continue limiting imports through the 1937 law, "our exports would not be less than before," and in fact would only cause the U.S. government public opinion problems while failing to restrict Mexican incursion into the market. In addition, labor shortages, high production costs, and "inferior quality" were all factors tending to make Florida's production disappear; thus any Mexican self-imposed limits would be in Florida's interest. In sum, any restrictions Mexico put upon itself without reciprocal action by Florida would be, in the Ambassador's view, more discriminatory than the Marketing Agreement mechanisms, even with their differential regulations for mature green and vine-ripe tomatoes.[66]

Ambassador Margaín pointed out that the U.S. Departments of State and Agriculture concurred in his opinion that the best solution would be one the producers themselves worked out, under the guidance of their respective governments. The ambassador then proposed that the market be regulated via price levels: when the price fell to a particular point, Mexico would cease exporting until the price reacted favorably to the decreased supply, in a manner similar to U.S. action in the cotton market. The price level would be set to allow both Mexican and Floridian producers to make a profit, keep Mexico's market supremacy, and let economic forces continue to work against Florida.[67] Mexican Secretary of Agriculture Juan Gil Preciado found the ambassador's proposal "acceptable in principal" and suggested a few additions of an administrative nature.[68]

One week before the bilateral negotiations began, SAG met with a commission comprised of two representatives each from the UNPH and AARC, along with two AARC technicians and a representative from Sonora. For the UNPH the bilateral meeting was important because it was "one of the first times" the problem received the importance it merited.[69] The meeting officially opened on September 23 with Foreign Secretary Carrillo Flores urging the U.S. delegation to view the tomato problem in the "simple panorama that we are your best clients."[70]

Little seems to have come of this meeting, and further talks were held. On November 11, 1969, Secretary Gil Preciado spoke with the U.S. Ambassador to Mexico about meat and tomatoes with the only result an announcement of future meetings.[71] Sinaloa producers met with the secretary on the 14th to discuss the present export season[72] (the Mexican producers had made the strategic decision to reduce acreage for the coming year), and a new meeting was held in Washington on the 24th. The Mexican producers appeared confident. It was clear, although USDA did not understand it at the moment, that even if the goal of the restrictions were not discriminatory, the effects were there for all to see: 90 percent of Mexican 6×7 exports had been stopped, compared with only 13 percent of Florida's production in the same size.[73] This new meeting seemed to offer more: SAG announced "bases" had been laid and announced another meeting in December.[74] Mexican producers' hopes were further lifted when U.S. Ambassador McBride paid a cordial visit to the Sinaloa Government, announcing that the Florida producers wished to reach an agreement.[75]

Three more trade meetings between the two countries were held during the 1969–70 season.[76] Ambassador McBride paid an informal visit to Culiacán at the invitation of UNPH to inspect the production and packing of tomatoes.[77] But as the talks dragged on, Mexican growers began to lose hope. Florida growers believed that they were in a position of strength and would accept nothing less than Mexico assuming a position as residual supplier.

In July of 1970, the UNPH president expressed fear that the U.S. government would exercise more control over Mexican imports via import quotas. Problems were also anticipated in light of an unexpected increase in Mexican acreage for 1970–71.[78] A few days later the local paper reported, with no mention of source, that since USDA's measures to protect the FTC had failed, it would institute an import quota. Such a quota would, the paper claimed, "automatically retire" Mexican producers from the market.[79]

In mid-July the Mexican government took the initiative and set an official quota for tomato exports to the U.S. market. This was precisely the measure against which the Mexican producers and the Mexican ambassador had argued a year earlier. The SAG directors of International Affairs and Agricultural Economics broke the news to producers during a three-day conference in Culiacán. The officials pointed out that the expansion of production was creating problems and that it would be in the economic interests of the producers themselves to avoid excessive production by means of a "healthy" regulation. Producers were warned that the past season had been a success only due to climatic factors in Florida and that a good season in Florida would have spelled disaster for Mexican producers.[80]

Pains were taken to make clear that although the United States itself had not set a quota on imports, if the trend toward increasing Mexican participation in the U.S. market remained unaltered, it could very well restrict access to avoid saturating domestic markets. The SAG officials conceded this to be a "legitimate" U.S. option. The director of agricultural economics noted that in the 1969–70 season Mexico exported 263,000 tons of tomatos for a 51 percent share of the winter-early spring market, a situation which the U.S. government "did not consider healthy." According to SAG, the U.S. government believed the optimal volume of imports should fluctuate between 160,000 and 180,000 tons; the Mexican government thus considered this to be a reasonable goal for planning, with a reserve in case climatic conditions warranted increased Mexican supplies. SAG consequently recommended that the producers reduce acreage 15 percent below the average of the previous five years and allow no new tomato producers; the Canadian and European markets remained unrestricted. Though the production decision was to be made by the producers, SAG reminded producers that it issued export permits and would use this power to enforce its recommendation since "the government of Mexico has the right to regulate and plan its agricultural production".[81] Legislation was then written to facilitate SAG's regulation of exports.[82]

Mexico later modified its official program of self-restriction for the 1971–72 season because the market demanded more tomatoes. Instead of tonnage limits to exports, a trigger price was set up (at $3.50 per box) below which increases in quality requirements would decrease supply and push prices back up above the trigger. This switch in tactics did not please the Florida producers, as evidenced by Congressman Dante B. Fascell's congressional comments that this constituted a step backward for U.S. efforts to limit tomato imports.[83] But the following year a further erosion in Mexican control occurred as Mexico sought to keep supply in line with an ever-increasing demand for Mexican tomatoes.

The Dumping Controversy. When the second tomato war began, Mexican producers believed that their previously set production targets already took into consideration the relationship between supply and demand. The Mexican secretary of agriculture and hydraulic resources (Secretaría de Agricultura y Recursos Hidraulicos, SARH), however, viewed the production decisions not from the perspective of supply and demand, but rather that of political pressures and conflicts with the U.S. government and growers. Consequently, invoking the 1970 legislation requiring SAG (now SARH) approval of export quotas, SARH authorized less than the amount requested by producers for both the 1978–79 and 1979–80 seasons.[84]

In contrast to the earlier controversy and due principally to the changed context of U.S.-Mexican relations,[85] the pressures for bilateral negotiations came chiefly from the U.S. side, including both government and citizenry. Mexican producers were steadfast against any negotiations while the threat of anti-dumping sanctions remained, arguing that their existence was a form of pressure on Mexican producers to reach an agreement.[86]

Spurred on by the early opinion of Treasury lawyers that a strict interpretation of the Anti-dumping Act could not avoid finding dumping on the part of the Mexicans, the Carter administration pressured Florida growers to take the issue to the bargaining table.[87] Even before the Floridians agreed to withdraw their petition to the Treasury, the U.S. Special Trade Representative's Office headed a bilateral task force to work out a compromise.[88] After months of pressure by the White House and Departments of Treasury and State and postponement of the first deadline for a preliminary decision by Treasury, Florida growers agreed, on the day a tentative determination was to have been given, to withdraw their petition for ninety days to give negotiations an opportunity to resolve the dispute.[89]

The Mexican side, however, was not united in its view as to the usefulness of negotiations. Growers, fearing negotiations would imply some legitimacy to the dumping charges and stimulate other producers to bring similar charges in hopes of forcing Mexico to negotiate restrictions, advocated staying away from the bargaining table until the Treasury ruled that the dumping legislation did not apply to perishable produce. In addition, they pointed out that the possibility of recourse to a dumping suit would handicap Mexico's bargaining abilities. Nevertheless, the Mexican government agreed to negotiate, but rejected solutions which shifted all costs to Mexico.[90]

Six meetings were held in Mexico City, Washington, and Miami; in the first two, August 14 and 28, only government representatives attended, and the discussions were of an exploratory technical nature. On September 17 the United States introduced the Florida proposal to the Mexican officials: quantitative limits were to be put on Mexican imports when the market price reached a certain level; temporary tariff increases were to be used to control the limits; and no proposals concerning Floridian limitations were forwarded. On September 28 the two producer groups met for the first time in the negotiations; U.S. government officials were present to insure respect for U.S. antitrust laws.[91]

Negotiations did not prosper as the basic disagreement revolved around not whether controls were needed but *who* was going to limit their supply in periods of excess supply. The positions of a decade ago continued unaltered: Mexican growers, proclaiming their "historical right" to the U.S. market, advocated equal limitations, while Floridian producers, arguing sovereignty rights, were steadfast in their opposition to restricting their supply. Negotiations broke off the day after the sixth meeting began when Florida growers resubmitted their petition to the Treasury on October 19, 1979.[92]

In summary, this section has shown that contrary to the conventional view of the unimportance of interest group pressures and initiatives for the setting and conduct of Mexico's foreign policy, the fact is that the Mexican government was willing to allow Sinaloa producers to guide its policy during the 1969–70 season of negotiations. When it appeared that the United States might increase the severity of its trade restrictions, however, the Mexican government abandoned its producers' position on the issue. At this point it made policy unilaterally and in defense of its long-term trade interests, leaving Mexican producers no alternative but to adhere to the government policy. Once it became clear that Florida could not supply the increased market share it inherited through Mexican self-restrictions, the Mexican government loosened controls and allowed its producers to set their own export policy once again in the early seventies.

Nevertheless, in 1979 the situation reverted back to one of government setting export quotas below producer requests. A variety of reasons have been forwarded to explain such an occurence, among them that the new agricultural policy of President José López Portillo required a quiet cutback on export production.* Nevertheless, if history is to provide some lessons, in this case a more likely scenario is one where SARH once again diminished exports to lessen U.S. fears about Mexican import quantities.

THE DIVERGENCE OF STATE AND GROWER INTERESTS

The winter vegetable case illustrates the dynamic relationship that exists between domestic and international political-economic forces which influences the political economy within a state and between states. The most important implication of the winter vegetable trade for Mexico's political economy has been the strengthening of the Sinaloa rural elite with respect to their relationship with both local and international actors.

---

*López Portillo repeatedly stated that export crops would not suffer under the new policy because their generation of employment and foreign exchange was needed.

The performance of the Sinaloan vegetable producers in these two arenas, and their role in influencing Sinaloa's political economy, presents a picture of invincible vegetable producers. Nevertheless, there is at least one arena in which producer interests take a backseat. In normal times the Mexican government allows the Sinaloan producers, through the UNPH, to set export policy. During periods of trade disputes, however, the government has stepped in to regulate exports. Thus during the tomato wars the agriculture secretary set export quotas in 1970–71, 1978–79, 1979–80, and 1980–81 below what the UNPH calculated the market would require from Mexico.*

How does one explain this independence of Mexican foreign economic policy from the Sinaloan rural elite in light of the almost unlimited support given them in the production phase? At this point one must again insert the vegetable trade in its broader context of U.S.-Mexico relations. Bilateral trade relations are crucial for Mexico, as over 60 percent of exports and imports are U.S.-related. Because of the diversified nature of Mexican exports before the petroleum boom, winter vegetable exports are of relatively small importance, even when they constitute one of the chief agricultural exports. Therefore, the Mexican government must place the defense of vegetable exports in the larger context of general trade vulnerability vis-à-vis the United States. Consequently it has apparently not wanted to push the U.S. too far on this issue; Mexican government vegetable export policy has sought to convince the United States that Mexican exports are complementary, not competitive, with U.S. production. This tactic requires holding Mexican exports down at crisis periods.

The winter vegetable case, therefore, suggests that Mexican foreign economic policy allows industry, in this case the well-organized rural elite of Sinaloa, to carry a great deal of weight in its formulation during normal periods. But when the "national interest" appears threatened, the state makes policy even if it is detrimental to the short-run interests of a particular industry.

---

*In the Culiacán offices of CAADES a computer programmed by the Wharton School analyzes the coming season and provides guidelines for production and export.

CONCLUSION

9

PENETRATING THE INTERNATIONAL MARKET: SOME COMPARATIVE EVIDENCE

This book presents an argument about the political nature of international competitiveness. The theoretical basis was developed in two steps. First, I built upon Ruggie's concept of embedded liberalism to argue that our understanding of the trade regime which evolved from embedded liberalism is heightened if we conceive of the regime as segmented. Segmented liberalism consists of a liberal segment, reliant primarily on market allocation, and an illiberal segment, more reliant on explicitly political interventions. It is the complementarity of the illiberal segment to the liberal counterpart which distinguishes an illiberal trade regime from a segmented liberal one. I then constructed an analytic framework for the examination of the factors leading to international competitiveness. This framework postulated that international competitiveness depends upon the interaction of three variables: the characteristics of the product in question, the structure of its international market, and the domestic allocation of resources. Each of these variables, as well as their interaction, were seen to respond to both economic and political forces. I also argued that the methodology of a tri-level analysis, in which local forces would be included along with international and national forces, was proper for the utilization of this theoretical perspective.

Using my argument about segmented liberalism and the determinants of international competitiveness, I explored two issues in the political economy of Southern penetration of Northern markets. These were (a) how could the South continue to export to the North products which fell outside the liberalization process; and (b) how could Southern private capital compete with Northern entrepreneurs both in production at home and in trade in the Northern market?

I used the Mexican fresh winter vegetable trade to illustrate the utility of my theoretical perspective and analytical framework to answer these questions. The biological characteristics of this product (which require a certain climate and large inputs of labor) limit large-scale U.S. production in the winter months to southern Florida. Since U.S. demand greatly outstrips Floridian production, imports play an important role in the market. Climate and production perishability make Mexico, Central America, and the Caribbean the logical foreign suppliers. Mexico evolved as virtually sole exporter because of U.S. foreign policy and domestic politics in Central America and the Caribbean.

As the only important U.S. producer, Florida growers' ability to raise nontariff barriers (NTB's) to imports depended upon creating alliances with domestic producers of other crops to pass multicrop legislation (as happened with the addition of Section 8(e) in 1954 to the 1937 Agricultural Marketing Agreement Act) or insulating decisions within the agricultural bureaucracy (as was the case in the first tomato war). When they attempted to pass very focused legislation in the 1970s, the Congressional votes failed to materialize. And when trade conflicts were pushed out of the bureaucracy and into the courts the pro-import transnational alliance could defeat the isolated Floridians. Finally, the U.S. executive branch found that the domestic incentives to control inflation and the foreign policy need for good relations with oil-rich Mexico (at a time when access to petroleum supplies was of concern) far outweighed the interests of a small group of domestic producers.

It is apparent that the U.S. fresh winter vegetable market belongs to the politically regulated segment of the liberal international trade regime because there has been no liberalization of tariff rates. But Florida growers have not had the political weight to increase the level of protection beyond that perceived necessary to ensure a significant market share (which seems to be around 40 percent to 50 percent) for U.S. producers. Variations in market share beyond these limits are explained by state macro and sectoral policies which influence the price of resources used in production (water, land, labor, and especially foreign exchange) and grower decisions which affect cost competitiveness (adoption of technological change).

In terms of the ability of Mexican growers to compete with foreign capital in the production of these crops, the framework again helps us. Once climate, labor, and perishability are controlled for, the characteristics of their production/marketing process make for low barriers to entry. In addition, the fresh winter vegetable agribusiness commodity system had been quite competitive at each level and unintegrated across levels. As chapters 2 and 7 demonstrated, the structure of the international trade in fresh winter vegetables is highly competitive on the finance and marketing side because of the low barriers to entry. On the production side, the local rural elite maintained effective control over lands most suitable for vegetable production, leading to conditions of oligopoly at this stage. This dual competitive structure developed because the state forbids foreign ownership of coastal land, thereby giving nationals firm-specific advantages in any industry in which access to land is vital.

This combination of competitiveness and oligopoly proved extremely favorable to Mexican growers. Competition explains the volatility of the Nogales distributorships as well as the ability of the cucumber producer in chapter 7 and the grower/distributor of the introduction to shift risk onto foreign capital.

From this vantage point the Mexican growers were poised to move against the interests of the U.S. companies. But first they had to extend their control beyond land and into the productive process itself. The most important step was to regulate supply, both to decrease risk in the market and to limit the ability of U.S. investors to circumvent the aggressive Mexican growers. As we have seen, state support of this private initiative also proved fundamental to success. As Mexican growers began to gain control over some elements of production and trade, the traditional instability of the market declined. As risk fell growers began to integrate forward into the competitive phases of the agribusiness commodity system. As is the case for Northern capital, national boundaries proved little obstacle to these aggressive Southern entrepreneurs. With integration into the marketing phase of the U.S. market, Mexican growers increasingly gained influence over the market.

Political decisions as to the allocation of resources and the rules by which private parties can interact are important even beyond the local-foreign capital relationship. In his study of Brazilian international coffee policy, Krasner demonstrated the importance of state control over the response of private producers to the improved market resulting from state action.[1] A similar situation holds for Mexican vegetables and spurred the state to act. Two important moments came when the majority of growers opposed first production and then trade controls. The state turned to its control over water and export licenses, respectively, to avoid grower short-run profit maximizing, which would have undermined the longer-term health of the industry.

But lest we overemphasize the success of the state in managing forces which influence production and trade, we need to recall that Mexico's position has been under serious strain since 1980. Protectionism in the international market has been marginal to this decline. The fundamental problem is found in Mexico's general macroeconomic policies, specifically those relating to the exchange rate, inflation, and internal growth. Chapter 7 demonstrated how policy made outside the arena of vegetable production brought the industry to its knees and undermined the ability of domestic capital to bargain with foreign entrepreneurs. It is now in the process of rebuilding, but one lesson in particular should stay with us: while state intervention can be crucial to the development of national control over production and trade in a particular industry, general macroeconomic policies can be the Achilles heel for entrepreneurs attempting to operate in international markets.

To begin to explore the transferability of this analytic framework from the Mexican vegetable case to other Southern countries and products, this conclusion examines the textile and apparel industry in South Korea and Colombia. The following analysis is neither comprehensive nor definitive; it suggests parallels as an invitation for other analysts to develop or dispute further.

Textiles and apparel were chosen as a point for comparison for theoretical and empirical concerns. Because these products belong to the manufacturing rather than agricultural sector, their analysis provides further evidence that the political economy of production and trade in agriculture is not theoretically distinct from that of manufactures. Textiles and apparel exports have also been fundamental to the rise of the newly industrializing countries. In addition, because of their successes, these products have been subject to Northern attempts to manage trade for the longest period of any Southern manufactures. Of crucial importance is the contrasting experiences in Southern performance in this trade which allows us to gain further insight into international competitiveness. Finally, comparative analysis is facilitated because of the extensive literature on the textile and apparel trade.

THE POLITICAL ECONOMY OF THE TEXTILE AND APPAREL TRADE

The proposed framework of analysis argues that product and production characteristics play fundamental roles in determining who can compete internationally. The textile and apparel industry in the North can be usefully differentiated into two general categories in accordance with their relative use of capital and labor.[2] In the clothing and knitting sectors production is labor-intensive and the product life cycle model serves us well in understanding why Southern countries have become such a dominant force in these sectors.[3] Spinning, weaving, and the synthetic fiber sectors, however, are capital-intensive due to recent major technological innovations. Yet even here we find an important Southern presence. This anomaly can still be partly explained by the product cycle once we recognize that the cycle is speeding up as a result of changes in both the production strategies of multinational corporations and the communications revolution.[4] The capital-intensive nature of the production process in spinning, weaving, and synthetic fibers thus gives an advantage to producers who are newcomers (such as South Korea in the late 1960s) or who renew their capital frequently (e.g., West Germany and Japan).[5]

These product characteristics helped make Southern textile producers very competitive in Northern markets by the late 1950s. Southern producers also had help from international politics and domestic policy. Internationally, Japan was the most efficient producer and thus bore the brunt of U.S. and European NTBs when the domestic political costs of embedded liberalism demanded attention. By restricting exports from Japan, the United States and Europe contributed to the rise of textile exports from other low-wage countries (including Hong Kong) which were initially not as competitive as Japan. Domestic policies also help Southern producers to take advantage of the product cycle. In South Korea the domestic textile industry had to be reconstructed after the Korean War (1950–1952). Interest group pressure combined with national interest to produce government policies that closed the domestic market to imports, while overvalued exchange rates reduced the cost of imported machinery and increased industry profits and U.S. economic aid financed imports. The result was a modernized South Korean textile industry whose capacity by 1957 outstripped domestic demand for all but chemical fibers and synthetics.[6]

My analytic framework argues that the structure of the international market will also play a major role in determining international competitiveness. In the textile and apparel case the issue of political access stands out. The international economic competitiveness of Southern textile producers brought protectionist responses from Northern governments concerned over the domestic political power of their declining textile sectors. Initially these were unilateral or bilateral measures taken on the margins of GATT. By the late 1950s, the Scandinavian countries, among the most stalwart Northern defenders of liberal trade,[7] imposed import restraints on textiles, including those from Colombia and South Korea. This management of textile trade by Northern states was never made conditional upon adjustment in Northern industry despite Southern efforts.[8] As each agreement expired it was renewed, and its scope expanded because Northern industry remained uncompetitive. My argument about the segmented nature of liberal trade would have anticipated this trend, but conventional liberal regime analysts are just beginning to ask whether thirty years of protection is enough to classify the textile arrangements as "illiberal protection".

Political access to Northern markets became a barrier to the expansion of Southern exports (actually to intra-North trade in textiles as well). But these constraints were not determinate. While they did impose an additional cost to doing business with the North, some countries (like South Korea) paid it and did well overall. The costs were basically two. First, the country had to invest time, money, and intellectual energy in devising bargaining strategies to limit restraints in each of the numerous bilateral and multilateral accords negotiated over the past three decades. Both South Korea and Colombia did so, the latter's textile negotiator even representing the coordinated Southern group in the discussions to renew the multifiber agreement in 1980–81. These negotiations could not keep Northern restraints from becoming increasingly restrictive over time, but they probably made them less restrictive than unilateral action on the part of the North.[9]

The second cost has been addressed differently by Southern exporters, as illustrated by the South Korean and Colombian cases. Continued success in penetrating Northern textile markets has depended upon staying one step ahead of the protectionists by switching production from a restricted category (e.g., cotton textiles in the early 1960s) to one not yet subject to restriction (textiles from man-made fibers until 1974). But there are political and economic costs to maintaining a flexible industrial structure which might or might not offset the benefits of adjustment programs.[10] As the Northern countries themselves discovered in the 1970s, adjustment can carry important political costs, as capital and labor are displaced or reorganized.[11] Many Southern countries have refused to pay these costs as well, with the result that the dynamism of their textile and apparel exports suffers. South Korea is one country which has adjusted to stay in Northern markets and Colombia one which has not.

The issue of adjustment in the Southern textile industry brings us to the third component in my framework for analyzing the political economy of international competitiveness: the domestic allocation of resources. As I noted in the introduction, in broad terms this depends upon state-society relations and the structure of the political system. For a particular product this relationship plays out in the context of the product's production requirements, its position in the international division of labor, and the overall development strategy of the country. Analysis of the South Korean and Colombian responses highlights the importance of domestic choices.

In the face of Northern import restraints South Korea has done remarkably well. From 1962 to 1975 the annual rate of increase of its textile and apparel exports was 52 percent.[12] Using figures that are not strictly comparable to the earlier period, Yoffie found the annual rate of increase for these South Korean exports to be 42 percent from 1975 to 1978, yielding $4.1 billion.[13] From Yoffie's work we know that such success depended upon "upgrading, bargaining for loopholes, cheating, and exploiting transnational ties."[14]

But what are the domestic politics of such a flexible textile and apparel industry? It has been argued that in South Korea we have a combination of a "strong" state and an entrepreneurial class with a long history.[15] Because most of Korea's heavy industry was located in the northern part of the country,[16] the textile and apparel industry played a crucial role in post-Korean War economic development. Analysis of adjustment in the textile and apparel industry calls for the examination of the relationship between the South Korean state and domestic textile entrepreneurs.

The state in South Korea is perceived to be strong because of its relative autonomy from social forces and its ability to extract resources and change the behavior of societal actors by its policies.[17] The strong state in South Korea is best understood as dating from the 1961 military coup; before that time domestic and international factors limited the insulation of government decision makers from societal forces.[18] Since the export-led development strategy which helped stimulate textile and apparel exports coincided with this strong state, many analysts support the argument that a strong state was fundamental to export success. Among the major policies seen facilitating international competitiveness were control over labor, the exchange rate, exemption from import restrictions for exporters, subsidies, and credit allocation. South Korean entrepreneurs also benefited from state regulation of foreign investment requiring joint ventures, local content, export performance, and prior screening. Haggard and Cheng see this as part of a bargain with local capital for its acquiescence to "microeconomic controls and political quiescence."[19] State leaders used their resources and policy tools to reward and facilitate flexibility by entrepreneurs to respond to international opportunities.[20]

It remains difficult, however, to discern whether the state led Korean entrepreneurs or if the latter used the state to help reach their domestic and foreign goals. Despite the export orientation of state leaders, societal forces were able to block further liberalization of the domestic economy in the late 1970s; the military coup of 1981 helped usher in a new liberalization phase, but even it was limited by opposition from domestic entrepreneurs.[21] The creation of General Trading Companies in 1975 is often used as an example of a state instrument used to alter firm behavior in accord with national interests. But South Korean traders had been pressing for their government to favor Korean over Japanese trading houses since the early 1970s.[22]

In the textile case, the Spinners and Weavers Association of Korea is the largest and strongest business association in the country and has used its great financial base and access to the government to promote favorable policies.[23] Since both state and textile interests were served by the export-oriented development project after the end of the "easy" phase of import substitution industrialization, causation is difficult to know without in-depth study, which has not been carried out. For example, when the South Korea government negotiated a bilateral restraint on textile exports to the United States in 1965, Korean firms violated that commitment. Analysts have been unable to tell us whether companies acted on their own until they upgraded product lines into non-restrained categories (as U.S. policymakers believed) or whether the South Korean state was cheating on its commitment.[24]

In sum, these points about producer responses suggest that the literature on South Korea's great flexibility in the textile sector (and elsewhere) has a large gap in it which limits understanding: an analysis of the political economy of Korean entrepreneurs' responses to the opportunities and constraints of the international market. Many analysts claim that the question is one of the relative weights of state and societal forces in setting economic policy. My own work agrees with this perspective, but the empirical question in many countries has not been answered because societal pressure on the state and response in the marketplace have not commanded as much attention as state policy. Expanding the analysis on the societal side, as well as that of the interaction between state and society, might or might not strengthen the statist argument for South Korea.*

Colombia faced the same Northern restraints to its textile and apparel trade as did South Korea. In terms of international bargaining, its response seems to have been similar to South Korea's.[25] And initially it made significant gains in increasing its clothing exports: export value increased from less than $1 million in 1964 to $83 million in 1973. Exports were concentrated in the United States and Europe (61 percent in 1975). Colombia appeared to be "the East Asian Latin American NIC" because of its manufactured export success. But after 1975 Colombian clothing

---

*David Freidman's dissertation, "The Misunderstood Miracle," which came to my attention after writing this conclusion, is a potentially devastating attack on the strong-state thesis for what has hitherto been perceived as a strong state par excellence, Japan. He examines production and trade in the critically important machine tool industry and the preferences of small entrepreneurs, big business, and MITI (Ministry of International Trade and Industry). Freidman demonstrates that, despite efforts by the alliance of big business and the state to consolidate control over the industry in their hands, small producers have successfully opposed such measures, survived, thrived, and are responsible for the adjustments which keep the industry internationally competitive.

exports stagnated and veered toward southern markets: in 1978 the United States and Europe received only 24 percent of these exports, while Venezuela and the Caribbean increased their share from 33 percent to 72 percent.[26]

If this decreased share of Northern markets were simply the result of international competitiveness leading to the penetration of diverse markets, it would signify a positive development. But the stagnation of exports suggests that diversification was largely a result of declining competitiveness in Northern markets.

How can we explain this negative development in light of both Colombia's initial success and South Korea's continued success? We have seen that adjustment to trade barriers was fundamental for South Korea. Did the political management of apparel imports by the North pose sufficiently high barriers that Colombia's state leaders and relevant interest groups found the costs of adjustment too high to pay? This does not seem to have been the case. The EEC has not imposed quotas on Colombian clothing exports. Of the sixty categories of clothing on which the United States imposed quotas, 70 percent had less than 10 percent of the quota filled during 1975–1977. For 1975–1976 only four categories filled quota allotments to at least two-thirds, and in 1976–1977 that number fell to two. Morawetz's in-depth study of the Colombian clothing industry found that in only two of the sixty categories did U.S. restraints prove to be determinant.[27]

In the Colombian case our second component in the framework for the analysis of international competitiveness provides little insight, and we move to the third component. It is in the domestic political economy that one finds the answers to the Colombian failure. Is the key variable here the economic ideology of the leaders in a strong state, as Haggard and Cheng argue for South Korea and I argue is true (but with a negative outcome) for Mexico?[28] Hardly. Colombian political leaders seem to have been committed to shifting out of ISI and diversifying exports since 1966.[29] But the Colombian state is weak, heavily penetrated by the two rival political parties (even here party leadership seems to have little control over the party itself), and with little capacity to mold societal demands.

The question becomes how a relatively weak state and exporters combat pressures from ISI-oriented interest groups. In 1966 the incoming Colombian president oversaw a switch in foreign exchange policy which allowed the currency to float downward (crawling peg) to avoid overvaluation. With this one move years of bias against exporters was removed, providing a significant stimulus to exports. In addition, a variety of export incentives were introduced. Those industries which depended upon ISI-inspired protectionism, such as textiles, were retained in the policy coalition by undertaking only very limited import liberalization. The coalition was rounded out by providing urban labor with a construction boom and apparently a significant influence over the organization of production at the shop floor.[30] Initial success was great, and nontraditional exports (including clothing) grew (in constant U.S. dollars) 25 percent per year from the pre-crawling peg year of 1965 to the year in which the crawl proved inadequate to avoid overvaluation, 1974.[31]

But this coalition proved to be economically unstable. One result was an increase in domestic inflation with the 1971 and 1972 rates doubling those of 1967–1970.[32] By 1974 international inflation added to domestic inflation and the rate of crawl of the exchange rate began to lag. Government policy responded with deflationary measures and reduced subsidies. Exporters now began to face a negative bias from exchange rate and subsidy policies which was not offset by the still modest measures of import liberalization undertaken.[33] For the clothing industry the protection afforded the domestic textile industry reduced the price and quality competitiveness of Colombian exports in the very competitive Northern market.[34]

Although the failure of the state to maintain an effective export promotion environment is an important element in the decline in Colombia's clothing exports to Northern markets, producers also have to share in some of the responsibility for both success and failure. Colombian clothing manufacturers have not been aggressive in pursuing the marketing contacts and fashion awareness necessary for penetrating Northern markets: this was true even in the boom years. To a large degree producers have been content with producing for a protected domestic market (its protection is presumably a result of clothing manufacturers' demands on policy-makers) and a less price- and quality-sensitive clothing market in Venezuela and the Caribbean.[35]

This brief examination of the textile and apparel trades, in which Southern countries have penetrated northern markets, bears out the analytic utility of the framework proposed in the introduction and illustrated in the Mexican fresh winter vegetable case. Both cases demonstrate the complexity of international competitiveness and dispel some of the simplified views of the export experience of the South. To those who argue that protectionism in the North severely limits southern possibilities for export, I demonstrate that growth in exports in regulated markets can still occur and bring substantial benefit in terms of foreign exchange and employment to the South. For analysts who focus on "getting prices right", I have shown that not only is economic competitiveness insufficient but, because of northern policies which derive from the very nature of the liberal trade regime, "getting prices right" may not even be necessary!

Ordinarily, it is necessary to perform well in each component of the framework. If producers and/or state policymakers guess wrong on the product cycle or do not have a comparative advantage in the Heckscher-Ohlin sense, political access to markets and the domestic allocation of resources are usually irrelevant. If, on the other hand, product characterisics favor production by the South, then economic competitiveness and the domestic allocation of resources become fundamental to international competitiveness. As Southern producers become economically competitive, political access to northern markets surfaces as a necessary component for international competitiveness. When domestic and/or foreign policy concerns lead to restrictions on economically efficient producers, market management can relegate economic competitiveness to a secondary role.

In addition to proposing a framework for the analysis of international competitiveness, I have argued that the international liberal trade regime is divided into market and politically guided segments. As the volume and influence of inefficient producers in both the North and South has grown, the managed trade segment of embedded liberalism has enlarged its scope.

In this context some policymakers and intellectuals look back on halcyon days and idealize the North's commitment to global liberalism. But such a false view of the international liberal trade regime imposes serious theoretical and practical costs. Theoretically, it distorts our understanding of international politics by suggesting that Northern governments were willing to allow the market to determine position in the international system via its impact on economic capabilities. In practical terms, such a misunderstanding of liberal trade endangers the liberal system by rejecting the management (both intra-North as well as North-South) necessary for continuation of the regime. Ironically, liberal idealists opposed to the concept of a segmented liberal trade regime could push the international trading system back into illiberalism.

NOTES

1. THE POLITICAL ECONOMY OF INTERNATIONAL COMPETITIVENESS: THEORY AND A FRAMEWORK FOR ANALYSIS

1. *Comercio Exterior*, March 1980, pp. 208–300; The World Bank, *World Development Report 1984*, p. 28.

2. Steven Sanderson, "Florida Tomatoes, U.S.-Mexican Relations, and the International Division of Labor," p. 39.

3. Asociación de Agricultores del Río Culiacán (AARC), *Boletín Agrícola* XXIII:2 (May–June 1979), 23(2):57.

4. Files, U.S. Department of Commerce.

5. Houthakker's statement is found in "Rebuttal Brief of Respondents Union Nacional de Productores de Hortalizas and West Mexico Vegetable Distributors Association," pp. 12–13; Simmons study is Richard L. Simmons, "A Comparison of Prices of Winter Vegetables in Canadian and U.S. Markets"; and King's testimony is in "Exhibits to Brief of Respondents Union Nacional de Productores de Hortalizas and West Mexico Vegetable Distributors Association in the United States Department of Commerce."

6. For example, C. Fred Bergsten, "Let's Avoid a Trade War," pp. 24–31.

7. Theodore H. Moran, *Multinational Corporations and the Politics of Dependence* is the pioneering study on bargaining relationships between multinationals and the Southern state; see also Peter Evans, *Dependent Development*; Gary Gereffi, *The Pharmaceutical Industry and Dependency in the Third World*; and Douglas Bennett and Kenneth Sharpe, "Agenda Setting and Bargaining Power: The Mexican State Versus Transnational Automobile Corporations."

8. Evans, *Dependent Development*.

9. David G. Becker, *The New Bourgeoisie and the Limits of Dependency*.

10. John S. Odell, "Latin American Trade Negotiations with the United States"; David B. Yoffie, *Power and Protectionism*.

11. Louis T. Wells, Jr., *Third World Multinationals*; Krishna Kumar and Maxwell G. McLeod, eds., *Multinationals from Developing Countries*.

12. Moran, *Multinational Corporations.*

13. See Robert Keohane, "The Theory of Hegemonic Stability and Changes in International Economic Regimes, 1967–1977" and the special issue of *International Organization* (Spring 1982), 36:2, which focuses on regimes.

14. Stephen D. Krasner, *Structural Conflict,* p. 5.

15. John Gerard Ruggie, "International regimes, transactions and change: embedded liberalism in the postwar economic order"; Vinod K. Aggarwal, *Liberal Protectionism.*

16. These figures are weighted by each sector's share of total consumption in manufacturing. William Cline, "Exports of Manufactures from Developing Countries: Performance and Prospects for Market Access," as cited in Robert Reich, "Beyond Free Trade," p. 786.

17. Vernon L. Sorenson, *International Trade Policy,* pp. 118–125; T. K. Warley, "Western Trade in Agricultural Products"; Warley points out that U.S. support for liberalization of farm products is highly selective; see also Dale E. Hathaway, "Agricultural Trade Policy for the 1980s."

18. Sorenson, *International Trade Policy,* p. 67; Paul A. Samuelson, *Economics,* p. 388.

19. Jimmye S. Hillman, *Nontariff Agricultural Trade Barriers;* Warley, "Western Trade," p. 294; for an analysis of U.S. and British agricultural policymaking, see Graham K. Wilson, *Special Interests and Policy-Making.*

20. D. Gale Johnson, "Food Production and Marketing: A Review of Economic Developments in Agriculture"; Bruce L. Gardner, "Commentaries"; and Hendrik S. Houthakker, "Commentaries."

21. L. N. Rangarajan, *Commodity Conflict,* Ch. 4 presents an overview of this issue in North-South commodity trade.

22. Sidney Dell, "Conditionality: The Political Economy of Overkill," pp. 32–33.

23. Peter Alexis Gourevitch, "Breaking with Orthodoxy: the politics of economic policy responses to the Depression of the 1930s," p. 96.

24. Stephen D. Krasner, *Defending the National Interest.*

25. John Gerard Ruggie, "International regimes, transactions, and change: embedded liberalism in the postwar economic order," p. 399 (emphasis in the original), pp. 387 and 392, respectively.

26. Charles Lipson, "The transformation of trade: the sources and effects of regime change," p. 429.

27. Krasner, *Structural Conflict.*

28. Lipson, "The transformation of trade."

29. For a discussion of these and other migration issues, see Clark W. Reynolds, "The U.S. Mexican Labor Market of the Future."

30. See Wayne A. Cornelius, "Immigration, Mexican Development Policy, and the Future of U.S.-Mexican Relations."

31. Robert Gilpin, *U.S. Power and the Multinational Corporation.*

32. John Zysman, *Governments, Markets and Growth*, ch. 1.

33. Yoffie, *Power and Protectionism*, p. 46; Vinod K. Aggarwal, *Liberal Protectionism*, pp. 44–54; for a similar argument about trade management, see Susan Strange, "The Management of Surplus Capacity: Or How Does Theory Stand Up to Protectionism 1970s Style" and Susan Strange and Roger Tooze, ed., *The International Politics of Surplus Capacity*.

34. Samuelson, *Economics*, p. 387.

35. Hillman, *Nontarriff Agricultural Trade Barriers*, p. 2.

36. Wells, Jr., "The Product Life Cycle."

37. Daniel Orr, *Property, Markets, and Government Intervention*, p. 216.

38. Certainly the suspension of Cuba's U.S. sugar quota helped producers in less efficient countries. See also Rangarajan, *Commodity Conflict*, ch. 5.

39. See, for example, James Kurth, "The Political Consequences of the Product Cycle: Industrial History and Political Consequences"; for a comprehensive study of the trade side of import substitution industrialization, see Ian Little, Tibor Scitovsky, and Maurice Scott, *Industry and Trade in Some Developing Countries*.

40. Ralph Davis, *The Rise of the Atlantic Economies*; Immanuel Wallerstein, *The Modern World System*; Robert Gilpin, *U.S. Power and the Multinational Corporation*; Krasner, "State Power and the Structure of International Trade." Some oil producing states (members of the Organization of Petroleum Countries, OPEC), attempted to use their energy resources to lead the way to a new international economic order. They failed because they neither controlled the dynamics of the global energy market nor the Northern domestic economic policies which made it possible to live with high energy prices. The keys to oil prices thus lay out of their hands. OPEC increased its vulnerability with its initial success and not only was not able to change the structure of the international political economy, but also lost its ability to play a major role in the present structure.

41. Odell, "Latin American Trade Negotiations."

42. Yoffie, *Power and Protectionism*.

43. Krasner, *Defending the National Interest*; Rangarajan, *Commodity Conflict*; Sorenson, *International Trade Policy*; Hillman, *Nontarif Agricultural Trade Barriers*; Warley, "Western Trade"; James Kurth, "The Political Consequences of the Product Life Cycle"; Stephen D. Krasner, "United States Commercial and Monetary Policy: Unraveling the Paradox of External Strength and Internal Weakness."

44. Odell, "Latin American Trade Negotiations"; Yoffie, *Power and Protectionism*.

45. Peter Katzenstein, ed., *Between Power and Plenty*, and his *Small States in World Markets*.

46. See Suzanne D. Berger, ed., *Organizing Interests in Western Europe*; Guillermo O'Donnell, *Modernization and Bureaucratic-Authoritarianism*; David Collier, ed., *The New Authoritarianism in Latin America*.

47. Katzenstein, "Conclusion: Domestic Structures and Strategies of Foreign Economic Policy," and his *Small States;* Zysman, *Governments, Markets and Growth;* Alfred Stepan, *State and Society.*

48. Peter Alexis Gourevitch, "International Trade, Domestic Coalitions, and Liberty: Comparative Responses to the Crisis of 1873–1896," pp. 307–308.

49. Zysman, *Governments, Markets, and Growth;* Bela Belassa, *The Newly Industrializing Countries in the World Economy;* O'Donnell, *Modernization and Bureaucratic-Authoritarianism;* Chalmers Johnson, *MITI and the Japanese Miracle,* p. 315, respectively.

50. Staple theory is briefly summarized in Michael Roemer, *Fishing for Growth,* ch. 1; Albert O. Hirschman, *The Strategy of Economic Development.*

51. The original formulation of this thesis is found in Bo Anderson and James D. Cockcroft, "Control and Cooptation in Mexican Politics."

2. AGRIBUSINESS AND THE U.S.–MEXICO FRESH WINTER VEGETABLE TRADE

1. John H. Davis and Ray A. Goldberg, *A Concept of Agribusiness,* p. 3.

2. Interview with one of the AARC field inspectors, Culiacán, 1983.

3. Interview with Francisco Campaña, a grower who is also a seed producer, Culiacán, 1983.

4. Ray A. Goldberg, *Agribusiness Management for Developing Countries—Latin America* Ch. 2; Edward W. McLaughlin and Thomas R. Pierson, "The Fresh Fruit and Vegetable Marketing System," p. 9.

5. *The Packer,* January 16, 1982, p. 17B. A producer may utilize his own label within this relationship; see the story on Luis Saenz Unger in the same issue, p. 7B.

6. See the Treasury Department's report on the relationship between Elva Carlota Podesta R. and Río Vista Limited, February 15, 1979, U.S. Department of Commerce files.

7. *The Packer,* January 22, 1983.

8. Interview with Patrick J. McCrory, of Arnold and Porter, legal counsel for UNPH, Washington, D.C., 1981.

9. Cited in NACLA, *Harvest of Anger: Agro-Imperialism in Mexico's Northwest,* p. 13.

10. McLaughlin and Pierson, "The Fresh Fruit and Vegetable Marketing System," p. 10.

11. *Ibid.,* pp. 10–11; they cite (a) Produce Newark, Delaware; and (b) *Chain Store Age Supermarkets* (April 1979).

12. *Ibid.,* p. 13.

13. *Ibid.,* pp. 14–25.

14. Figures are for the 1977–78 season. UNPH, *VIII convención anual 1978,* table 5, p. 98.

15. Confidential interviews with two different brokers who worked for supermarket chains and a distributor, all in Nogales, Arizona, 1983.

16. *Ibid.*

17. Field notes, Nogales, Arizona, 1983.

18. Steven Sanderson, "Florida Tomatoes, U.S.-Mexican Relations, and the International Division of Labor," p. 32.

19. This information on growers' groups comes from the file compiled by the U.S. Department of the Treasury in the process of investigating the anti-dumping suit filed by Florida growers. I consulted it when it merged with the file of the U.S. Department of Commerce when jurisdiction was transferred; it represents perhaps the most valuable source of information on the structure of production in Sinaloa.

20. Interview, Manuel Ortega, Culiacán, 1979.

21. Interview with Rubén Meraz Figueroa, author of a book on credit for agriculture *(Criterios financieros sobre crédito agrícola)* which was published by CAADES, Culiacán, 1980.

22. Interview, Mario Haroldo Robles, general manager of the national union, Unión Nacional de Productores de Hortalizas (see ch. 7), Culiacán, 1979; Interview, Javier Rodriguez, Mexican Trade Institute (Instituto Mexicano de Comercio Exterior), Mexico City, 1981; Interviews conducted in 1983 at various distributorships in Nogales, Arizona, and examination of the files of the U.S. Department of Commerce (gathered for the investigation of the dumping suit discussed in ch. 9) linked individual producers with the distributorships they owned.

23. For example, Sanderson, "Florida Tomatoes." He in fact labels Arizona distributors as part of the "commercial element of the U.S. bourgeoisie" on p. 39; James Austin, *Agribusiness in Latin America*, pp. 250–253.

24. For example, Ruth Rama and Raúl Vigorito, *El complejo de frutas y legumbres en México*, pp. 153–154; NACLA, *Harvest of Anger*, p. 11; and F. H. Beck, "Como controla la agroindustria la producción de verduras en el noroeste de Mexico," p. 123.

25. Goldberg, *Agribusiness Management*, p. 83.

26. Leonidas P. Bill Emerson, Jr., *Preview of Mexico's Winter Vegetable Production for Export*, pp. 70–74.

27. Goldberg, *Agribusiness Management*, p. 22.

28. McLaughlin and Pierson, "The Fresh Fruit and Vegetable Marketing System," pp. 5–8.

29. G. A. Zepp, *U.S. Winter Fresh Tomato Price and Quantity Projections for 1985*, pp. 1–12.

30. For example, one study noted that during the years of the Bracero program, these workers provided 85 percent of the harvest labor in California tomatoes during the peak portion of the season. David Runsten and Phillip LeVeen, "Mechanization and Mexican Labor in California Agriculture," p. 37; see also pp. 22–29 for a discussion of immigrant labor in California agriculture.

31. Regional market shares from 1962–63 to 1973–74 are found in Ernest B. Smith, "Florida's and Mexico's Shares of the U.S. Fresh Winter Vegetable Market," *The Vegetable Situation* (February 1976) pp. 41–42.

32. Zepp, *U.S. Winter Fresh Tomato Price*, p. 12.

33. R. L. Simmons et al., *Mexican Competition for the U.S. Fresh Winter*

Vegetable Market, p. 11; Emerson, *Preview of Mexico's Winter Vegetable Production*, p. 5.

34. Emerson, *Preview of Mexico's Winter Vegetable Production*, passim.

35. *The Packer*, January 16, 1982.

36. USDA, Foreign Agricultural Service, Horticultural and Tropical Products, WANG DOC. NO. 1935H; internal document, June 13, 1983.

37. G. A. Zepp, "Trend and Outlook for Florida Tomato Competition," pp. 5–6.

38. Simmons et al, *Mexican Competition*, p. 42; see also Teunis DeBoon, "Influence of Trade Barriers: The Florida and Mexico Experience with Winter Cucumbers," cited in Ernest B. Smith and Chris O. Andrew, *Cucumber Production, Distribution, and Competition for the U.S. Market: A Southern State's Perspective*, Economic Information Report 97, Food and Resource Economics Department, University of Florida, Gainesville, and Economics, Statistics and Cooperatives Service, USDA, 1978.

39. G. A. Zepp and R. L. Simmons, *Producing Fresh Winter Vegetables in Florida and Mexico*, p. 10; R. L. Simmons and Carlos Pomareda, "Equilibrium Quantity and Timing of Mexican Vegetable Exports," pp. 477–478.

40. John R. Brooker and James L. Pearson, *The Winter Vegetable Fresh Tomato Industry*, p. 2.

41. Maury E. Bredahl et al., *Technical Change, Protectionism, and Market Structure*, pp. 35–38.

42. *Ibid.*

43. See table 6.3 in ch. 6.

44. *The Packer*, January 24, 1981 and January 16, 1982.

45. Zepp and Simmons, *Producing Fresh Winter Vegetables*, pp. 20–39.

46. *The Packer*, January 16, 1982.

47. *The Packer*, January 16, 1982; I would like to thank Paul Bush of *The Packer* and a group of investigators from the Universidad Autonoma de Sinaloa for pointing out the relationship between vegetable production and DEPRODIT.

48. Timothy G. Taylor, *Costs and Returns from Vegetable Crops in Florida*, pp. 9, 10, 13, 14, 18–23.

49. *Ibid.*

50. Edward V. Jesse and Aaron C. Johnson, Jr., *Effectiveness of Federal Marketing Orders for Fruits and Vegetables*, p. 3.

51. *Ibid.*, p. 27.

3. THE STATE-GROWER ALLIANCE: CONVERGENT AND DIVERGENT INTERESTS

1. For an interesting discussion, see John Ikenberry, "The State and Strategies of International Adjustment."

2. Peter Smith, *Labyrinths of Power*.

3. David R. Mares, "Explaining Choices of Development Strategies"; see

also Susan Kaufman Purcell, "Decision-Making in an Authoritarian Regime: Theoretical Implications from a Mexican Case Study," p. 30.

4. Albert O. Hirschman, "The Turn to Authoritarianism in Latin America."

5. Jorge I. Domínguez, "Introduction," pp. 10–11; Susan Kaufman Purcell and John F. H. Purcell, "State and Society in Mexico: Must a Stable Polity be Institutionalized?"

6. John F. H. Purcell and Susan Kaufman Purcell, "Mexican Business and Public Policy."

7. Alfred Stepan, *The State and Society*, p. 69. The major works on corporatism include Philippe C. Schmitter, "Still the Century of Corporatism?" and "Modes of Interest Intermediation and Models of Societal Change in Western Europe"; and Peter J. Katzenstein, *Small States*.

8. Schmitter, "Modes of Interest Intermediation," p. 13.

9. David Collier, "Who Does What, to Whom and How," p. 493.

10. Peter J. Katzenstein, "Small European States" and *Small States*.

11. The cultural approach to corporatism is found in Howard Wiarda, ed., *Politics and Social Change in Latin America*.

12. Mares, "Explaining Choice of Development Strategy."

13. Ian Little, Tibor Scitovsky, and Maurice Scott, *Industry and Trade*.

14. Standard works on Mexico's political and economic history include Clark W. Reynolds, *The Mexican Economy*; Roger D. Hansen, *The Politics of Mexican Development*; Robert E. Scott, *Mexican Government in Transition*; L. Vincent Padgett, *The Mexican Political System*; Frank Brandenberg, *The Making of Modern Mexico*; José Luis Reyna and Richard S. Weinert, eds., *Authoritarianism in Mexico*; Raymond Vernon, *The Dilemma of Mexico's Development*; René Villarreal, *El desequilibrio externo en la industrialización de México (1929–1975)*; and the multiple volume series *Historia de la Revolución Mexicana*, coordinated by Luis González.

15. S. Kenneth Shwedel, "After the Fall."

16. *Ibid.*

17. *Ibid.*

18. *Ibid.*; Billie R. DeWalt, "Mexico's Second Green Revolution," analyzes the role of sorghum in Mexican agriculture.

19. David R. Mares, "The Evolution of U.S.-Mexican Agricultural Relations."

20. *Comercio Exterior* (March 1985), p. 298.

21. Leonides P. Bill Emerson, Jr., *Preview of Mexico's Vegetable Production for Export*, p. 13.

22. Banco Nacional de Comercio Exterior, "Las fluctuaciones de los precios internacionales del algodón y sus repercusiones en la economía mexicana," p. 230.

23. Interview with a confidential source at AARC, 1980.

24. This information comes from interviews with two of the farmers involved in these meetings: Juan José Villa, 1980; Emilio Gastelum Gaxiola, 1980.

25. Reynolds, *The Mexican Economy*, table 3.3, p. 98; table 3.5, p. 102; and table 3.6, p. 103.

26. Lorenzo Meyer, *El conflicto social y los gobiernos del Maximato*, p. 184.

27. Mexico, *PP*, "Ley sobre cámaras agrícolas, que en lo sucesivo se denominarán asociaciones agrícolas," and Francisco Javier Gaxiola, Jr., *El Presidente Rodríguez*, pp. 248–251.

28. Mexico, *PP*, "Reglamento de la ley de asociaciones agrícolas."

29. Interview with Francisco Campaña, 1980.

30. Confederación de Asociaciones Agrícolas del Estado de Sinaloa (CAADES), *Boletín Informativo* (July 1960), vol. 1, no. 1.

31. *Ibid.*

32. Wayne A. Cornelius, "Nation Building, Participation and Distribution," John F. W. Dulles, *Yesterday in Mexico*.

33. Interview with former (1964–1970) Sinaloa Governor Leopoldo Sánchez Celis, 1981.

34. Sinaloa Governor's Proclamation, "Decreto Num. 117: Ley de asociaciones agrícolas," *Periódico Oficial*, January 30, 1937, pp. 2–7.

35. Interviews with founding fathers Gastelum Gaxiola and Villa indicate that the early meetings of the Culiacán association were attended by 20 to 30 farmers.

36. Interview with Campaña.

37. Luis Medina, *Del cardenismo al avilacamachismo*, p. 57, note 61.

38. Interview with Sánchez Celis; Arturo Murillo M., *Los años no bastan*, p. 206.

39. Ingeniero Guillermo Liera B., *Sinaloa: estudio económico-social*, p. 99.

40. Reynolds, *The Mexican Economy*, p. 103.

41. *Ibid.*, p. 139.

42. Interview with Sánchez Celis.

43. Information on this series of events from interviews with Campaña and Sánchez Celis.

44. Sinaloa Governor's Proclamation, "Decreto Num. 112: Ley de asociaciones agrícolas," *Periódico Oficial*, August 23, 1954.

45. Interview with Campaña.

46. *Excelsior*, clipping in AARC Archives, periodical file, n.d.

47. Merilee S. Grindle, *Bureaucrats, Politicians, and Peasants in Mexico*, pp. 30–69.

48. Interview with Manuel Ortega, 1980.

49. Interview with Manuel Ortega, 1982.

50. Liera B., *Sinaloa*, p. 185.

51. Sinaloa Governor's Proclamation, "Decreto Num. 112."

52. AARC, "Informe sobre presidentes," *Boletín Bimestral* (1963), n.p.

53. Interviews with founding fathers Gastelum Gaxiola and Villa.

54. AARC, *Estatutos*, ch. 2.

55. Interviews with Manuel Ortega and Humberto Carrizoso, 1980.

56. Interview with Manuel Ortega, 1980.

57. AARC, "Informe de labores correspondientes al bienio 1977–1978," *Boletín Agrícola* (January–February 1979), 23 (1): 12. No figures could be located for the period before 1964, but in 1957 an association meeting was scheduled three times before finally convening with an attendance of 32, *Ibid.* "Informe" (August 1957) AARC Archives, presidential file.

58. SARH, Gerencia del Estado de Sinaloa, "Padrón de Usuarios, Distrito No. 10, Concentrado," Culiacán, Sinaloa.

59. Because of the sensitivity of this issue for AARC, my sources are confidential.

60. Interview with Rubén Meraz Figueroa, 1980.

61. Benito Tarriba Ungar, "Características generales de producción y mercadeo del tomate para exportación a los paises de Norteamerica en el Valle de Culiacán, Sinaloa."

62. *SS* January 16, 1961.

63. *El Debate de Culiacán*, AARC Archives, periodical file, n.d., 1978 file.

64. AARC, *Boletín Agrícola* (May and June 1961), 5(3):4; *ibid.* (July–December 1977), 21 (3-5): 10.

65. *Ibid.* (February 1962), 6(1):20.

66. *Ibid.* (November–December 1968), vol. 12, no. 6. These certificates, signed by the Mexican president, are designed to guarantee the security of tenure to those private farmers in possession of one, even in the face of ongoing land reform. See ch. 5 for a discussion of conflicts over land tenure in Sinaloa.

67. *Ibid.* (March–April 1972), vol. 16, no. 2.

68. *Ibid.* (January-February 1979), vol. 23, no. 1, reproduced in "Informe de labores correspondientes al bienio 1977–1978."

4. COMPETITION FOR WATER

1. There does not appear to exist any written history of the Culiacán branch of the Almada family; this information was obtained from interviews in Culiacán during 1979.

2. México, Secretaría de Recursos Hidráulicos (herein SRH), *Presa Adolfo López Mateos*, p. 8.

3. Adolfo Orive Alba, *La irrigación en México*, pp. 36–37.

4. Florencio Posadas Segura, "El proletariado agrícola en el estado de Sinaloa," pp. 8–9.

5. Mario Gil, *La conquista del Valle del Fuerte*, *passim*.

6. Cynthia Hewitt de Alcantara, *Modernizing Mexican Agriculture*, p. 18.

7. SRH, *Prontuario estadístico del estado de Sinaloa*, p. 185.

8. CAADES, *Análisis de la situación agrícola en el estado de Sinaloa*, 1965.

9. Báldemar Rubio et al., "Algunas conclusiones sobre la evolución del padrón de cultivos en Sinaloa."

10. Interview with Manuel Ortega, 1980.

11. See the discussion in Billie DeWalt, "Mexico's Second Green Revolution."

12. Statistics from SARH office in Culiacán.

13. *Ibid.*

14. Báldemar Rubio, et al., *1976: las invasiones de tierra en Sinaloa*, pp. 151, 153.

15. Sergio Reyes Osorio, et al., *Estructura agraria y desarrollo agrícola en México*, p. 884.

16. *Proceso* 2, November 13, 1976, cited in Carlos Arcos Cabrera and Gonzalo Varela Petito, "Los empresarios agrícolas y el estado Mexicano, 1964-1976," p. 15.

17. *Ibid.*

18. CAADES, *Análisis*, 12(87): 303.

19. Department of Economic Development, State of Sinaloa, wall display.

20. All of these figures are from SARH, "Producción y valor de los cultivos del ciclo agrícola: 1976-1977."

21. Emilio López Zamora, *El Agua, la tierra*, passim.

22. *Sol de Sinaloa*, n.d., AARC periodical Archives.

23. See Mexico, *PP*, "Ley federal de aguas de 30 de diciembre de 1971."

24. Arthur Maass and Raymond L. Anderson, . . . *and the Desert Shall Rejoice*, chs. 2-4.

25. SARH, Comité Directivo, Distrito de Riego Nos. 10 y 74, *Boletín del Comité Directivo Agrícola* (July and August 1965), 5(39):24.

26. "Acuerdos del Comité Directivo de Abril 21 de 1977," SARH Archives in Culiacán, Sinaloa.

27. "Acuerdos del Comité Directivo Agrícola," Acto #8, December 1978. SARH Archives in Culiacán, Sinaloa.

28. SARH, Comité Directivo, Distrito de Riego Nos. 10 y 74, *Boletín del Comité Directivo Agrícola* (July-December 1977), 15(102-103):19-20.

29. See CDA notes for 1978, SARH Archives in Culiacán, Sinaloa.

30. SARH, Comité Directivo, Distrito de Riego Nos. 10 y 74, *Boletín del Comité Directivo Agrícola* (September-October 1971), 11:75.

31. *Ibid.* (September and October 1968), 8(57):1.

32 Mexico *PP*, "Ley federal de aguas," Título Quinto.

33. See the discussion of illegal tampering with the *padrón* in the Mexicali Valley in López Zamora, *El agua, la tierra*, pp. 41-46.

34. Interviews with ejidatarios and canal keeper.

35. Interview with Ing. Salomón of SARH.

36. Reyes Osorio et al, *Estructura agraria*, pp. 461-464.

37. Mexico, *PP*, "Ley federal de aguas," Artículo Segundo:13.

38. Letter, "Comité Estatal Ejecutivo, Unión General de Obreros y Cam-

pesinos de México al C. Ing. Lázaro Ramos Esquer, Representante General de Agricultura y Recursos Hidráulicos en el Estado," November 15, 1979.

39. See the minutes of the CDA meetings in the SARH Archives, Culiacán, Sinaloa.

40. David Ronfeldt, *Atencingo*, ch. 8.

41. For a discussion of patron-client relationships, see Merilee S. Grindle, *Bureaucrats, Politicians, and Peasants*, pp. 30–34.

42. SARH, Comité Directivo Agrícola, Distrito de Riego Nos. 10 y 74, "Acuerdos . . ." 1978, SARH Archives, Culiacán, Sinaloa. Note that this water, since it is not yet controlled by a dam, tends to dry up just as the rice needs the final watering; water from the Culiacán and Humaya systems was explicitly placed off-limits to these producers.

43. For a discussion of the relationship between social mobility and political participation, see Samuel P. Huntington and Joan M. Nelson, *No Easy Choice*.

44. See Roger D. Hansen, *The Politics of Mexican Development*.

45. SARH, Comité Directivo, Distrito de Riego Nos. 10 y 74, "Comisión de Cuotas y Presupuestos," SARH Archives in Culiacán, Sinaloa.

46. SARH, Gerencia del Estado de Sinaloa, "Producción y valor."

47. AARC, *Boletín Agrícola* (July–December 1977), 21 (3-5):8.

48. SARH, Comité Directivo, Distrito de Riego Nos. 10 y 74, "Acuerdos del Comité Directivo Agrícola," Acta 16, July 8, 1976.

49. Banco Nacional de México, "Planeación en el campo," in *Exámen de la situación económica de México* (June 1978), 54(631): 263.

5. ACCESS TO LAND

1. *Sol de Sinaloa* (herein *SS*), February 14, 1958.

2. Atilano Bon Bustamante, president, AARC, "Informe de labores que rinde el presidente de la asociación de agricultores" (March 16, 1958).

3. *SS*, March 9, 1958.

4. *SS*, April 2, 1958. A similar process took place with respect to the distribution of lands expropriated in Cananea, Sonora (the other half of UGOCM's policy for collective action in 1958), where CNC members received the benefits of actions which the UGOCM paid for. Sergio Reyes Osorio et al., *Estructura Agraria*, p. 505.

5. *SS*, April 12, 1958.

6. *Ibid*.

7. *SS*, May 5, 1958.

8. *SS*, April 19 and 22, 1958.

9. *SS*, January 8, 1959.

10. *SS*, February 8, 1959.

11. *SS*, July 28, 1959.

12. *SS*, August 9, 1959.

13. Rosa Elena Montes de Oca, "The State and the Peasants"; Armando Bartra, "Seis años de lucha campesina."

14. Carlos Arcos Cabrera and Gonzalo Varela Petito, "Los empresarios agrícolas," pp. 138–139, and Steven Sanderson, *Agrarian Populism and the Mexican State*, pp. 187–190. Sanderson makes no mention of the UGOCM occupations.

15. See the discussion of this case in Arcos Cabrera and Varela Petito, "Los empresarios agrícolas," pp. 144–146.

16. Báldemar Rubio et al., *1976: Las invasiones de tierra*, p. 29.

17. CAADES, *La defensa de la tierra*, p. 3.

18. *Ibid.*, pp. 7, 8, 11, and 17; Rubio, et al., *1976: Las invasiones de tierra*, pp. 30–31.

19. Rubio et al., *1976: Las invasiones de tierra*, p. 46.

20. *Ibid.*, p. 78.

21. *Ibid.*, pp. 86–87.

22. *Ibid.*, pp. 104–105; *Tribuna del yaqui*, September 5–8, 1976, cited in Arcos Cabrera and Varela Petito, "Los empresarios agrícolas," p. 162.

23. Rubio et al, *1976: Las invasiones de tierra*, pp. 104–105.

24. *Ibid.*, p. 118.

25. *Excelsior*, November 27, 1976.

26. Rubio et al., *1976: Las invasiones de tierra*, pp. 120–121, lists 5,600 hectares for the CNC, 2,571 hectares for the UGOCM, and 1,303 hectares for the CCI, which only total 9,474 hectares.

27. Sanderson, *Agrarian Populism*, p. 199.

28. Lázaro Rubio Félix, *Cuando tomamos la tierra*, pp. 99–100.

29. *Ibid.*, pp. 100, 103.

30. *Ibid.*, pp. 107, 116.

31. *Excelsior*, April 1, 3, 4, 1957.

32. Rubio Félix, *Cuando tomamos la tierra*, pp. 104–129.

33. Of the 81 only 47 had been officially censused, indicating 3,382 applicants in these petitions. *Ibid.*, pp. 117–118.

34. Karl Schmitt, *Communism in Mexico*, p. 180.

35. Rubio Félix, *Cuando tomamos la tierra*, p. 129.

36. *Ibid.*, p. 133.

37. *SS*, January 31, 1958.

38. *SS*, February 2, 1958.

39. Rubio Félix, *Cuando tomamos la tierra*, pp. 158–166, 173; see also *SS*, February 11, 1958.

40. *SS*, July 14 and August 27, 1958.

41. *SS*, September 2, 1958; López had been jailed along with other UGOCM leaders for their role in the land occupations in Cananea, Sonora.

42. *SS*, March 3 and 4, 1959.

43. *SS*, March 5, 1959.

44. *SS*, March 3 and 6–10, 1959.

45. *SS*, July 25 and 26, 1959.

46. *SS*, July 30 and August 9, 1959; on the exclusivity of rights, see September 8, 1959.

47. *SS*, December 6, 1959.

48. *SS*, October 21, 1959.

49. *SS*, January 30, 1959.

50. *SS*, March through October 1960.

51. Moisés González Navarro, *La confederación nacional campesina*, p. 157; Reyes Osorio, *Estructura agraria*, p. 632.

52. For a discussion of the Pacto de Ocampo, see Montes de Oca, "The State and the Peasants."

53. *Noroeste*, February 18, 1976.

54. See Rubio et al., *1976: las invasiones de tierra*, p. 69, and fig. 1.

55. *Ibid.*, pp. 69, 78–79, 105–106; *Diario de Culiacán*, July 24, 1976; and *Noroeste*, October 8, 1976.

56. *SS*, January 25, 1958.

57. *SS*, January 28, 1958.

58. *SS*, February 2, 1958.

59. *Ibid.*

60. *Ibid.*

61. *SS*, February 12, 1958.

62. *SS*, February 13, 1958.

63. *Ibid.*

64. *SS*, February 14, 1958.

65. *SS*, February 15, 1958.

66. *SS*, February 14, 1958.

67. Bon Bustamante, "Informe de labores," 1958. At the then current exchange rate of 12.50:1 this equaled U.S.$120,000.

68. *SS*, October 3 and 22, 1959.

69. *SS*, November 18, 1959.

70. *Proceso #2*, November 13, 1976, cited in Arcos Cabrera and Varela Petito, "Los empresarios agrícolas," p. 15.

71. AARC, *Boletín Mensual* (April 1964), 2(12):14; CAADES, *Análisis de la situación agrícola*, February 15, 1967, p. 84.

72. *SS*, July 29, 1969.

73. *SS*, July 10, 1971; in December the Liga also called for such investigations.

74. *SS*, December 7, 1969.

75. *SS*, March 11, 1970.

76. Rubio et al., *1976: Las invasiones de tierra*, p. 32.

77. *Ibid.*, p. 39.

78. *Debate de Culiacán*, June 8, 1976; *Noroeste*, June 8, 1976.

79. Rubio et al., *1976: Las invasiones de tierra*, pp. 98–99.

80. *Ibid.*, p. 41.

81. Rubio et al., *1976: Las invasiones de tierra*, pp. 39, 40, 42, 46.

82. *Ibid.*, p. 51.

83. *Ibid.*
84. *SS*, February 22, 1976.
85. Rubio et al., *1976: Las invasiones de tierra*, p. 65.
86. *Noroeste*, June 8, 1976; *SS*, June 23, 1976.
87. *Noroeste*, July 9, 1976; *Debate de Culiacán*, June 14, 1976.
88. Rubio et al., *1976: Las invasiones de tierra*, pp. 96–98.
89. *Ibid.*, p. 104.
90. *Noroeste*, November 16, 1976.
91. Gustavo Esteva et al., *La batalla en el México rural*, table 8, pp. 230–231. Only 64 percent of lands formally distributed between 1935 and 1976 have actually been turned over to the campesinos at all; those who receive their lands the same day would be a small subset of the actual beneficiaries.
92. CAADES, *La defensa de la tierra*, pp. 7–8.
93. Rubio et al., *1976: Las invasiones de la tierra*, p. 32.
94. *Noroeste*, February 28, 1976.
95. Rubio et al., *1976: Las invasiones de la tierra*, p. 60.
96. Sanderson, *Agrarian Populism*, p. 192.
97. Rubio et al., *1976: Las invasiones de la tierra*, pp. 66–68.
98. *Ibid.*, pp. 102–103.
99. *Ibid.* These authors claim the SRA and Pacto de Ocampo leaders rejected this solution. While that may have been the case, had President Echeverría wanted to accept the offer, these representatives would have obviously gone along.
100. *Noroeste*, November 15, 1976.
101. *SS*, November 16, 1976.
102. See the analysis in David R. Mares, "Explaining Choice of Development Strategies."

6. MANAGING LABOR COSTS

1. Voss, *On the Periphery of Nineteenth Century Mexico.*
2. Posadas Segura, "El proletariado agrícola," pp. 10 and 40.
3. For an example, see "Confederación de Asociaciones Agrícolas del Estado de Sinaloa to Asociación Agrícola del Río Culiacán," December 6, 1966. AARC Archives.
4. Posadas Segura, "El proletariado," p. 131. He also lists a cotton-cotton cycle (Guasave–Ciudad Obregón–Mexicali), but omitted Mexicali in the tomato-cotton cycle. See also Carlota Botey, J. L. Heredia, and M. Zepeda, *Los jornaleros agrícolas migratorios: una solución organizativa* (Mexico: Secretaría de Reforma Agraria, 1975), summarized in Luisa Paré, *El proletariado agrícola en México*, pp. 109–121.
5. SRH, *Prontuario estadístico del estado de Sinaloa*, p. 106 For a discussion of the problem of counting jornaleros at the national level, see Reyes Osorio, *Estructura agraria*, pp. 333–346, and Altimar, "La medición de la población económicamente activa en México, 1950–1970."

6. CAADES, "Estudio socio-económico de los trabajadores estacionales del campo en el Valle de Culiacán—la vivienda, un problema específico," *Análisis de la situación agrícola* (January–February 1975), 13(93):50–59; Posadas Segura, "El proletariado agrícola," pp. 104–106; see also his "Trabajo y producción de los proletarios agrícolas migratorios en Sinaloa."

7. Sergio Reyes Osorio et al., *Estructura agraria y desarrollo agrícola en México*, p. 343.

8. Bartra, *Notas sobre la cuestión campesina: México, 1970–1976*, p. 41.

9. Francisco Schnabel, "Vivienda transitoria para trabajadores migrantes del campo," *Vivienda* (Mexico: INFONAVIT, 1976), pp. 4–5, cited in Posadas Segura, "El proletariado," pp. 123–124.

10. Kevin Jay Middlebrook, "The Political Economy of Mexican Organized Labor, 1940–1979," p. 137, m. 42.

11. AARC, "Informe de labores," January 27, 1957, p. 6. AARC Archives.

12. *SS*, May 8, 9, August 8, and September 1, 1958.

13. *SS*, December 22, 1958.

14. *SS*, for example January 1 and 26, 1959.

15. *SS*, May 2, 23, 1958.

16. Vizcarra demanded that contracts be signed with his FTS-affiliated union directly and not with the FTS. *SS*, January 9, 1959.

17. *SS*, August 8, September 1, 1958. AARC requested that CAADES intervene before the governor on this matter as early as July 15, 1957. AARC, "Informe de labores," August 11, 1957, p. 11. AARC Archives, president's file.

18. *SS*, November 14, 1958.

19. *SS*, January 24, 1959.

20. *SS*, December 10, 1958.

21. *Ibid.*

22. *SS*, January 9, 1958.

23. *SS*, January 6, 1959.

24. *SS*, January 26–28, 1959.

25. *SS*, February 3, 1959.

26. *SS*, February 5, 1959.

27. For example, José Luis Reyna and Raul Trejo Delarbe, eds., *La clase obrera en la historia de México*.

28. "Sindicato de Obreros Legumbreros y Conexos to Sr. Luis Gaxiola Clouthier, Presidente, Asociación de Agricultores del Río Culiacán," September 5, 1962. AARC Archives.

29. *Excelsior*, February 22, 1979.

30. Jorge Delgado Cortés and Benito García, "Registro Cronológico de las Luchas de los Obreros Agrícolas Migratorios en Sinaloa," p. 34.

31. *Ibid.*, p. 39.

32. Interview with Felipe González Gurrola, Legal Adviser, FIOACS, 1983, and corroborated with confidential interviews with grower representatives in 1979 and 1983.

33. CAADES, *Boletín Informativo* (February–March 1958).

34. *SS*, May 3 and 18, 1958, respectively.

35. *SS*, January 4, 1959.

36. *Ibid.*

37. *SS*, January 6, 1959.

38. *SS*, January 21, 22, 25, 26, 27 and February 22, 1959.

39. *SS*, January 30, 1959.

40. *SS*, January 31, 1959.

41. *SS*, February 2, 1959.

42. *SS*, February 11, 1959.

43. *SS*, February 16, 1959.

44. See chapter 7 and *SS*, March 4, 1959.

45. *SS*, November 19, 1959.

46. AARC,"Informe de labores," February 15, 1959, p. 14; AARC Archives, presidential file.

47. *SS*, November 29, 1961.

48. AARC Archives contained these documents.

49. *Excelsior*, February 22, 1979.

50. Confidential interview, 1979.

51. *SS*, September 21, 1978.

52. *SS*, June 15, 1978; *El Noroeste*, December 17, 1978; see also January 8 and May 23, 1979; *El Diario de Culiacán*, January 1 and May 6, 1979.

53. *El Debate de Culiacán*, October 2, 1979.

54. Interview, Humberto Carrizosa, Acting Chief of the Department of Economic Studies, AARC, 1983.

55. *SS*, February 2, 1979.

56. *Ibid.* February 4, 1980.

57. Interview with Felipe González Gurrola, Legal Advisor, FIOACS, 1983.

58. G. A. Zepp and R. L. Simmons, *Producing Fresh Winter Vegetables in Florida and Mexico*, p. 10.

59. *The Packer*, January 24, 1981.

60. *SS*, April 24, 1958.

61. *SS*, January 9, 1958; on January 10, Vizcarra said he was not a UGOCMista, but he did not say he had never been one. His reputation twenty years later was so tainted that interviews with both the Culiacán branch of the FTS rural union and the community in which he lived turned up only vague name recognition, despite his notoriety in the late 1950s and early 1960s.

62. Interview with Francisco Campaña, 1983.

63. Interview in the offices of the Sindicato Nacional de Trabajadores Asalariados del Campo, Culiacán, 1979.

64. *SS*, November 11 and December 3 and 10, 1958.

65. *SS*, December 10, 1958.

66. *SS*, March 4, 1959.

67. *SS*, November 19, 22, 1959.
68. *SS*, March 4, 1959.
69. *SS*, January 20, 1959.
70. *SS*, January 20, 30 and February 13, 14, 16, 24, 1960.
71. *SS*, April 24, 1960.
72. *SS*, May 4, 7, 11, 13, 1960.
73. *SS*, November 16, 1961.
74. Luisa Paré, *El proletariado agrícola en México*, pp. 213–224.
75. Field observations by the author; interview with Antonio Quevedo, reporter for *El Noroeste*, 1983; and *Excelsior*, February 23, 1979.
76. *Excelsior*, February 23, 1979.
77. Interview with González Gurrola, 1983; *Excelsior*, February 22, 1979.
78. Interview with Quevedo, 1983.
79. Interview with Posadas Segura, 1983.
80. *SS*, August 8, 1958.
81. *SS*, January 31, 1959.
82. See, for example, *SS*, November 22, 1959.
83. Interview with Quevedo, 1983.
84. Interview with Posadas Segura, 1983; *Excelsior*, February 23, 1979.
85. For example, *Proceso #365* (October 31, 1983), pp. 6–11.
86. Interviews with Carrizosa and Quevedo, 1983.
87. Interviews with Carrizosa and González Gurrola, 1983.

7. SUBORDINATION OF FOREIGN INVESTMENT

1. The quote is from Steven Sanderson, "Florida Tomatoes, U.S.-Mexican Relations, and the International Division of Labor," p. 39.
2. Gil, *La conquista del Valle del Fuerte*, pp. 165–184.
3. Emerson, Jr., *Preview of Mexico's Winter Vegetable Production*, pp. 32–34.
4. CAADES, "Reglamento para la siembra, empaque, seleccion, tráfico y distribución de tomate, frutas, legumbres y verduras para el mercado de exportación que se produzcan en el estado de Sinaloa," *Boletín Informativo*, 1(11):10. This source does not indicate who initiated the CAADES effort, and interviews were also unsuccessful in determining its origin. Neither the AARC nor CAADES archives turned up a copy of the 1955 CAADES regulations which AARC approved, and interviews twenty-five years after the fact also proved useless on this point.
5. For example, *SS*, May 28, June 15 and 22, 1958.
6. AARC, *Boletín Agrícola* (January 1960), 4(1):13.
7. AARC Archives, Tomato File.
8. For example, *SS*, April 4, 1958, in which AARC is reported to have fined a grower 5,000 pesos for repeated violations of quality stipulations.
9. AARC, *Boletín Agrícola* (May–June 1961), 5(3):32.
10. AARC, *Boletín Agrícola*, May 9, 1957, 1(1):4.

11. *Ibid.*

12. *Ibid.* (June 1959), 3(20):7–8.

13. AARC, "Informe anual," 2d semester of 1961. AARC Archives.

14. Interview with Francisco Campaña, Culiacán, 1980.

15. UNPH, "Acta Constitutiva de la Unión Nacional de Productores de Hortalizas," 1961, p. 1.

16. *Ibid.*

17. *Ibid.*

18. UNPH, *IX Convención anual* (1979) pp. 2–7.

19. *Excelsior*, November 25, 1980.

20. AARC, "Informe anual," 2d semester of 1961, in which the president of AARC communicates to Culiacán growers that their strategic position is safeguarded and that the costs of regulating the market are being spread over a larger group.

21. "La producción de hortalizas en la república Mexicana" in AARC Archives, files (1960–1965).

22. Interview with Humberto Carrizosa, Culiacán, 1983.

23. Interview with Campaña, 1980.

24. UNPH, *X Convención Anual*, November 20–22, 1980, p. 130, for the Sinaloa share and AARC sources for information on the special fund. Note that this fund does not represent 100 percent of what is collected by the UNPH taxes on sales; public UNPH records do not disaggregate this figure, so it is difficult to tell the exact weight of the Sinaloa actions. But the threat this posed to the UNPH is clear if we take this as a warning by Sinaloa growers to other members of the organization.

25. AARC, *Boletín Agrícola* (April–May, 1961), 5(2–3):n.p.

26. *SS*, June 26, 1981.

27. AARC, *Boletín Agrícola*. "Informe de labores" (January 1961), vol. 5, no. 1.

28. *SS*, June 18, 1961.

29. AARC, *Boletín Agrícola* (May–June 1961), 5(3):34, and *SS*, June 26, 27, 1961. The newspaper reports that area would be reduced 45 percent, but AARC's bulletin reports that all growers would be limited to a maximum of 45 hectares.

30. Circular from AARC to tomato producers, dated March 27, 1962. AARC Archives; see also *SS*, March 28, 1962.

31. "Agencia General en Sinaloa, Agente General, Secretaría de Agricultura y Ganadería to Asociación de Agricultores del Río Culiacán," dated September 14, 1963. AARC Archives.

32. Minutes from AARC meeting of September 15, 1963 (AARC Archives), indicate that they requested an increase of 1,000 hectares of staked tomatoes to accommodate tomato growers who had not planted in the previous season. The request was also justified on the basis of economic efficiency, as Culiacán's production was reported to be the most efficient. The governor granted them an increase of 500 hectares; noted in "Informe de labores que por

conducto de su presidente, Señor Alfredo Careaga Cebreros, rinde el Consejo de Administración, 1963–64," AARC, *Boletín Agrícola* (January–February 1965), 9(1):11.

33. Article 1 of the 1963–64 program notes that its jurisdiction will be statewide with respect to area controls and national as regards quality controls. AARC Archives.

34. "Unión Nacional de Productores de Hortalizas to Confederación de Asociaciones Agrícolas del Estado de Sinaloa," July 20, 1967. CAADES Archives.

35. See, for example, AARC's complaints in "Asociación de Agricultores del Río Culiacán to Unión Nacional de Productores de Hortalizas," May 29, 1964. AARC Archives.

36. CAADES, "Estudio para determinar la superficie de siembra de tomate de exportación para el estado de Sinaloa, en la temporada 1967–68," *Análisis de la Situación Agrícola de Sinaloa*, n.d. 49:231–252.

37. CAADES, "Panorama Horticola 1967/68," *Análisis de la situación agrícola de Sinaloa*, n.d., 50:125. The concern over maintaining the formal existence of regulation until growers came to accept its desirability comes through clearly in a letter from CAADES to AARC in reference to the latter's dispute of certain quality controls. CAADES notes that the regulations are not perfect but that all try to make them the most efficient possible. CAADES then says, "We implore (rogamos) you to collaborate with us so that the idea that it is necessary to give the commission authority is generalized." Confederación de Asociaciones Agrícolas del Estado de Sinaloa to Asociación de Agricultores del Río Culiacán, February 9, 1967. AARC Archives.

38. AARC Archives.

39. *SS*, February 18, 1962.

40. *SS*, December 22, 1962.

41. Calculated from table 7.3.

42. "AARC to Sr. Julio Ernesto Teisser," dated October 25, 1961. AARC Archives, Tomato Files.

43. For individual limits, see *Boletín Agrícola* (May–June 1967), 11(3):59; for packinghouse limits, see *Boletín Agrícola* (September–October 1972), 16(5):380.

44. The number of groups is taken from notes of the "Junta de Delegados Legumbreros," dated August 20, 1965, in the AARC Archives; the number of packing sheds is from the *Boletín Agrícola* (January–February 1965), 9(1):10.

45. AARC, "Permisos de siembra de tomate, ciclo agrícola 67–68," cited in Carlos A. Castro Sanchez, "El tomate Sinaloense: el problema de restricción de sus exportaciones," undergraduate economics thesis, ITESM, 1969, cited by Jaime Benito Tarriba Unger, "Características generales de la producción y mercadeo de tomate para exportación a los paises de Norteamérica, en el Valle de Culiacán, Sin." Growers have become sophisticated about presenting the "correct" public image, leading them to, among other things, list all of the names of those people to whom production permits are granted,

rather than the actual producer. This fact, and the sensitive material to which both of these authors had access, gives these undergraduate theses an important place in any analysis of winter vegetable production for export.

46. Glenn D. Meyers, "Centralized Planning of Mexican Vegetable Exports and Its Impact on the U.S. Market and the Florida Industry," May 15, 1978. Draft prepared for the Florida growers in the dumping suit; *passim*, but see especially pp. 18–22; I would like to thank Linda Jo Froman for providing me with a copy of this study.

47. UNPH, "Circular muy urgente a nuestros organismos miembros productores de tomate, pepino y chiles bell pepper," n.d. AARC Archives.

48. "Comisión de Control para Exportaciones de Tomate." AARC Archives.

49. AARC, *Boletín Agrícola* (January–February 1968), 12(1):2,3; and "Valle Culiacán: producción de tomate por temporada," September 15, 1967. AARC Archives.

50. AARC, *Boletín Agrícola* (July–August 1963), 7(4):12, 19–21.

51. Calculated from AARC, *Boletín Agrícola* (July–August, 1964), 8(4):30.

52. Simmons et al., *Mexican Competition for the U.S. Fresh Winter Vegetable Market*, p. 20.

53. Letter, CAADES to AARC, dated January 10, 1962. AARC Archives. See also *SS*, March 6, 1961.

54. *SS*, December 2, 1961.

55. That the treasurer of the Sinaloa government participated in such a fashion is suggested by the letter he sent to customs agents once CAADES rescinded its policy on the company. He instructs the agents that they should now ignore whether or not the cargo complies with the permits of the agricultural associations or the company. "Tesorero General del Estado to Inspectores de Hacienda, El Espinal, Elota, Sinaloa," April 6, 1962. AARC Archives.

56. The AARC Archives contain many letters from CAADES to AARC and AARC to individual growers requesting that they abide by the agreement and sign contracts with the company.

57. CAADES circular, dated February 19, 1962. AARC Archives.

58. *Diario Oficial*, June 7, 1971, p. 6.

59. For example, CAADES circular No. 29, dated February 19, 1972. AARC Archives.

60. For example, Glenn D. Meyers, "Centralized Planning," pp. 18–22, 101–107.

61. Confidential interview with an AARC official, Culiacán, 1983.

62. Calculated from a confidential internal CAADES document.

63. *Ibid.*

64. "El consumo de tomate en los Estados Unidos de Norteamerica," 1965. AARC Archives.

65. CAADES, *Análisis de la situación agrícola de Sinaloa* (September 1964), 2(17):5.

66. "Unión Nacional de Productores de Hortalizas to Asociación de Agricultores del Río Culiacán," July 19, 1966. AARC Archives.

67. UNPH, *Asamblea General Ordinaria* (1968), p. 49. UNPH Archives.

68. Interview with Ariel García Mascareño, Marketing Manager, UNPH. Culiacán, 1979.

69. Food Business Associates, "Nature's Winter Sunshine from Sunny Mexico," p. 113.

70. *The Packer*, January 16, 1982, p. 17B.

71. For example, UNPH, *XII Convención anual* (1982), p. 31.

72. Confidential interview with a manager for a grower-owned distributor, Nogales, Arizona, 1983.

73. See the stories on Brownie Brokerage and FoodSource in *The Packer*, January 22, 1983. The latter has set up a Mexican affiliate, FoodSource, S.A., to promote its controlled-atmosphere process for seagoing containers.

74. AARC, *Boletín Agrícola* (January–February 1972), 16(1):198.

75. *The Packer*, January 22, 1983, p. 7B.

76. UNPH, *XII Convención anual* (1982), pp. 30, 33.

77. Interview with Ariel García Mascareño.

78. Richard L. Simmons, "Costs of Production and Marketing Staked Tomatoes, Bell Peppers, Cucumbers and Eggplant in Culiacán, 1978–1979," pp. 12 and 49, respectively.

79. AARC, "Circular," dated November 30, 1960, which informs growers that the comission in charge of the domestic market set a minimum price for sales. AARC Archives.

80. Confidential interview, Culiacán, 1983.

81. "México: Mercado Potencial de Hortalizas Frescas," presented at the Asamblea General Ordinaria, UNPH, Guadalajara, October 1965; reprinted in *Boletín Agrícola* (September–October, 1965), 9(5):41–44; see also "Solución a la ponencia México: mercado potencial de hortalizas," April 1965. AARC Archives.

82. "Informe especial de problemas que observamos de interés únicamente para los horticultores, en la comisión que se nos confirió de 26 de abril al 7 de mayo de 1967"; AARC Archives; also AARC, *Boletín Agrícola* (January–February 1968), 12(1):213.

83. See the notes from the "Junta de Delegados Legumbreros," dated November 23, 1967, and "Circular No. 9: reglamento para empaque y embarque de hortalizas para consumo nacional," dated January 30, 1969, but noting that the regulations had been in effect since December 28, 1967. AARC Archives.

84. "Informe de Labores . . . correspondiente al año de 1969," reprinted in AARC, *Boletín Agrícola* (January–February 1970), 14(1):208. AARC, "Circular #7: a los jefes de grupos legumbreros," dated January 22, 1969; see point no. 9. AARC Archives.

85. AARC, "Circular #7," point no. 7.

86. "Informe que rinde la comisión sobre las gestiones realizadas en la

Cd. de Guasave, Sinaloa, el día 5 de febrero de 1969, con los representantes legumbreros de la AARSP." AARC Archives.

87. "Acuerdos tomados por el comité regulador de tomate para consumo nacional en reunión celebrada en la AARC el día 12 de febrero de 1969 a las 16 horas." AARC Archives.

88. *The Packer*, January 16, 1982.

89. *Ibid.*

90. For example, *Noroeste*, January 15, 1979, for the remarks of the president of the committee which regulates Sinaloa's supply to the national market.

91. UNPH, *XII Convención Anual* (November 1982).

92. This information comes from an informal discussion with an official of the Banco Nacional de México, which was asked to study the potential in the Mexican market.

93. *SS*, June 15, 1958.

94. "Reglamento para el envió de tomate 'pinto' y 'verde' a Estados Unidos y Canada," reprinted in AARC, *Boletín Agrícola* (July–August 1963), 7(4):21.

95. Letter, "West Mexico Vegetable Distributors Association to Asociación de Agricultores del Río Culiacán," May 4, 1968. AARC Archives.

96. *SS*, February 6, 1961.

97. AARC, *Boletín Mensual*, Special Number (March 1965), p. 18.

98. Interview with Francisco Campaña; AARC, *Boletín Informativo*, (February–March 1958), 1(10):7, 38; CAADES, *Boletín Mensual* (April 1964), 2(12):17.

99. *SS*, February 6, 1962.

100. A letter from AARC to the national export bank notes that "in some cases" this is so. "Asociación de Agricultores del Río Culiacán to Banco Nacional de Comercio Exterior," dated February 20, 1962. AARC Archives. The local press also contains reports of growers on bank boards of directors; in only one case did I notice reference to a bank project or group which watches over the vegetable export market. *SS*, February 27, 1962.

101. Conversation with Maury Bredahl, author of one of the major agricultural economic studies of the winter vegetable market, who cited a dinner conversation with a manager who had been with the company since its inception.

102. See the AARC document, "Gerencial general pone a consideración de la Asamblea Especializado de Legumbreros de la CAADES el siguiente: proyecto de reglamento de financiamiento, siembra, selección, empaque, embarque, tráfico, cruce y distribución de hortalizas de exportación, para el estado de Sinaloa," dated 1965. AARC Archives, "Hortalizas Generales, 1960–1965" file.

103. "Bases generales para la distribución de las superficies de tomate en el Valle de Culiacán en la temporada 1966–67," Point No. 10. AARC Archives.

104. "Reglamento para superficies, siembra, solicitudes, empaque, em-

barque y cruce de hortalizas," Ch. 2, Article 3.f; reprinted in AARC, *Boletín Agrícola* (July–August 1968), 12(4):356–359.

105. See the accusation by a high UNPH official in *SS*, April 21, 1979.

106. In the first tomato war U.S. distributors attempted to limit their contributions to one-third that of Mexican growers, which the UNPH rejected. Letters: "West Mexico Vegetable Distributors Association to Unión Nacional de Productores de Hortalizas," August 7, 1969, and "Unión Nacional de Productores de Hortalizas to West Mexico Vegetable Distributors Association," August 11, 1969. AARC Archives.

107. See the proposal by distributors in the letter "West Mexico Vegetable Distributors Association to Asociación de Agricultores del Río Culiacán," June 18, 1969, and the reply by CAADES in the letter, "Confederación de Asociaciones Agrícolas del Estado Sinaloa to West Mexico Vegetable Distributors Association," July 3, 1969. AARC Archives.

108. *The Packer*, January 16, 1982.

109. *Ibid.*, January 22, 1983.

110. See UNPH, "Circular a organismos miembros," dated October 12, 1967, which mentions both the UNPH to the ejido credit bank (Banco Nacional de Crédito Ejidal) letter of August 9, 1967, and the bank's reply of September 27, 1967; Ref: (25) Gerencia Num:18976. AARC Archives.

111. Ray A. Goldberg, *Agribusiness Management for Developing Countries*, p. 83.

112. Calculated from Maury Bredahl et al., *Technical Change, Protectionism, and Market Structure*, pp. 105, 110–113, for the five major vegetables.

113. *SS*, October 23, 1978.

114. Tarriba Unger, "Características generales de producción y mercadeo," p. 26.

115. *The Packer*, January 22, 1983.

8. TRANSNATIONAL ALLIANCES IN INTERNATIONAL TRADE

1. Robert O. Keohane and Joseph S. Nye, Jr., eds., "Transnational Relations and World Politics."

2. AARC, *Boletín Agrícola* (May–June 1979), 23(3):57.

3. Florida Tomato Committee (FTC), *Annual Report, 1968–1969*, p. 1.

4. Senator Spessard L. Holland, United States Senate Committee on Agriculture and Forestry, in a letter to J. S. Peters, FTC, June 3, 1969. AARC Archives, Tomato file.

5. *Ibid.*

6. *Federal Register* (January 4, 1969), 34(3):128.

7. U.S. District Court for the District of Columbia, *Stipulation and Order of Dismissal Without Prejudice*, September 18, 1975.

8. FTC, *Annual Report, 1973–1974*, p. 1.

9. Communication with Linda Jo Froman, Harvard Business School.

10. Confidential interview with Department of Commerce official.

11. *Ibid.*

12. Ray A. Goldberg, *Agribusiness Management for Developing Countries*, pp. 344–345.

13. Food Business Associates, "Mejorando el mercado," p. 180.

14. Food Business Associates, *UNPH 1979 Promotion Handbook*, p. 111.

15. Of course, the United States itself has not always followed the spirit of the laws it sets to govern imports into its own economy when the issue is U.S. exports to the world economy; thus the cotton export subsidies utilized by the United States in the 1950s clearly constituted U.S. dumping on the world market. The cotton case is discussed in David R. Mares, "The Evolution of U.S.-Mexican Agricultural Relations."

16. Masaoka-Ishikawa and Associates in a letter to West Mexico Vegetable Distributors Association, February 24, 1969. AARC Archives, Tomato file.

17. Ingeniero Manuel J. Clouthier, President, AARC, in a letter to U.S. Senator Barry Goldwater, February 10, 1969. AARC Archives, Tomato file.

18. Masaoka-Ishikawa and Associates in a letter to West Mexico Vegetable Distributors Association, May 28, 1970. AARC Archives, Tomato file.

19. *Ibid.*

20. Florida Tomato Committee, "News Release," February 17, 1969. AARC Archives, Tomato file.

21. *SS*, March 11, 1972.

22. U.S. House of Representatives, 91st Congress, 1st Session, H.R. 9656, March 27, 1969, and 93d Congress, 1st Session, H.R. 5413, March 8, 1973, respectively.

23. U.S. House of Representatives, Committee on Ways and Means, *Certain Tariff and Trade Bills, Hearings*, 96th Congress, 2d Session, March 17, April 17, May 8, 1980, pp. 336–339.

24. *New York Times*, June 15, 1979, pp. D1, 3.

25. *Ibid.*

26. West Mexico Vegetable Distributors Association in a letter to Unión Nacional de Productores de Hortalizas, April 29, 1969. AARC Archives, Tomato file.

27. Food Business Associates, *UNPH 1979 Promotional Handbook*, p. 111.

28. FTC, *Annual Report, 1971–1972*, p. 11.

29. Fred Kahn, "Legal and Analytical Options in the Determination of Less Than Fair Value Sales of Certain Fresh Winter Vegetables from Mexico."

30. *Wall Street Journal*, July 19, 1979, p. 40.

31. *Ibid.*, and *New York Times*, September 9, 1979, pp. 1, 52.

32. Letter, "Memorandum al Sr. Lic. José López Portillo, Presidente de la República, sobre la Acusación de 'Dumping' a las Hortalizas de México en los Estados Unidos," June 1979. Reprinted in UNPH, *IX Convención Anual*

(November 1979), pp. 12–24; and "Memo of Conversation," dated June 19, 1979. U.S. Department of Commerce, Public Files, respectively.

33. *Wall Street Journal*, July 19, 1979, p. 40.

34. "Memorandum al Sr. Lic. José López Portillo."

35. Richard L. Simmons, "A Comparison of Prices of Winter Vegetables."

36. Kahn, "Legal and Analytical Options in the Determination of Less Than Fair Value Sales."

37. "Brief of Respondents Unión Nacional de Productores de Hortalizas and West Mexico Vegetable Distributors Association in the United States Department of Commerce," p. 11.

38. *Ibid.*

39. Professors Houthakker and Nordhous were former advisors on agricultural economics to the U.S. president in their capacities as members of the Presidential Council of Advisors; Professor King was president of the American Agricultural Economics Association.

40. "Exhibits to Brief of Respondents Unión Nacional de Productores de Hortalizas and West Mexico Vegetable Distributors Association."

41. "Rebuttal Brief of Respondents."

42. *Ibid.*, pp. 12–13.

43. FTC, *Annual Report, 1968–1969*, pp. XVI, XXXV–XXXVI.

44. *Ibid.*

45. FTC, *Annual Report, 1970–1971.*

46. U.S. Court of Appeals, District of Columbia Circuit, *Walter Holm & Company et al., Appellants, v. Clifford M. Hardin, Individually and as Secretary of the United States Department of Agriculture et al."* (No. 24848). Argued January 26, 1969. Decided March 19, 1969; cited in *Federal Register,* Part I (April 5, 1972), 37(65):6857–6867.

47. *Federal Register*, 37(65).

48. U.S. District Court for the District of Columbia (No. 2142-72) *Consumers Union of United States, Inc., Consumer Federation of California, Consumer Federation of Illinois, and Consumer Association of the District of Columbia v. the Honorable Earl L. Butz, Secretary of the United States Department of Agriculture, Richard E. Lyng, Ervin L. Peterson, and Floyd Hedlund.* In the same court (No. 2154-72) *Coast Marketing Co., William S. Wright, Inc., West Mexico Vegetable Distributors Association v. same defendants.*

49. FTC, *Annual Report, 1972–1973*, p. VII.

50. FTC, *Annual Report, 1973–1974*, p. 1.

51. U.S. District Court for the District of Columbia (No. 2142-72).

52. Interview with Patrick J. McCrory of Washington law firm Arnold and Porter.

53. John H. Shenefield, Assistant Attorney General, Antitrust Division, Department of Justice, in a letter to Robert H. Mundhein, Esquire, General Counsel, Department of the Treasury, July 16, 1979. U.S. Department of Commerce Archives.

54. See David R. Mares, "La política norteamericana en el comercio de hortalizas" and David R. Mares, "México y los Estados Unidos."

55. See Mares, "Mexico y los Estados Unidos."

56. Mike M. Masaoka, Masaoka-Ishikawa, in a letter to Sr. Alfredo Careaga Cebreros, Presidente, Unión Nacional de Productores de Hortalizas, March 3, 1969. AARC Archives, Tomato file.

57. *Ibid.*

58. Masaoka-Ishikawa and Associates, in a letter to Mr. A. B. Conrad, Secretary-Manager, West Mexico Vegetable Distributors Association, February 24, 1969. AARC Archives, Tomato file.

59. Untitled document. AARC Archives, Tomato file.

60. Letter, "Memorandum que presentan la Unión Nacional de Productores de Hortalizas, la Confederación de Asociaciones Agrícolas del Estado de Sinaloa y la Asociación de Agricultores del Río Culiacán a la Secretaría de Agricultura y Ganaderia, en relación a las restricciones impuestas a las importaciones de tomate por el Departamento de Agricultura de los Estados Unidos de Norteamerica," April 15, 1969. AARC Archives, Tomato file.

61. Fernando González Avila, Agente General en Sinaloa, Secretaría de Agricultura y Ganadería in a letter to C. Don Juan Gil Preciado, Secretario de Agricultura y Ganadería, January 12, 1969. AARC Archives, Tomato file.

62. *Ibid.*

63. "Informe de Lic. Margaín" (January 17, 1969). AARC Archives, Tomato file.

64. Secretaría de Agricultura y Ganadería in a letter to Agente General en Sinaloa, Secretaría de Agricultura y Ganadería, June 12, 1969. AARC Archives, Tomato file.

65. Embajador Lic. Hugo B. Margaín in a letter to Antonio Carrillo Flores, Secretario de Relaciones Exteriores, June 30, 1969. AARC Archives, Tomato file.

66. *Ibid.*

67. *Ibid.*

68. Juan Gil Preciado, Secretario de Agricultura y Ganadería, in a letter to Antonio Carrillo Flores, Secretario de Relaciones Exteriores, June 23, 1969. AARC Archives, Tomato file.

69. *SS*, November 10, 11, 15, 1969.

70. *SS*, October 23, 1969.

71. *SS*, November 11, 1969.

72. *Ibid.*

73. *SS*, November 23, 1969.

74. *SS*, November 27, 1969.

75. *SS*, December 4, 1969.

76. *SS*, March 7, 1970.

77. *SS*, April 18, 1970.

78. *SS*, July 3, 1970.

79. *SS*, July 6, 1970.

80. *SS*, July 18 and 19, 1970.

81. *SS*, July 20, 1970.

82. *Diario Oficial*, October 6, 1970, pp. 2–3.

83. U.S. House of Representatives, Committee on Foreign Affairs, *United States-Mexican Trade Relations, Hearings*, 92d Congress, Second Session, February 24, 1972, p. 2.

84. UNPH, *Boletín Bimestral #33*, pp. 1340, 1362, for 1978–1979 and personal communication from UNPH official for 1979–1980, 1980–1981.

85. See Mares, "México y los Estados Unidos" and "La política norteamericana."

86. UNPH, "Informe de labores, 1979," November 1979, p. 15. UNPH Archives.

87. On pressure from the Treasury, see the *New York Times*, June 15, 1979, pp. D1, 3, and the *Wall Street Journal*, July 19, 1979, p. 40; for the Special Trade Representative's role, see the *Washington Star*, July 20, 1979, pp. E10, 12; and for State's intervention with the growers, see the *New York Times*, September 9, 1979, pp. 1, 52; see also the *New York Times*, October 27, 1979, p. 29.

88. *Wall Street Journal*, July 19, 1979, p. 40.

89. *New York Times*, October 27, 1979, p. 29.

90. UNPH, "Informe de labores, 1979," p. 17. UNPH Archives.

91. *Ibid.*

92. *Ibid.*

9. PENETRATING THE INTERNATIONAL MARKET: SOME COMPARATIVE EVIDENCE

1. Krasner, "Manipulating International Commodity Markets: Brazilian Coffee Policy, 1906 to 1962."

2. Dolan, "European Restructuring and Import Policies for a Textile Industry in Crisis," p. 586; Chris Farrands, "Textiles and Clothing," p. 80.

3. For a discussion of the product life cycle see Louis Wells, Jr., ed., *The Product Life Cycle*.

4. Vernon, "The Product Cycle Hypothesis in a New International Environment."

5. Farrands, "Textiles and Clothing," p. 80.

6. Kim, "The Growth and Structural Change of Textile Industry," pp. 214–215.

7. Aggarwal, *Liberal Protectionism*, p. 74; on the liberalism of the Scandinavian countries, see Peter J. Katzenstein, *Small States in World Markets*.

8. Aggarwal, *Liberal Protection*, for the U.S., U.K., and E.E.C.; for the Canadian case, see Rianne Mahon and Lynn Krieger Mytelka, "Industry, the State, and the New Protectionism: Textiles in Canada and France," pp. 551–581; despite the proliferation of studies on North-South state bargaining

over the textile arrangements and domestic politics in the North, there has been very little attention paid to domestic politics in the South in this issue.

9. Yoffie, *Power and Protectionism, passim*; Aggarwal, *Liberal Protectionism, passim*.

10. Yoffie, *Power and Protectionism, passim*.

11. For an introduction to the discussion of industrial policy in the North, see William Diebold, *Industrial Policy as an International Issue*.

12. Kim, "The Growth and Structural Change of Textile Industry," p. 121.

13. Yoffie, *Power and Protectionism*, p. 166.

14. *Ibid.*, p. 167.

15. Haggard and Moon, "The South Korean State in the International Economy"; Stephan Haggard and Tun-jen Cheng, "State Strategies, Local and Foreign Capital in the Gang of Four"; Cumings, "The Origins and Development of the Northeast Asian Political Economy: Industrial Sectors, Product Cycles, and Political Consequences."

16. Cumings, "Origins and Development," p. 23.

17. Haggard and Moon, "The South Korean State" p. 141.

18. Cumings, "Origins and Development," p. 27.

19. Haggard and Cheng, "State Strategies," p. 35.

20. Haggard and Moon, "The South Korean State"; Haggard and Cheng, "State Strategies"; Cumings, "Origins and Development."

21. Haggard and Moon, "The South Korean State," p. 161.

22. *Ibid.*, p. 167.

23. J. Kim, *The Korean Cotton Manufacturing Industry* (Ann Arbor: University Microfilms, 1966), pp. 11–13; as cited in Yung Bong Kim, "The Growth and Structural Change of Textile Industry," pp. 214–215.

24. Yoffie, *Power and Protectionism*, p. 116.

25. Aggarwal, *Liberal Protectionism, passim*.

26. Morawetz, *Why the Emperor's New Clothes Are Not Made in Colombia*; market share figures from p. 20 and export value from p. 75; 1978 figures are for first half of year.

27. *Ibid.*, pp. 122–126; EEC data are to 1981.

28. Haggard and Cheng, "State Strategies"; Haggard and Moon, "The South Korean State"; David R. Mares, "Explaining Choice of Development Strategies."

29. Díaz Alejandro, *Colombia*, ch. 1; Richard Nelson et al., *Structural Change in a Developing Country*, ch. 7; Thomas L. Hutcheson and Daniel M. Schydlowsky, "Colombia," p. 123.

30. Barry and Thoumi, "Import Substitution and Beyond: Colombia"; Morawetz, *Why the Emperor's New Clothes*, blames management and culture for labor's reluctance and ability to change the work flow, but this is more a function of labor's institutional and political strength to block productivity changes which may adversely affect employment.

31. Barry and Thoumi, "Import Substitution," p. 99.

32. Díaz Alejandro, *Colombia*, pp. 16–17.

33. Belassa, "The Newly Industrializing Countries After the Oil Crisis," pp. 57–61.

34. Morawetz, *Why the Emperor's New Clothes*, pp. 92–106.

35. *Ibid., passim.*

SELECT BIBLIOGRAPHY

PRIMARY SOURCES

Published

AARC (Asociación de Agricultores del Río Culiacán). *Boletín Agrícola.* Various issues. Culiacán.

AARC. *Boletín Bimestral.* Various issues. Culiacán.

AARC. *Boletín Mensual.* Various issues. Culiacán.

AARC. *Estatutos.* Culiacán, 1969.

CAADES. (Confederación de Asociaciones Agrícolas del Estado de Sinaloa) *Análisis de la situación agrícola en el estado de Sinaloa.* Various issues. Culiacán.

CAADES. *Boletín Informativo.* Various issues. Culiacán.

El Debate de Culiacán

El Diario de Culiacán

Excelsior

Florida Tomato Committee. *Annual Reports.* Various issues.

Mexico. Dirección General de Estadística. *IV Censo agrícola, ganadero y ejidal, 1960; Resumen General.* Mexico: Talleres Gráficos de la Nación, n.d.

Mexico. PP. (Presidential Proclamation). "Ley federal de aguas de 30 de diciembre de 1971." *Diario Oficial* (January 11, 1972). Mexico: Talleres Gráficos de la Nación, 1972.

Mexico. PP. "Ley federal de reforma agraria de 22 de marzo de 1971." *Diario Oficial* (May 1, 1971). Mexico: Talleres Gráficos de la Nación, 1971.

Mexico. PP. "Ley sobre cámaras agrícolas, que en lo sucesivo se denominarán asociaciones agrícolas." *Diario Oficial* (August 27, 1932). Mexico: Talleres Gráficos de la Nación, 1932.

Mexico. PP. "Reglamento de la ley de asociaciones agrícolas." *Diario Oficial* (April 13, 1934). Mexico: Talleres Gráficos de la Nación, 1934.

Mexico. Secretaría de Agricultura y Recursos Hidráulicos. Comité Directivo.

Distrito de Riego No. 10 y 74. *Boletín del Comité Directivo Agrícola.* Culiacán, Sinaloa.

Mexico. SRH (Secretaría de Recursos Hidráulicos). *Crecimiento agropecuario comparativo de los entidades federativos, 1940–1970.* Mexico: Secretaría de Recursos Hidráulicos, 1973.

Mexico. SRH. *Presa Adolfo López Mateos.* Culiacán: Secretaría de Recursos Hidráulicos, n.d.

Mexico. SRH. Gerencia del Estado de Sinaloa. *Prontuario Estadística del Estado de Sinaloa.* Culiacán: Secretaría de Recursos Hidráulicos, 1976.

New York Times

Noroeste

The Packer. St. Louis.

Proceso

Sinaloa. GP (Governor's Proclamation). "Decreto Num. 112: Ley de asociaciones agrícolas del Estado de Sinaloa." *Periódico oficial* (August 23, 1954). Culiacán: n.p., 1954.

Sinaloa. GP. "Decreto Num. 117: Ley de asociaciones agrícolas." *Periódico oficial* (January 30, 1937). Culiacán: n.p., 1937.

Sinaloa. SDE (Secretaría de Desarrollo Económico). *Plan Básico de Desarrollo 1977–1982.* Culiacán: Secretaría de Desarrollo Económico, 1977.

Sinaloa. SDE. *Sinaloa en cifras 1978.* Culiacán: Secretaría de Desarrollo Económico, 1978.

Sol de Sinaloa

U.S. Congress. House of Representatives. Committee on Ways and Means. *Certain Tariff and Trade Bills, Hearings*, before a subcommittee of the Committee on Ways and Means, 96th Congress, 2d Session, 1980.

U.S. Congress. House of Representatives. Committee on Foreign Affairs. *United States-Mexican Trade Relations Hearings*, before a subcommittee of the Committee on Foreign Affairs, 92d Congress, 2d Session, 1972.

U.S. Congress. House of Representatives. *Fresh Fruits and Vegetables Market Sharing Act of 1969*, H.R. 9656, 91st Congress, 1st Sess., March 27, 1969; and *Fresh Fruits and Vegetables Market Sharing Act of 1973*, H.R. 5413, 93d Congress, 1st Sess., March 8, 1973.

U.S. Court of Appeals, District of Columbia Circuit. "*Walter Holm & Company, et al., Appellants, v. Clifford M. Hardin, Individually and as Secretary of the United States Department of Agriculture, et al.*" (No. 24848). Argued January 26, 1969. Decided March 19, 1969.

U.S. Department of Agriculture. *Vegetable Outlook and Situation*, October 1982.

U.S. Government. *Federal Register.*

Unión Nacional de Productores de Hortalizas (UNPH). *Convención Anual.* Various years. Culiacán.

Wall Street Journal

Washington Post

Washington Star

Unpublished

AARC (Asociación de Agricultores del Río Culiacán). Archives.

AARC. "Las necesidades de crédito para la horticultura." Paper presented at the General Assembly of the Unión Nacional de Productores de Hortalizas. Guadalajara, 1965.

Bon Bustamante, Atilano. "Informe de labores que rinde el presidente de la Asociación de Agricultores." Culiacán, 1958. Mimeograph.

"Brief of Respondents Unión de Productores de Hortalizas and West Mexico Vegetable Distributors Association in the United States Department of Commerce." February 29, 1980. Mimeograph.

Campaña, Francisco, President, Campaña y Asociados. Interviews, 1980 and 1983.

Carrizosa, Humberto, economist, Department of Economic Studies, AARC. Interviews, 1980 and 1983.

Clouthier, Manuel J., President, Confederacíon Patronal de la República Mexicana. Interview, 1980.

Confederación de Asociaciones Agricultores del Estado de Sinaloa (CAADES). Archives.

Esquerra, Quinto Jaime, State Legislator and President, Asociación de la Pequeña Propiedad del Municipio de Culiacán. Interview, 1980.

"Exhibits to Brief of Respondents Unión Nacional de Productores de Hortalizas and West Mexico Vegetable Distributors Association in the United States Department of Commerce." February 19, 1980. Mimeograph.

FBA (Food Business Associates). "Mejorando el Mercado." Circa 1974. Mimeograph.

FBA. "Nature's Winter Sunshine from Sunny Mexico." Mimeograph.

FBA. *UNPH 1979 Promotion Handbook.*

Friedman, David Bennett. "The Misunderstood Miracle: Politics and the Development of a Hybrid Economy in Japan" Ph.D. Dissertation, Massachusetts Institute of Technology, 1986.

García Mascareño, Ariel, Marketing Manager, UNPH. Interview, 1979.

García Meza, María Idalia, Technical Assistant, Department of Economic Studies, AARC. Interview, 1980.

Gastelum Gaxiola, Emilio, founding father, AARC. Interview, 1980.

González Gurrola, Felipe, Legal Advisor, FIOACS. Interview, 1983.

González Sánchez, Arturo, Director General of Bilateral Economic Relations, Secretaría de Relaciones Exteriores. Interview, 1982.

Kahn, Fred. "Legal and Analytical Options in the Determination of Less Than Fair Value Sales of Certain Fresh Winter Vegetables from Mexico." October 1979. Mimeograph.

Meraz Figueroa, Rubén, financial analyst and author. Interview, 1979.

Mexico. SARH (Secretaría de Agricultura y Recursos Hidráulicos). Comité Directivo. Distrito de Riego No. 10 y 74. "Comisión de Cuotas y Presupuestos." Culiacán, Sinaloa, n.d. Mimeograph.

Mexico. SARH. Gerencia del Estado de Sinaloa. "Padrón de usuarios, Distrito de Riego No. 10, Concentrado." Culiacán, Sinaloa, n.d. Manuscript.

Mexico. SARH. Gerencia del Estado de Sinaloa. "Producción y valor de los cultivos del ciclo agrícola: 1976–1977." Culiacán, n.d. Manuscript.

Meyers, Glenn D. "Centralized Planning of Mexican Winter Vegetable Exports and Its Impact on the U.S. Market and the Florida Industry." May 15, 1978, draft. Prepared for the Florida growers in the dumping suit.

Miller Urias, Fausto Renato, Chief, Department of Economic Studies, CAADES. Interview, 1979.

McCrory, Patrick J., Arnold and Porter. Interview, 1981.

Ortega, Manuel, Chief, Department of Economic Studies, AARC. Interviews, 1979, 1980, and 1982.

Posadas Segura, Florencio, Instituto de Investigaciones Económicas y Sociales, Universidad Autónoma de Sinaloa. Interview, 1983.

Quevedo, Antonio, reporter for *Noroeste*. Interview, 1983.

Ramos Cantoral, Francisco, Director General, Dirección General de Economía Agrícola, SARH. Interview, 1980.

Ramos Esquer, Lázaro, Representative in Sinaloa, SARH. Interview, 1979.

"Rebuttal Brief of Respondants Unión Nacional de Productores de Hortalizas and West Mexico Vegetable Distributors Association." Presented to U.S. Department of Commerce n.d. Mimeograph.

Robles, Mario Haroldo, General Manager, UNPH. Interview, 1980.

Rodríguez, Javier, Instituto Mexicano de Comercio Exterior. Interview, 1980.

Roíz, Enrique, Chief, Economic Studies, CAADES. Interview, 1979.

Salamon, Ingeniero, Jefe de Unidad, SRH. Interview, 1979.

Sánchez Celis, Leopoldo, ex-Governor of Sinaloa. Interview, 1981.

Secretaría de Agricultura y Recursos Hidráulicos (SARH), Comité Directivo. Distrito de Riego No. 10 y 74. "Acuerdos del Comité Directivo." Culiacán, n.d. Mimeographed.

SARH, "Cuotas de Servicio" various years. Culiacán. Mimeographed.

SARH, Distrito de Riego No. 10. "Producción y valor de los cultivos del ciclo agrícola" various years. Culiacán. Mimeographed.

Secretaría de Recursos Hidráulicos (SRH), Comité Directiva de Agricultura. Culiacán. Archives.

Simmons, Richard L. "A Comparison of Prices of Winter Vegetables in Canadian and U.S. Markets" n.d. Mimeographed.

Simmons, Richard L. "Costs of Production and Marketing Staked Tomatoes, Bell Peppers, Cucumbers and Eggplant in Culiacán, 1978–1979," USDA contract 53-319 x-8-02462. January 1979.

Unión Nacional de Productores de Hortalizas. Archives.

U.S. Department of Agriculture. Foreign Agricultural Service. "Horticultural and Tropical Products," WANG DOC. NO. 1935H. Internal document. June 13, 1983.

U.S. Department of Commerce. Files.

U.S. Department of Justice, Antitrust Division. "Memorandum from John

H. Shenfield, Assistant Attorney General, to Robert H. Mundhein, Esquire, General Counsel, Department of the Treasury." Washington, D.C., July 16, 1979.

U.S. District Court for the District of Columbia. *Coast Marketing Co., William S. Wright, Inc., West Mexico Vegetable Distributors Association v. the Honorable Earl L. Butz, Secretary of the United States Department of Agriculture, Richard E. Lyng, Ervin L. Peterson and Floyd Hedlund.* No. 2154-72.

U.S. District Court for the District of Columbia. *Consumer's Union of United States, Inc., Consumer Federation of California, Consumer Federation of Illinois, and Consumer Association of the District of Columbia v. the Honorable Earl L. Butz, Secretary of the United States Department of Agriculture, Richard E. Lyng, Ervin L. Peterson and Floyd Hedlund.* No. 2142-72.

U.S. District Court for the District of Columbia. *Stipulation and Order of Dismissal Without Prejudice.* September 18, 1975.

Villa, Jaime, farmer. Interview, 1980.

Villa, Juan José, founding father, AARC. Interview, 1980.

Zepp, G. A. "Trend and Outlook for Florida Tomato Competition." Paper presented at the Florida Tomato Institute, Naples, Florida. September 10, 1981.

Secondary Sources

Aggarwal, Vinod K. *Liberal Protectionism.* Berkeley: University of California Press, 1985.

Ai Camp, Rodrigo. *Mexican Political Biographies.* Tucson, Ariz.: University of Arizona Press, 1976.

Altimar, Oscar. "La medición de la población económicamente activa en México, 1950–1970." *Demografía y Economía* (1974), 7:1.

Anderson, Bo and James D. Cockcroft. "Control and Co-optation in Mexican Politics." In James D. Cockcroft, Andre Gunder Frank, and Dale L. Johnson, *Dependence and Underdevelopment.* Garden City, N.Y.: Anchor Books, 1972.

Arcos Cabrera, Carlos and Gonzalo Varela Petito. "Los empresarios agrícolas y el estado Mexicano, 1964–1976." Licenciatura Thesis, Facultad Latinoamericana de Ciencias Sociales, Mexico, circa 1978.

Austin, James. *Agribusiness in Latin America.* New York: Praeger, 1974.

Banco Mexicano de Comercio Exterior. *Comercio Exterior.*

Banco Nacional de México. *Exámen de la situación económica de México.*

Barry, Albert and Francisco Thoumi. "Import Substitution and Beyond: Columbia." *World Development* (1977), vol. 5, nos. 1/2.

Bartra, Armando. *Notas sobre la cuestión campesina. (Mexico 1970–1976).* Mexico: Editorial Macehual, S.A., 1979.

Bartra, Armando. "Seis años de lucha campesina." *Investigación Económica (Nueva Epoca)* (July–September 1977), vol. 36, no. 3.

Beck, F. H. "Como controla la agroindustria la producción de verduras en el noroeste de México." *Problemas del Desarrollo* (August–October, 1977), 8:31.

Becker, David G. *The New Bourgeoisie and the Limits of Dependency.* Princeton: Princeton University Press, 1983.

Belassa, Bela. *The Newly Industrializing Countries in the International Economy.* New York: Pergamon Press, 1981.

Bennett, Douglas and Kenneth Sharpe. "Agenda Setting and Bargaining Power: The Mexican State Versus Transnational Automobile Corporations." *World Politics* (October 1979), 32:1.

Berger, Suzanne, ed. *Organizing Interests in Western Europe: Pluralism, Corporatism, and the Transformation of Politics.* Cambridge, Eng.: Cambridge University Press, 1981.

Bergsten, C. Fred. "Let's Avoid a Trade War." *Foreign Policy* (Summer 1976), vol. 23.

Brandenburg, Frank. Introduction by Frank Tannenbaum. *The Making of Modern Mexico.* Englewood Cliffs, N.J.: Prentice-Hall, 1964.

Bredahl, Maury E. et al. *Technical Change, Protectionism, and Market Structure.* Agricultural Experiment Station Technical Bulletin 249, University of Arizona, College of Agriculture, 1983.

Brooker, John R. and James L. Pearson. *The Winter Fresh Tomato Industry— A Systems Analysis.* Economic Research Service, U.S. Department of Agriculture, in cooperation with the University of Florida, Agricultural Economic Report No. 330, 1976.

Brown, Lyle C. "General Lázaro Cárdenas and Mexican Presidential Politics." Ph.D. Dissertation, University of Texas at Austin, 1964.

Burbach, Roger and Patricia Flynn. *Agribusiness in the Americas.* New York: Monthly Review and North American Congress on Latin America, 1980.

Cardoso, Fernando Henrique and Enzo Faletto. *Dependency and Development in Latin America.* Berkeley and Los Angeles: University of California Press, 1979. Expanded and amended version of Spanish edition, 1971.

Castell Cancino, Jorge and Fernando Rello Espinosa. "Las desaventuras de un proyecto agrario: 1970–1976." *Investigación Económica (Nueva Epoca)*, (July–September 1977), vol. 36, no. 3.

Ceceña Cervantes, José Luis, Fausto Burgueño Lomeli, and Silvia Millan Echeagaray. *Sinaloa: crecimiento agrícola y desperdicio.* Mexico: Universidad Nacional Autónoma de México, Instituto de Investigaciones Económicas, 1973.

Centro de Investigaciones Agrarias. *Los distritos de riego del noroeste: tenencia y aprovechamiento de la tierra.* Mexico: Instituto Mexicana de Investigaciones Económicas, 1957.

Collier, David. "Overview of the Bureaucratic-Authoritarian Model." In

David Collier, ed., *The New Authoritarianism in Latin America*. Princeton: Princeton University Press, 1979.

Collier, David. "The Bureaucratic-Authoritarian Model: Synthesis and Priorities for Future Research." In David Collier, ed., *The New Authoritarianism in Latin America*. Princeton: Princeton University Press, 1979.

Collier, David and Ruth Berins Collier. "Who Does What, to Whom, and How: Toward a Comparative Analysis of Latin American Corporatism." In James M. Malloy, ed., *Authoritarianism and Corporatism in Latin America*. Pittsburgh: University of Pittsburgh Press, 1977.

Confederación de Asociaciones Agrícolas del Estado de Sinaloa (CAADES). *La defensa de la tierra: historia de una crisis, noviembre–diciembre 1975*. Culiacán, circa 1976.

Contreras, Ariel José. *México 1940: industrialización y crisis política*. 2nd ed. Mexico: Siglo Veintiuno Editores, 1980.

Córdova, Arnaldo. *La ideología de la Revolución Mexicana: la formación del nuevo régimen*. 2nd ed. Mexico: Ediciones Era, 1973.

Córdova, Arnaldo. "La transformación del PNR en PRM: el triunfo del corporativismo en México." In James W. Wilkie, Michael C. Meyer, and Edna Monzón de Wilkie, eds., *Contemporary Mexico: Papers of the IV International Congress of Mexican History*, vol. 29 of Johannes Wilbert, ed., *Latin American Studies Series*. Berkeley: University of California Press, 1976.

Cornelius, Wayne. "Nation Building, Participation and Distribution: The Politics of Social Reform under Cárdenas." In Gabriel A. Almond, Scott C. Flanagan, and Robert J. Mundt, eds., *Crisis, Choice and Change*. Boston: Little, Brown, 1973.

Cumings, Bruce. "The Origins and Development of the Northeast Asian Political Economy: Industrial Sectors, Product Cycles, and Political Consequences," *International Organization*. (Winter 1984), vol. 38, no. 1.

Davis, John H. and Ray A. Goldberg. *A Concept of Agribusiness*, Boston: Harvard Graduate School of Business Administration, 1957.

Davis, Ralph. *The Rise of the Atlantic Economies*. Ithaca, N.Y.: Cornell University Press, 1981.

Delgado Cortés, Jorge and Benito García. "Registro cronológica de las luchas de los obreros agrícolas migratorios en Sinaloa." *Ciencia y Universidad* (July 1980), 4:13.

Dell, Sidney. "Conditionally: The Political Economy of Overkill." In John Williamson, ed., *IMF Conditionality*. Washington, D.C.: Institute for International Economics, 1983.

DeWalt, Billie. "Mexico's Second Green Revolution" *Mexican Studies* (Winter 1985), vol. 1, no. 1.

Díaz-Alejandro, Carlos F. *Colombia: Foreign Trade Regimes and Economic Development*, vol. 9. New York: National Bureau of Economic Research, 1976.

Diebold, William. *Industrial Policy as an International Issue*. New York: McGraw-Hill, 1980.

Dolan, Michael B. "European Restructuring and Import Policies for a Textile Industry in Crisis." *International Organization* (Autumn 1983).

Domínguez, Jorge I. "Introduction." In Jorge I. Domínguez, ed., *Mexico's Political Economy: Challenges at Home and Abroad*. Beverly Hills: Sage Publications, 1982.

Dulles, John F. W. *Yesterday in Mexico*. Austin, Tex.: University of Texas Press, 1967.

Emerson, Leonidas P. Bill, Jr. *Preview of Mexico's Vegetable Production for Export*. Washington, D.C.: USDA, FAS M-297, 1980.

Esteva, Gustavo et al. *La batalla en el México rural*. Mexico: Siglo Veintiuno Editores, 1980.

Evans, Peter. *Dependent Development: The Alliance of Multinational, State and Local Capital in Brazil*. Princeton: Princeton University Press, 1979.

Farrands, Chris. "Textiles and Clothing." In Susan Strange and Roger Tooze, eds. *The International Politics of Surplus Capacity*. London: George Allen & Urwin, 1981.

Gardner, Bruce L. "Commentaries." *Food and Agricultural Policy*. Washington, D.C.: American Enterprise Institute for Public Policy Research, 1977.

Gaxiola, Francisco Javier, Jr. *El Presidente Rodríguez*. Mexico: Editorial 'Cultura,' 1938.

Gereffi, Gary. *The Pharmaceutical Industry in the Third World*. Princeton: Princeton University Press, 1983.

Gereffi, Gary and Peter Evans. "Transnational Corporations, Dependent Development, and State Policy in the Semi-Periphery: A Comparison of Brazil and Mexico." *Latin American Research Review*, vol. 16, no. 3. 1981.

Gil, Mario. *La conquista del Valle del Fuerte*. Mexico: Imprenta Técnica Moderna, S.A., 1957.

Gilpin, Robert. "Economic Interdependence and National Security in Historical Perspective." In Klaus Knorr and Frank Tager, eds., *Economic Issues and National Security*. Lawrence: The Regents Press of Kansas for the National Security Education Program, 1977.

Gilpin, Robert. *U.S. Power and the Multinational Corporation*. New York: Basic Books, 1975.

Goldberg, Ray A. *Argibusiness Management for Developing Countries— Latin America*. Cambridge, Mass.: Ballinger, 1974.

Gómez-Jara, Francisco A. *El movimiento campesino en México*. Mexico: Editorial Campesina, 1977.

González Navarro, Moisés. *La Confederación Nacional Campesina: un grupo de presión en la reforma agraria mexicana*. Mexico: Universidad Nacional Autónoma de México, 1977.

González Pacheco, Cuauhtémoc. *Organización campesina y lucha de clases. La Confederación Nacional Campesina*. Volume in *Libros preliminares de la investigación* of the Instituto de Investigaciones Económicas. Mexico: Universidad Nacional Autónoma, n.d.

Gourevitch, Peter Alexis. "Breaking with Orthodoxy: The Politics of Economic Policy Responses to the Depression of the 1930s." *International Organization.* (Winter 1984), 38:1.

Gourevitch, Peter Alexis. "International Trade, Domestic Coalitions and Liberty: Comparative Responses to the Crisis of 1873–1896." *Journal of Interdisciplinary History* (Autumn 1977), vol. 8.

Greenberg, Martin Harry. *Bureaucracy and Development.* Lexington, Mass.: Heath Books, 1971.

Grindle, Merilee S. *Bureaucrats, Politicians, and Peasants in Mexico.* Berkeley: University of California Press, 1977.

Haggard, Stephan and Tun-jen Cheng. "State Strategies, Local and Foreign Capital in the Gang of Four," n.d.

Haggard, Stephan and Chung-in Moon, "The South Korean State in the International Economy: Liberal, Dependent or Mercantile?" In John Gerard Ruggie, ed., *The Antinomies of Interdependence: National Welfare and the International Division of Labor.* New York: Columbia University Press, 1983.

Hansen, Roger D. *The Politics of Mexican Development.* Baltimore: Johns Hopkins University Press, 1974.

Hathaway, Dale E. "Agriculture Trade Policy for the 1980s." In William R. Cline, ed., *Trade Policy in the 1980s.* Washington, D.C.: Institute for International Economics, 1983.

Hernes, Gudmund and Arne Selvik. "Local Corporatism." In Suzanne Berger, ed., *Organizing Interests in Western Europe: Pluralism, Corporatism, and the Transformation of Politics,* pp. 103–119. Cambridge, Eng.: Cambridge University Press, 1981.

Hewitt de Alcántara, Cynthia. *Modernizing Mexican Agriculture: Socioeconomic Implications of Technological Change, 1940–1970.* Geneva: United Nations Research Institute for Social Development, 1976.

Hillman, Jimmye S. *Nontariff Agricultural Trade Barriers.* Lincoln, Nebr.: University of Nebraska Press, 1978.

Hirschman, Albert O. "The Political Economy of Import-Substituting Industrialization in Latin America." *The Quarterly Journal of Economics* (February 1968), 82:1.

Hirschman, Albert O. *The Strategy of Economic Development.* New Haven: Yale University Press, 1958.

Hirschman, Albert O. "The Turn to Authoritarianism in Latin America and the Search for Its Economic Determinants." In David Collier, ed., *The New Authoritarianism in Latin America.* Princeton: Princeton University Press, 1979.

Houthakker, Hendrik S. "Commentaries." *Food and Agricultural Policy.* Washington, D.C.: American Enterprise Institute for Public Policy Research, 1977.

Huizer, Gerrit. *La lucha campesina en México.* Mexico: Centro de Investigaciones Agrarias, 1970.

Huizer, Gerrit. *Peasant Unrest in Latin America: Its Origins, Forms of Expression and Potential.* Amsterdam: Academisch proefschrift, 1970.

Huizer, Gerrit. *The Revolutionary Potential of Peasants in Latin America.* Lexington, Mass.: Lexington Books, 1972.

Huntington, Samuel P. and Joan M. Nelson. *No Easy Choice: Political Participation in Developing Countries.* Cambridge, Mass.: Harvard University Press, 1976.

Hutcheson, Thomas L. and Daniel M. Schydlowsky. "Columbia." In Bela Belasso & Associates, eds., *Development Strategies in Semi-Industrial Economies.* Baltimore: Johns Hopkins University Press for the World Bank, 1982.

IPADE, "CAADES, la guerra del tomate," Anexo 7, n.d.

Jesse, Edward V. and Aaron C. Johnson, Jr. *Effectiveness of Federal Marketing Orders for Fruits and Vegetables.* USDA, ESS, Agricultural Economic Report No. 471.

Johnson, Chalmers. *MITI and the Japanese Miracle.* Stanford, Calif.: Stanford University Press, 1982.

Johnson, D. Gale. *Farm Commodity Programs: An Opportunity for Change.* Washington, D.C.: American Enterprise Institute, 1973.

Johnson, D. Gale. "Food Production and Marketing: A Review of Economic Developments in Agriculture." *Food and Agricultural Policy.* Washington, D.C.: American Enterprise Institute, 1977.

Just, Richard and Wen Chern. "Tomatoes, Technology, and Oligopsony." *Bell Journal of Economics* (Autumn 1980).

Katzenstein, Peter J., ed. *Between Power and Plenty: Foreign Economic Policies of Advanced Industrial States.* Madison: University of Wisconsin Press, 1978.

Katzenstein, Peter J. *Small States in World Markets.* Ithaca, N.Y.: Cornell University Press, 1985.

Katzenstein, Peter J., "The Small European States in the International Economy: Economic Dependence and Corporatist Politics." In John Gerard Ruggie, ed., *The Antinomies of Interdependence: National Welfare and the International Division of Labor,* pp. 91–130. New York: Columbia University Press, 1983.

Kaufman, Robert. "Mexico and Latin American Authoritarianism." In José Luis Reyna and Richard S. Weinert, eds., *Authoritarianism in Mexico.* Vol. 22 of *Inter-American Politics Series.* Philadelphia: Institute for the Study of Human Issues, 1977.

Kaufman Purcell, Susan. "Decision-Making in an Authoritarian Regime: Theoretical Implications from a Mexican Case Study." *World Politics.* (October 1973), 26:1.

Kaufman Purcell, Susan and John F. H. Purcell. "State and Society in Mexico: Must a Stable Polity be Institutionalized?" *World Politics.* (January 1980).

Keeler, John T. S. "Corporatism and Official Union Hegemony: The Case of French Agricultural Syndicalism." In Suzanne Berger, ed., *Organizing Interests in Western Europe: Pluralism, Corporatism, and the Transformation of Politics*, pp. 185–208. Cambridge: Cambridge University Press, 1981.

Keohane, Robert O. "The Theory of Hegemonic Stability and Changes in International Economic Regimes, 1967–1977." In Ole Holsti et al., eds., *Changes in the International System*. Boulder, Colo.: Westview, 1980.

Keohane, Robert O. and Joseph S. Nye, Jr. "Transnational Relations and World Politics: A Conclusion." In Robert O. Keohane and Joseph S. Nye, Jr., eds., *Transnational Relations and World Politics*, pp. 371–398. Cambridge, Mass.: Harvard University Press, 1970.

Kim, Yung Bong. "The Growth and Structural Change of Textile Industry." In Chong E. Park, ed., *Macroeconomic and Industrial Development in Korea*. Seoul: Korean Development Institute, 1980.

Krasner, Stephen D. "United States Commercial and Monetary Policy: Unravelling the Paradox of External Strength and Internal Weakness." In Peter J. Katzenstein, ed. *Between Power and Plenty: Foreign Economic Policies of Advanced Industrial States*. Madison: University of Wisconsin Press, 1978.

Krasner, Stephen D. *Defending the National Interest: Raw Materials Investments and United States Foreign Policy*. Princeton: Princeton University Press, 1978.

Krasner, Stephen D. "Manipulating International Commodity Markets: Brazilian Coffee Policy, 1906 to 1962." *Public Policy* (Fall 1973), 21:4.

Krasner, Stephen D. "Structural Causes and Regime Consequences: Regimes as Intervening Variables." *International Organization* (Spring 1982), 36:2.

Krasner, Stephen D. *Structural Conflict*. Berkeley: University of California Press, 1985.

Kumar, Krishna and Maxwell G. McLeod, eds., *Multinationals from Developing Countries*. Lexington, Mass.: Lexington Books, 1981.

Kurth, James. "The Political Consequences of the Product Cycle: Industrial History and Political Consequences." *International Organization* (Winter 1979), vol. 33.

Liera B., Ingeniero Guillermo. *Sinaloa: estudio económico-social*. Mexico: Editorial Evolución, 1943.

Lindblom, Charles. *Politics and Markets*. New York: Basic Books, 1977.

Linz, Juan. "Totalitarianism and Authoritarian Regimes." In Fred I. Greenstein and Nelson W. Polsby, eds., *Handbook of Political Science*, vol. 3. Reading, Mass.: Addison-Wesley, 1975.

Lipson, Charles. "The Transformation of Trade: The Sources and Effects of Regime Change." *International Organization*. (Spring 1982), 36:2.

Little, Ian, Tibor Scitovsky, and Maurice Scott. *Industry and Trade in Some Developing Countries*. London: Oxford University Press for the Development Centre of the Organization for Economic Cooperation and Development, 1970.

López Zamora, Emilio. *El agua, la tierra: los hombres de México.* Mexico: Fondo de Cultura Económica, 1977.

Maass, Arthur and Raymond L. Anderson. . . .*and the Desert Shall Rejoice.* Cambridge: Harvard University Press, 1978.

McLaughlin, Edward W. and Thomas Pierson. "The Fresh Fruit and Vegetable Marketing System: A Research Summary." Agricultural Economics Staff Paper 83-44, Department of Agricultural Economics, Michigan State University, East Lansing. Presented at the 1983 Annual Produce Conference, Fresno, California, August 1983.

Mahon, Rianne and Lynn Krieger Mytelka. "Industry, the State and the New Protectionism: Textiles in Canada and France." *International Organization* (Autumn 1983), 37:4.

Malloy, James M., ed. *Authoritarianism and Corporatism in Latin America.* Pittsburgh: University of Pittsburgh Press, 1977.

Mares, David R. "Agricultural Trade: Domestic Interests and Transnational Relations." In Jorge I. Domínguez, ed., *Mexico's Political Economy: Challenges at Home and Abroad.* Beverly Hills: Sage Publications, 1982.

Mares, David R. "Explaining Choice of Development Strategies: Suggestions from Mexico, 1970–1982." *International Organization* (Autumn 1985), 39:4.

Mares, David R. "La política norteamericana en el comercio de hortalizas: Washington frente a México en 'las guerras del tomate.' " In Carlos Rico F., ed., *El proceso de toma de decisiones en el gobierno norteamericano frente a México.* Mexico: Siglo XXI, forthcoming.

Mares, David R. "México y los Estados Unidos: el vínculo entre el comercio agrícola y la nueva relación energética." *Foro Internacional* (July–September 1981), vol. 85.

Mares, David R. "The Evolution of U.S.-Mexican Agricultural Relations: The Changing Roles of the Mexican State and Mexican Agricultural Producers." *Working Papers in U.S.-Mexican Studies*, no. 16. Program in United States-Mexican Studies, University of California, San Diego, 1981.

Medina, Luis. *Del cardenismo al avilacamachismo.* Vol. 18 of *Historia de la Revolución Mexicana.* Coordinated by Luis González. Mexico: El Colegio de México, 1978.

Meyer, Lorenzo. *El conflicto social y los gobiernos del maximato.* Vol. 13 of *Historia de la Revolución Mexicana.* Coordinated by Luis González. Mexico: El Colegio de México, 1978.

Meyer, Lorenzo. "Historical Roots of the Authoritarian State in Mexico." In José Luis Reyna and Richard S. Weinert, eds., *Authoritarianism in Mexico.* Vol. 2 of *Inter-American Politics Series.* Philadelphia: Institute for the Study of Human Issues, 1977.

Middlebrook, Kevin Jay. "The Political Economy of Mexican Organized Labor, 1940–1978." Unpublished Dissertation, Harvard University, 1981.

Montes de Oca, Rosa Elena. "The State and the Peasants." In José Luis

Reyna and Richard S. Weinert, eds., *Authoritarianism in Mexico*. Vol. 2 of *Inter-American Politics Series*. Philadelphia: Institute for the Study of Human Issues, 1977.

Moran, Theodore H. *Multinational Corporations and the Politics of Dependence: Copper in Chile*. Princeton: Princeton University Press, 1974.

Morawetz, David. *Why the Emperor's New Clothes Are Not Made in Colombia*. New York: Oxford University Press for The World Bank, 1981.

Murillo M., Arturo. *Los años no bastan*. Mexico: B. Costa Amic, 1978.

Nacional Financiera, S.A. *Statistics on the Mexican Economy*. Mexico: Nacional Financiera, 1977.

Nelson, Richard et al. *Structural Change in a Developing Country*. Princeton: Princeton University Press, 1971.

North American Congress on Latin America (NACLA). "Harvest of Anger: Agro-Imperialism in Mexico's Northwest." *Latin American and Empire Report*. (July–August 1976), vol. 10, no. 6.

Odell, John S. "Latin American Trade Negotiations with the United States." *International Organization* (Spring 1980).

O'Donnell, Guillermo A. "Corporatism and the Question of the State." In James M. Malloy, ed., *Authoritarianism and Corporatism in Latin America*. Pittsburgh: University of Pittsburgh Press, 1977.

O'Donnell, Guillermo A. *Modernization and Bureaucratic-Authoritarianism: Studies in South American Politics*. Berkeley: Institute of International Studies, University of California, 1973.

Orive Alba, Adolfo. *La irrigación en México*. Mexico: Fondo de Cultura Económica, 1960.

Orr, Daniel. *Property, Markets, and Government Intervention*. Pacific Palisades, Calif.: Goodyear Publishing, 1976.

Padgett, L. Vincent. *The Mexican Political System*, 2nd ed. Boston: Houghton Mifflin Company, 1976.

Paré, Luisa. *El proletariado agrícola en México*. Mexico: Siglo Veintiuno, 1977.

Partido Revolucionario Institucional. *Sinaloa*. Mexico: Instituto de Estudios Económicos, Políticos y Sociales, circa 1976.

Petras, James F. "Cambios en la estructura agraria de la América Latina." In Antonio García, ed., *Desarrollo agrario y América Latina*. Mexico: Fondo de Cultura Económica, 1981.

Petras, James F. "The Latin American Agro-Transformation from Above and Outside: The Social and Political Implications." In Lawrence R. Alschuler, ed., *Dependant (sic) Agricultural Development and Agrarian Reform in Latin America*. Ottawa: Ottawa University Press, 1981.

Posadas Segura, Florencio. "El proletariado agrícola en el estado de Sinaloa." Masters Thesis, Facultad Latinoamericana de Ciencias Sociales, Sede en México, June 1983.

Posadas Segura, Florencio. "Trabajo y producción de los proletarios agrícolas migratorios en Sinaloa." *Ciencia y Universidad* (July 1980), 4:13.

Purcell, John F. H. and Susan Kaufman Purcell. "Mexican Business and

Public Policy." In James M. Malloy, ed., *Authoritarianism and Corporatism in Latin America.* Pittsburgh: University of Pittsburgh Press, 1977.

Rama, Ruth and Fernando Rello. "La transnacionalización de la agricultura mexicana." In Nora Lustig, ed., *Panorama y perspectiva de la economia mexicana.* Mexico: El Colegio de México, 1980.

Rama, Ruth and Raúl Vigorito. *El complejo de frutas y legumbres en México.* Mexico: Nueva Imagen, 1979.

Rangarajan, L. N. *Commodity Conflict.* Ithaca, N.Y.: Cornell University Press, 1978.

Reich, Robert. "Beyond Free Trade." *Foreign Affairs* (Spring 1983).

Restrepo Fernández, Ivan. "El caso de los jornaleros agrícolas en México." Revista del México Agraria (1972), 5:3.

Reyes Osorio, Sergio et al. *Estructura agraria y desarrollo agrícola en México: estudio sobre las relaciones entre la tenencia y uso de la tierra y el desarrollo agrícola de México.* Mexico: Fondo de Cultura Económica, 1974.

Reyna, José Luis. "El movimiento obrero en el ruizcortinismo: la redefinición del sistema económica y la consolidación política." In José Luis Reyna and Raúl Trejo Delarbre, eds., *La clase obrera en la historia de México: de Adolfo Ruiz Cortines a Adolfo López Mateos (1952–1964).* Mexico: Instituto de Investigaciones Sociales, Universidad Nacional Autónoma de México, 1981.

Reyna, José Luis and Richard S. Weinert, eds. *Authoritarianism in Mexico.* Vol. 2 of *Inter-American Politics Series.* Philadelphia: Institute for the Study of Human Issues, 1977.

Reynolds, Clark W. *The Mexican Economy: Twentieth Century Structure and Growth.* New Haven: Yale University Press, 1970.

Reynolds, Clark W. "The U.S. Mexican Labor Market of the Future." *Project on United States-Mexico Relations,* Working Paper No. 2, 1982.

Roemer, Michael. *Fishing for Growth.* Cambridge, Mass.: Harvard University Press, 1970.

Ronfeldt, David. *Atencingo: The Politics of Agrarian Struggle in a Mexican Ejido.* Stanford, Calif.: Stanford University Press, 1973.

Rothstein, Robert R. *Global Bargaining: UNCTAD and the Quest for a New International Order.* Princeton: Princeton University Press, 1979.

Rubio, Báldemar. "Algunos conclusiones sobre la evolución del padrón de cultivos en Sinaloa." Culiacán, 1978. Manuscript.

Rubio, Báldemar et al. *1976: las invasiones de tierra en Sinaloa.* Culiacán: Universidad Autónoma de Sinaloa, 1978.

Rubio Félix, Lázaro. *Cuando tomamos la tierra.* Mexico: Federación Editorial Mexicano, 1976.

Rubio Félix, Lázaro. *Sinaloa, campo de sangre: la quinta columna nazi en acción.* Mexico: Federación Editorial Mexicana, 1978.

Ruggie, John Gerard. "International Regimes, Transactions, and Change: Embedded Liberalism in the Postwar Economic Order." *International Organization.* (Spring 1982), 36:2.

Runsten, David and Phillip LeVeen. "Mechanization and Mexican Labor in California Agriculture." *Monographs in U.S.-Mexican Studies*, num. 6. Program in United States-Mexican Studies, University of California, San Diego, 1981.

Samuelson, Paul A. *Economics*. 8th ed. New York: McGraw-Hill, 1970.

Sanderson, Steven. *Agrarian Populism and the Mexican State*. Berkeley: University of California Press, 1981.

Sanderson, Steven. "Florida Tomatoes, U.S.-Mexican Relations, and the International Division of Labor." *International Economic Affairs* (Winter 1981).

Sanderson, Steven. "The Receding Frontier: Aspects of the Internationalization of U.S.-Mexican Agriculture and Their Implications for Bilateral Relations in the 1980s." *Working Papers in U.S.-Mexico Studies*. Center for U.S.-Mexico Studies, University of California, San Diego, 1981.

Schmitt, Karl. *Communism in Mexico: A Study in Political Frustration*. Austin, Tex.: University of Texas Press, 1965.

Schmitter, Philippe C. "Modes of Interest Intermediation and Models of Societal Change in Western Europe." *Comparative Political Studies* (April 1977), vol. 10, no. 1.

Schmitter, Philippe C. "Still the Century of Corporatism?" *Review of Politics* (January 1974), vol. 36.

Schumacher, August. "Agricultural Development and Rural Empire: A Mexican Dilemma." *Working Papers in U.S.-Mexican Studies*, no. 21. Program in United States-Mexican Studies, University of California, San Diego, 1981.

Shwedel, S. Kenneth. "After the Fall: Structural Change and Policy in Mexican Agriculture since 1965." June 1985 draft.

Scott, Robert E. *Mexican Government in Transition*. Rev. ed. Urbana, Ill.: University of Illinois Press, 1964.

Simmons, Richard L. and Carlos Pomareda. "Equilibrium, Quantity and Timing of Mexican Vegetable Exports." *American Journal of Agricultural Economics* (August 1975).

Simmons, Richard L. et al. *Mexican Competition for the U.S. Fresh Winter Vegetable Market*. Agricultural Economic Report 348, USDA, Economic Research Service, 1976.

Smith, Ernest B. "Florida's and Mexico's Shares of the U.S. Fresh Winter Vegetable Market." *The Vegetable Situation* (February 1976).

Smith, Ernest B. and Chris Andrew. *Cucumber Production, Distribution and Competition for the U.S. Market: A Southern State's Perspective*. Economic Information Report 97, Food and Resource Economics Department, University of Florida, Gainesville, and Economics, Statistics and Cooperatives Service, USDA, 1978.

Smith, Peter. *Labyrinths of Power*. Princeton: Princeton University Press, 1979.

Sorenson, Vernon L. *International Trade Policy*. East Lansing: Michigan State University, International Business and Economics Studies, 1975.

Stavenhagen, Rodolfo. "Los jornaleros agrícolas." *Revista del México agrario* (1967), 1:1.

Stepan, Alfred. *The State and Society: Peru in Comparative Perspective.* Princeton: Princeton University Press, 1978.

Strange, Susan. "The Management of Surplus Capacity: Or How Does Theory Stand Up to Protectionism 1970s Style?" *International Organization* (Summer 1979), 33:3.

Strange, Susan and Roger Tooze. "Introduction." In Strange and Tooze, eds., *The International Politics of Surplus Capacity.* London: George Allen & Unwin, 1981.

Suárez, Blanca. "Comentario." In Nora Lustig, ed., *Panorama y perspectiva de la económia mexicana.* Mexico: El Colegio de México, 1980.

Tarriba Unger, Benito. "Características generales de producción y mercadeo del tomate para exportación a los países de Norte América en el valle de Culiacán, Sinaloa." Licenciatura Thesis, Escuela Nacional de Agricultura, Chapingo, 1975.

Taylor, Timothy G. *Costs and Returns from Vegetable Crops in Florida, Season 1980–81, with Comparisons.* Economic Information Report 159, Institute of Food and Agricultural Sciences, University of Florida, Gainesville, June 1982.

Tello, Carlos. *La política económica en México, 1970–1976.* 2nd ed. Mexico: Siglo Veintiuno Editores, 1979.

Torres Angulo, José. *La lucha por la tenencia de la tierra en Sinaloa.* Mexico: Imprenta Venecia, 1975.

Trejo Delarbre, Raúl. "Los trabajadores y el gobierno de Adolfo López Mateos (1958–1964)." In José Luis Reyna and Raúl Trejo Delarbre, eds., *La clase obrera en la historia de México: de Adolfo Ruiz Cortines a Adolfo López Mateos (1952–1964).* Mexico: Instituto de Investigaciones Sociales, Universidad Nacional Autónoma de México, 1981.

Venezian, Eduardo L. and William K. Gamble. *The Agricultural Development of Mexico: Its Structure and Growth since 1950.* New York: Frederick A. Praeger, 1969.

Vernon, Raymond. *The Dilemma of Mexico's Development: The Roles of the Private and Public Sectors.* Cambridge, Mass.: Harvard University Press, 1963.

Vernon, Raymond. "The Product Cycle Hypothesis in a New International Environment." In John Adams, ed., *The Contemporary International Economy.* 2nd ed. New York: St. Martin's Press, 1985.

Villarreal, René. *El desequilibrio externo en la industrialización de México (1929–1975): un enfoque estructuralista.* Mexico: Fondo de Cultura Económica, 1976.

Voss, Stuart F. *On the Periphery of Nineteenth Century Mexico: Sonora and Sinaloa, 1810–1877.* Tucson, Ariz.: University of Arizona Press, 1982.

Walsh Sanderson, Susan. "Peasants and Public Policy: Agricultural Development and Politics in Mexico: 1916–1980." New York: Academic Press, forthcoming.

Warley, T. K. "Western Trade in Agriculture Products." "International Economic Relations of the Western World, vol. 1. In Andrew Shonfield, ed., *Politics and Trade*. London: Oxford University Press for the Royal Institute of International Affairs, 1976.

Weinert, Richard S. "The State and Foreign Capital." In José Luis Reyna and Richard S. Weinert, eds., *Authoritarianism in Mexico*. Vol. 2 of *Inter-American Politics Series*. Philadelphia: Institute for the Study of Human Issues, 1977.

Wells, Louis T., Jr. "International Trade: The Product Life Cycle Approach." In Louis T. Wells, Jr., ed., *The Product Life Cycle and International Trade*. Boston: Graduate School of Business Administration, Harvard University, 1972.

Wells, Louis T., Jr. *Third World Multinationals: The Rise of Foreign Investment from Developing Countries*. Cambridge, Mass.: MIT Press, 1983.

Wiarda, Howard J. *Politics and Social Change in Latin America*. n.p.: University of Massachusetts Press, 1974.

Wilson, Graham K. *Special Interests and Policy-Making*. London: Wiley, 1977.

World Bank. *World Development Report 1984*. Washington, D.C.: World Bank, 1984.

Yeats, Alexander J. "Agricultural Protectionism: An Analysis of its International Economic Effects and Options for Institutional Reform." *Trade and Development* (Winter 1981), no. 3.

Yoffie, David B. *Power and Protectionism*. New York: Columbia University Press, 1983.

Zepp, G. A. *U.S. Winter Fresh Tomato Price and Quantity Projections for 1985*. Washington, D.C. USDA, ESS-4, 1981.

Zepp, G. A. and R. L. Simmons. *Producing Fresh Winter Vegetables in Florida and Mexico: Costs and Competition*. Washington, D.C.: USDA, Economics, Statistics and Cooperatives Service-72, 1979.

Zysman, John. *Governments, Markets, and Growth*. Ithaca, N.Y.: Cornell University Press, 1983.

INDEX